May you always be a positive leader – & thus be the change you want to see in the world.

Becoming the Transformative Church

Beyond Sacred Cows, Fantasies, and Fears

Joy in the journey –
Kay Collier McLaughlin
November 2013

KAY COLLIER McLAUGHLIN

Morehouse Publishing

NEW YORK · HARRISBURG · DENVER

Morehouse Publishing, 4775 Linglestown Road, Harrisburg, PA 17112
Morehouse Publishing, 19 East 34th Street, New York, NY 10016
Morehouse Publishing is an imprint of Church Publishing Incorporated.
www.churchpublishing.org

Cover design by Laurie Klein Westhafer
Page design by Beth Oberholtzer

Library of Congress Cataloging-in-Publication Data

A catalog record is avaiable from the Library of Congress.

ISBN-13 : 978-0-8192-2883-3 (pbk.)
ISBN-13 : 978-0-8192-2884-0 (ebook)

Printed in the United States of America

To Virginia Varden Newsome,
beloved granddaughter whose gifts for leadership
are a light to her generation . . .

Contents

FOREWORD

Caging the Bloody Tiger

It was not long into my new life as a priest some 25 years ago that I noticed all was not as I thought it would be or should be in the congregation I was serving. It wasn't that there was something wrong with the congregation particularly. Its rector, for whom I worked, was an exceptional preacher and charismatic leader recognized throughout the diocese as a rising star. It was a strong congregation with wonderful people as members. But when those wonderful people got together for church . . . my goodness, they behaved in ways that did not make sense to me. The rector had issues of his own, quite irrespective of his many capabilities. Either they all had to be crazy or I did, I thought. Or, maybe both.

I probably would have gone through the rest of my ordained life trying to figure out who was crazy and responding accordingly, or more likely gone back to my former life as a lawyer, had it not been for my providential introduction to the work of Rabbi Edwin Friedman. I studied with him until his death in 1996. As a bishop, I participated in a colleague group of other bishops interested in, if not saved by, family systems theory. I continue to work at thinking systemically and applying what I've learned to the new challenges I face, which in the end always turn out to be about leadership.

Among Rabbi Friedman's writings is a collection of stories called *Friedman's Fables*. I have found all of them important as I have sought to get beyond the "someone must be crazy here" line of thinking in church leadership, but one of them strikes me as particularly relevant to Kay Collier McLaughlin's work. The story at issue is "The Friendly Forest."[1]

"The Friendly Forest" is the story of a lamb that, together with the other animals, lived happily frolicking in the Friendly Forest. One day, a tiger came to live in the forest. The tiger's presence was welcomed by the other animals but left the lamb understandably uncomfortable. The other ani-

---

1. "The Friendly Forest," in *Friedman's Fables* (New York, Guilford Press, 1990), 25–28.

v

mals assured the lamb that all would be well. It was not long, however, before the tiger began to growl and behave menacingly. The lamb complained. Each time she did, however, the other animals made excuses for the tiger. Growling and threatening gestures, after all, are just the nature of tigers.

Finally, the other animals proposed a meeting between the tiger and the lamb to work things out. After all, the animals in the Friendly Forest were reasonable creatures. Surely some accommodation was possible. The lamb, however, was apprehensive. What, she wondered, would she have to give up in a potential compromise? Something seemed wrong with the idea that the threatened creature would have to tolerate the invasive behavior of the threatening creature as part of any such compromise. The other animals, being reasonable, were convinced that communication was the answer.

Communication, of course, is a high value in church circles, too.

The story concludes with what I have always thought was an exceptionally wise observation. Friedman puts this wisdom in the mouth of an animal he describes as one of the less subtle and perhaps more uncouth animals in the forest (a description in which I have taken some comfort from time to time). "I never heard of anything so ridiculous," it said. "If you want a lamb and a tiger to live in the same forest, you don't try to make them communicate. You cage the bloody tiger."

The light began to go on for me.

I have spent 25 years thinking about how to cage the tiger running loose in the friendly forest; tigers, I have found, are almost always present in the friendly forest that is the Church. Indeed, as in the Friendly Forest, churches tend to attract, and indeed delight, in having a tiger or two. Churches also tend to have what is perhaps an unreasonable faith in being reasonable.

I have tried a number of strategies along the way, some more successful than others and many of which left me a bit bloody and bruised. The struggle, though, has been less with the tiger itself and more with trying to keep myself from a line of thinking that insisted on seeing some one individual as the problem, the crazy one. I knew Ed Friedman's thinking well enough to know that identifying the crazy one wasn't the answer. Diagnosing the insanity gets us nowhere, although it may leave us falsely reassured for a little while.

Through another providential turn of events, I became blessed to work with Kay Collier McLaughlin as a member of my staff when I was the Bishop of Lexington. As it turned out, I had the opportunity to learn, through our work together in leadership development in the diocese, the answer to the question of how to cage the bloody tiger—and live to tell the tale.

From my perspective, the pages of this insightful little book are about that conundrum for leaders—how to cage the tiger and defend against the invasive and boundary-less elements in churches, whether congregations or a diocese (or, I hope, an entire international church), without seeing the problem as about individuals. In other words, about who is crazy and who is not.

The answer has to do with being more interested in what is strong and healthy than in what is weak and dysfunctional, even at the risk of appearing uncompassionate. As Kay and I would often speak of it, to use a Pauline metaphor, the answer is in strengthening the body's own immune system rather than providing the solution from outside. But the body needs a little help to strengthen itself to deal with its own threats, an immunization if you will, or at least a vitamin supplement. In speaking of "The Friendly Forest," Rabbi Friedman himself asked this question: "To what extent is evil (or any disease) an independent force, and to what extent are its destructive effects the result of immunological failure?"[2] Kay's insight has to do with how to stay focused on the immunological challenge and make that work for the whole. That is what leaders do. They are the immune system.

That is what this book is about: how leadership can act to strengthen the body to protect itself. It isn't about providing answers to problems so much as it is intended to stimulate thinking for facing problems and meeting challenges. It doesn't provide the game plan. It invites the reader into the experiences of the author in thinking through the game plan. Leadership, after all, is not in following a recipe for dealing with what has happened in the past. It is about thinking clearly for whatever might come along. Sooner or later, there will not be a recipe adequate to a new challenge. Leadership is about thinking at the highest level one can and having the fortitude to take risks and apply that thinking, sometimes against long odds. Leadership is about the ability to think as clearly and non-reactively as possible. That is what good leaders are called to do.

This is a book about leadership in that sense. I have greatly benefitted from the fact that Kay and I had the opportunity to do a lot of that thinking together over the eleven years we worked as colleagues, and I am extremely pleased that Kay has the talent to share some of that thinking with the rest of the church.

The things this book describes are, as so many discoveries are, to some extent a matter of serendipity. In this case the serendipity has to do with the coming together of a number of factors. One of them was that, after a number of years with little turnover among clergy in the diocese, all at once we had a significant number of openings due to planned retirements and the normal rate of priests moving on to take new positions. It presented an unprecedented learning laboratory.

---

2. *Friedman's Fables: Discussion Questions* (New York, Guilford Press, 1990), 6.

Another aspect of the serendipity we experienced together had to do with the realization that our congregations were more alike than might first be imagined, despite what appeared to be important differences of location, economics, and demographics. Big churches are not really all that different from small churches. Categories like that are more excuses for not doing the necessary thinking than aids to it. Family-size congregations are not really all that different from pastoral size ones, pastoral size from program size, and corporate size from all the others because all of them, after all, are made up of human beings. Black congregations are, in many important respects, not all that different from white congregations, rural congregations from urban congregations, or as was the case in our diocese, Appalachian congregations from Blue Grass congregations. The key differential in congregational well-being is not any sociological factor or, for that matter, how wonderful the members are or are not. The key is, as we learned over and over, leadership. And it didn't really matter whether the leadership came from male clergy or female clergy, young clergy or old clergy, experienced clergy or novice clergy, and perhaps most heretical of all, whether it came from clergy or from laypeople. What matters is that it had to come from somewhere.

We realized that in some cases we were facing an endless revolving door. If that was ever going to change, we needed to bring some new thinking to the equation. Again, heresy entered the thought process. It turns out that the most demanding leadership challenges sometimes suggest allocating the best leadership resources in others than the most financially well-resourced congregations. The difficulty is that the free-market system of clergy placement makes this difficult. New thinking was necessary. It turns out that leadership for a short period of time is better than having the Sunday Eucharist covered for a long period of time. More heresy. It turns out that inexperienced-with-imagination is better than experienced-and-tired. Still more heresy. Long tenure was not the answer. Leadership was. Heresy upon heresy.

Some of the serendipity had to do with realizing that many of our congregations faced the same kinds of challenges—and that those challenges had to be reframed from problems to opportunities if those congregations were to be successful. Congregations had to, and it turns out they can, be taught to focus on giving their best gifts away to others. And when they are retaught to give rather than hoard, they are much more likely to thrive.

In some cases, we realized that until certain underlying issues from the past were addressed, it would be impossible to make progress. In a number of cases, we realized that paying attention to interim ministry was at least as important, and sometimes more important, than the eventual "permanent" call. Of course, we also realized that permanent was an unhelpful myth in and of itself. In all cases, what I realized is that setting Kay free to do what she was so good at doing, developing leadership resources, was the best thing my office could possibly do. And it paid off in big ways for our diocese.

Now Kay has done the work necessary to share what we learned with the rest of the church. It is a pleasure for me to commend that work, and her, to others. What you will find here is not a "one-size-fits-all" approach or pronouncements from the expert of the day. What you will find here is not necessarily even reasonableness, which may be the greatest heresy in church life of all, for as Rabbi Friedman said about the Friendly Forest, "an unreasonable faith in reasonableness is a condition that makes terrorism possible."[3] What you will find is an invitation to do your own work, and resources on which to draw to enhance it, to cage the bloody tigers in your congregational and diocesan life. Maybe even in your own. And that is something much more valuable. And interesting.

The Rt. Rev. Stacy F. Sauls
December 2012

---

3. *SF Sauls notes from studies with Ed Friedman from 1990–96.*

Acknowledgments

- To the Rev. Dr. W. Robert Insko and the Rev. William Yon, who brought leadership training to the Diocese of Lexington and taught me that knowing myself and "drawing back the curtain" to reflect on experience are major components of all learning. And to the Rev. Dr. Joel P. Henning who lived it all with us—all are with me still.

- To Dr. Pearl Rutledge, the Gestalt Training Center of Central Kentucky, and countless hours in airports, restaurants, workshops, and friendship over the years as we continue the "outrageous adventure" of leadership development.

- To the Rt. Rev. Stacy F. Sauls, Sixth Bishop of the Diocese of Lexington, who modeled extraordinary differentiated leadership and offered me the incredible learning laboratory of the Diocese of Lexington.

- To the Diocesan Leadership Team, who "get it" and give countless hours helping others "get it."

- To Benjamin "Bungee" Bynum, who is taking leadership development to the next level in his personal journey, recognizing his ministry and pursuing the training to continue the work for future generations.

- To the nominating committees and convenors of the Diocese of Lexington 2010–2012, who did it right, and got the results.

- To the Rev'ds LaRae Rutenbar, Ron Pogue, Joan Pritcher, Nicolette Papanek, Joe Pennington, Phillip Haug, Larry Minter, and David Perkins, deans and rectors in the interim who led with integrity and skill.

- To the Rev'ds Laurie Brock, Amy Dafler Meaux, Carol Wade, Philip Linder, Jeffrey Queen, Jessee Neat, Christina Brannock-Wanter, Elise Johnstone, Peter D'Angio, Brian Cole, T. J. Azar, and Paul Brannock-Wanter—the faces on the Transition office door come to life in life-giving ways.

- To Canon Sam McDonald, the Rev. Richard Burden, and the Network for Pastoral Leadership and Sustaining Healthy Congregations—Richard Burden, Bruce Swinehart, Tim Fleck, Cindy Duffus, Janey Wilson, Chris Arnold, Coke McClure, Peter Doddema, Dominic Moore, Joe Mitchell, and Marshall Jolly, who live it all out every day.

- To my colleagues at Mission House and in our diocesan outposts at the Cathedral Domain, St. Agnes House and Barnes Mountain, who put up with reams of newsprint, smelly magic markers, and more—Bryant Kibler, Holli Powell, Ellen Darnall, Allison Asay Duvall, Cindy Sigmon, Andy Sigmon, and Susan McDonald.

- To the Rt. Rev. Chilton Knudsen, Interim Assisting Bishop, for adding her own exemplary leadership.

- To the Rt. Rev. Doug Hahn, Seventh Bishop of Lexington, for joining his experience and wisdom to the journey.

- To Jackie Henkelman-Bahn, Roy Oswald, David Sawyer, and the Center for Emotional Intelligence and Human Interaction.

- To Bob Gallagher, Ann Holtz, and trainers of the Leadership Training Institute of the Episcopal Church.

- To the Mid-Atlantic Association for Training and Consulting, trainers, and participants who spoke in tongues I understood and offered hope over many years.

- To Morton Kelsey, Esalen Institute and the Hero's Journey; Irving and Miriam Polster; Dr. Arthur Traub, the Association for Psychological Type.

- To Roy Persons, PhD and colleagues of The Union Institute, who validated the dream and provided years of unprecedented growth and learning.

- To Solo Flight staff and communities—at Christ Church Cathedral, Lexington, Kanuga and Roslyn—Whitty, Bruce, Corky, Skip, David, Jan, Michele, Laurie, Tom, Joe, and more . . . and all solo flyers over the years who have played a major role in my spiritual journey

- To the other rich "learning laboratories" in which I have been privileged to work, and the colleagues with whom and from whom I have learned and grown: Suzuki Talent Education, University of Kentucky Circles of Power Women's Leadership Initiative, Morehead State University Leadership initiatives, the Blanton Collier Sportsmanship Group, the Kentucky Pro Football Hall of Fame, and to decades of small group participants.

- To all those bishops, priests, transition officers, communicators, lay leaders, and others in the Episcopal Church system, and leaders in academic, athletic, and corporate systems who were part of important conversations that resulted in this book.

- To Heike and Irwin Pickett and the Homestead in Fish Creek, Wisconsin for precious writing sanctuaries; to my sister Jane Collier Hansen for assisting in the process of securing permissions and providing meals and companionship on the journey; to my family for constant support and love; my incredibly understanding husband and creative life partner Raymond, to my daughters Diane and Laura, and my amazing grandchildren Virginia, Drew, and MaryChun, that we pass on a better church and world to them.

- To my readers, who offered invaluable perspectives on this work at various stages: Kenton Ball, Benjamin Bynum, David Codell, Jane Fitzpatrick, The Rev. Deacon Mary Kilborn-Huey, Ned Meekins, Dr. David Sawyer, The Rev. Bruce Swinehart, Tracey Werner-Wilson, and Mary T. Yeiser.

- To Nancy Bryan, my gifted and amazing editor at Church Publishing, who "got it," got me, and whose talent for insuring that an author's authentic voice is heard is a treasure.

- To "my people"—the ongoing supportive community of fellow travelers with whom I journey and for whom I am continually grateful . . . Pearl, Jane, Whitty, Carolyn, Jane, MaryLouise, Chris, Ann.

As storyteller, counselor, and trainer, my reflective process is joined by the qualitative research methodologies of phenomenology and heuristics. Names of churches and individuals represent no specific individual; rather, they utilize the phenomenological approach of "clustering" to represent characters who embody the characteristics revealed in numerous situations. Did the situations really happen? You bet, and lest anyone feel their terminal uniqueness, that they alone have the lock on a particular situation—know that the behaviors represented in vignettes are themselves patterns within our church that await our attention and correction. An appearance in this manuscript indicates that a version of this story has been told by several individuals, speaking from different parts of the church and the country.

As this manuscript moves forward in the publication process, I am aware of the conversations that *could* have been, had time allowed. I am grateful for the chain of conversations, as one connection moved organically to the next. It is my hope that many more conversations will join those reflected in this book, adding their voices across our church, and those of other people and organizations who are interested in transformative leadership. While the language of this book was born in the system of the Episcopal Church, the theories and practices of transformative leadership belong to all who would claim them.

Gratefully, and with hope—
Kay

Introduction

Sometimes the clarion call comes over bacon and eggs.

The setting was rather ordinary—a small restaurant in the Chevy Chase neighborhood in Lexington, Kentucky, where granddaughter Virginia and I were having an early dinner, sandwiched between her play rehearsal and an evening dance lesson. It was catch-up time over her favorite bacon-and-eggs kind of meal, as she had just returned from an international youth leadership event for rising high school juniors held in Chicago. An interesting meal was a sure thing—time with my eldest grandchild and the opportunity to hear what was being offered to high schoolers today as "leadership development."

"Tell me . . ." opened a door on much more. We stopped long enough to place our orders. By the time the waitress returned with our meals, we might physically have been sitting in the booth at Josie's, but Virginia was mentally and emotionally in a small group in Illinois and I was traveling with her. A nibble of bacon and there was more, the words spilling out, wrapped in the transformation that had taken place since I had seen her just ten days before. The eggs were turning cold by the time she stopped to take a breath.

"I guess you had to be there to really understand," she said.

"I just was," I told her, smiling.

I could feel it in my bones as Virginia spoke. Four hundred young men and women from twenty countries had shared their cultures through music and art, had sung songs together, and listened to inspirational speakers tell of their life journeys—often through unbelievable odds. They had gone into sections of Chicago where visitors do not usually go and worked. They had reflected on their experiences in small groups. And they had physically built a wall—a huge wall on the stage of the auditorium, piled with "stones" of judgment, prejudice, fear—all of the things they carried with them at this stage of their lives that could fester as years passed. They had looked in the

1

face the things that divide and polarize. And then, together, they had physically torn that wall down; allowing their experiences of the "other"—the face-to-face encounters, the times of working together and playing together—to cut through all of the differences that might have separated them. Her eyes shone with the intensity of each experience as she related them.

Not only was I "there" in the sense of feeling myself tearing down the experiential wall of bias and prejudice with the teenagers on that Chicago stage, I was also "there" in a leap from Virginia's youth leadership experience to my own deep, internal knowing that the designers of this training had the courage not only to name the dysfunctional and destructive practices that limit human understanding and true progress, but to offer new ways to transform lives—year after year after year.

The experience accompanied me through the evening, as I dropped Virginia at her dance class, invaded my sleep, and woke with me the next morning. I knew that I was traveling with a very twenty-first century young woman as she described an experiential learning/reflective small group process. Her stories both transported me back to 1968 and my first experience in transformative leadership development, and powerfully linked the ongoing work in which I was involved into a call that was as clear as the face of the young woman who, at fifteen years of age, had embraced a mission to save as much of the world as she could possibly embrace.

The writer in me had toyed with the idea of putting the concepts of leadership development that undergird my work in church systems on paper, but the trainer in me always rebelled. After all, how could I take the experiential and make it live on paper in a way that compelled without limiting, that captured essence without becoming prescriptive? How would I write about transformation without crossing the line, labeling the hard work ahead without frightening?

With the memory of Virginia's face across that table, I knew that it was time. One of the "bibles" of my trade is *A Failure of Nerve: Leadership in the Age of the Quick Fix* by Edwin H. Friedman. In the introductory chapter, "The Problem with Leadership," Rabbi Friedman says:

> I believe there exists throughout America today a rampant sabotaging of leaders who try to stand tall amid the raging anxiety—storms of our time. It is a highly reactive atmosphere pervading all the institutions of our society—a regressive mood that contaminates the decision-making processes of government and corporations at the highest level, and on the local level seeps down into the deliberations of neighborhood, church, synagogue, hospital, library, and school boards. It is "something in the air" that affects the most ordinary family, no matter what its ethnic background. And its frustrating effect on leaders is the same no matter what their gender, race, or age.

It is my perception that this leadership-toxic climate runs the danger of squandering a natural resource far more vital to the continued evolution of our civilization than any part of the environment. We are polluting our own species. The more immediate threat to the regeneration, and perhaps even the survival of American civilization is internal, not external. It is our tendency to adapt to its immaturity. To come full circle, this kind of emotional climate can only be dissipated by clear, decisive, well-defined leadership. For whenever a "family" is driven by anxiety, what will also always be present is a failure of nerve among its leaders.[4]

Virginia restored this leader's nerve. She had just begun a marvelous, outrageous adventure that had already changed her life. And as I watched and listened, I knew that those of us who work with these same concepts could no longer afford the luxury of having the Virginias of our time move into the adult world only to have their idealism, their creativity, their energy, their passion killed by *our* failure of nerve. The experience of transformative leadership is not a sentimental memoir, but an ever-evolving, integrative journey from where each of us began to where the Virginias of today (and the systems of today) are, and where they might go in the future—if we step up to the plate and name what we know.

It is one thing to be with others on a leadership journey experiencing theories come to life and become foundational in decision making, recognizing in the moment why no "prescription" for how to lead prepares one to turn on a dime, knowing by "prepared instinct" what must be done next. It is another to set down the steps that have gotten at least this one person there.

Like Virginia, my life changed forever in a week-long residential training. I have known for half a century how to replicate that experience, to train others in such a setting. And, I have been hounded by the title of a little book, *How to Survive in Suburbia When My Heart Is in the Himalayas*.[5] Anyone can survive and thrive in the Himalayas, when "being" is all there is to do. The trick is how to bring it down from the mountaintop, to survive in the middle of suburbia, in the check-out line, the traffic, the office, etc.

The problem is, there are fewer and fewer folks able to get to the metaphorical Himalayas—be they a retreat center ten miles away or a corporate conference center a thousand miles away. For some, it's the five days that are impossible. For others, the dollars or the distance. Time, dollars, distance, and lack of intention combine for an excuse to continue being the

---

4. Edwin H. Friedman, *A Failure of Nerve: Leadership in the Age of the Quick Fix* (New York: Seabury, 1999, 2007), 2.

5. This small paperback book from the late 1960s or early 1970s is currently not listed in any online or out-of-print resources, but has continued to resonate in the author's mind over the decades since it was read.

way we've always been in any system—and in our more hopeful moments, wishing there was a way to change things.

Since the early 1970s, I have worked in the field of "training" within the Episcopal Church, and in corporate and educational systems. Some might refer to this work as "consulting." To me, the difference is this: "Training," in the sense that I use the word here, is based on foundational coursework in applied behavioral science, originating from the work of Kurt Lewin,[6] and returns to the core ingredients in its practices, continually adding the best of other complementary theories, such as Appreciative Inquiry, Emotional Intelligence, Typology, and Family Systems, to its resources.

Critical to understanding the chapters ahead is this tenet: Proven theories, not prescriptions, lead to sound practices within a system. It is the incorporation of sound theories of leadership development, practiced and internalized in the DNA, that allow the healthy practices that promote relationships and creativity, and free the people of God for mission and ministry.

In the first decade of the new millennium, while serving on the staff of the Episcopal Diocese of Lexington (Kentucky) under the Rt. Rev. Stacy F. Sauls, I was asked to utilize these methodologies in strengthening existing diocesan leadership and in situations of conflict resolution. As the work evolved, Bishop Sauls saw an opportunity for the work of leadership development for laity and clergy and the re-structuring of the process for transition ministries (previously known as "deployment") to lead to healthy behaviors across the system.

In retrospect, it is clear that an unusual set of circumstances, including mandatory retirements and the election of a local priest as bishop in another diocese, had led to the "normal" turnover of five to six clergy per year being more than doubled. Thirteen back-to-back transition processes in congregations ranging in size from pastoral (50–150 average Sunday attendance) to corporate (401-plus average Sunday attendance) provided a research laboratory that might never have been recognized had time and space separated these transitions. The back-to-back processes revealed patterns that were consistent regardless of the size of congregations. Early on, Bishop Sauls and I listed what we believed to be essential ingredients of a transition process in the Episcopal Church, and what rationale was behind the normative practices regarding those essentials. Our list included a column for "Lived Experience" and a column for "Alternative Recom-

---

6. Lewin was a modern pioneer of Organizational and Applied Psychology, and influenced Fritz Perls and Abraham Maslow. Major works: *The Complete Social Scientist: A Dynamic Theory of Personality*, 1999; *Resolving Social Conflicts*, 1978; and *Field Theory and Social Service*, 1964.

mendations/Practices," when the lived experience differed from the original rationale.

We realized that the work of transition touched every part of the system in some way—pointing out the truly integrative nature of the system, and the need for all parts of the system to be as connected in understandings of leadership and behaviors as in liturgy and mission.

In truth, the work of transition touches all of us today—both in the church and in our larger lives and the culture. The larger story is of the leadership challenge for a time of perpetual change, when all of our organizational cultures must be based on the expectation of change, not on improving last year's model or re-using methods that have worked before.

Effective leadership may begin with an individual who is a self-differentiated leader,[7] but building healthy leadership and sustaining it requires intention and a common vision, vocabulary, and practice throughout the system. It requires utilizing the energy within the system in creative engagement with those who have the greatest potential to strengthen the system at every level, rather than expending toxic or negative energy on those who consciously or unconsciously sabotage. One of the most important things a self-differentiated leader can do, both for his/her own sanity and effectiveness in the system, is strengthen the leadership at all levels. Above all, being a self-differentiated and effective leader requires having the courage—the nerve—to be *prepared to **recognize and name** dysfunctional and destructive behaviors that limit a system and to know possible alternative behaviors,* all the while remaining connected to the people. Strengthening leadership at all levels is one of the important ways of staying connected. Mature people need to be connected to other mature people. The importance of maturity is difficult to exaggerate. Immaturity sees self-differentiation as controlling, tyrannical, and selfish. We are too often governed by the perceptions of the immature.

In far too many systems, leaders are appointed, called, or promoted to managerial or supervisory positions because they:

a. have performed well in their current area, but have no special training or skills with human relations;

b. know a particular *content* well, but have no knowledge of or experience with *process*;

c. have longevity, wealth, "connections," or other kinds of environmental power;

---

7. "Self-differentiated leader" is a term that will be used throughout this book to describe an individual who is possessed of particular attributes; see glossary, page 159.

d. appear to be the 'quick-fix' answer to a current need (or antithesis to the last leader);

e. are "sweet . . . and say they love Jesus, so we slap a collar on them";

f. allow the group to *avoid* conflict by taking responsibility for someone else's feelings (e.g., asking unhappy parishioners to run for vestry or serve on the nominating committee).

From academia to religion to corporate America, this kind of unprepared leadership struggles mightily and often fails, due to lack of understanding of themselves, others, and the basic concepts of human systems, group development and dynamics, and conflict resolution. From academia to religion to corporate America, we accept dysfunctional behavior which thwarts progress, failing to pull back the curtain and reflect on the repetition of patterns that continue, as Friedman would say, "generation to generation." Such failure is a moment of truth for leaders: do they trust their own nerve or not?

The good news is that the outrageous adventure is transportable from the Himalayas to everyday life. And the skills themselves are transferable from church bodies to offices, homes, and families. Every hour of time, every bit of emotional and spiritual energy, every dollar invested in leadership development is an investment in people and structure which may be difficult to quantify, but pays huge dividends for today and tomorrow.

Virginia was inspired and challenged by her leadership development experience in the Hugh O'Brian Youth Leadership (HOBY) program to found a 501(c)(3) the summer she was 15. *heARTS* 4ARTS (www.heARTS4ARTS .org) is an organization that brings art supplies and supplemental programs to schools that have had budget cuts for the arts, or little funding for the arts, in Kentucky and across the world. Two years into the program, there are *heARTS* "ambassadors" in numerous states from New York to California, and project leaders in many more. Contributions have been made to schools and orphanages as far away as Mexico, South Africa, Haiti, and Guatemala. Virginia was named Young Philanthropist of the Year by the local chapter of fundraising professionals. One of her HOBY counselors, a teacher from Ohio, traveled to Lexington to be present for the award ceremony.

"Gamma has the HOBY bug," Virginia informed Eric, as we chatted after the ceremony. "As one who has spent much of her life in leadership development of some kind, I am excited about what HOBY is doing," I said to the young man. "What keeps you involved?"

"I'm a teacher," he said, "and this is teaching at its very best, as far as I'm concerned. It's a grand adventure every time. I still believe that it's possible to make the kind of contributions that can change the world—and it's incredible to be a part of seeing young people catch that idea, year after year. And besides—it's FUN!"

I knew there could be much more to say, but Eric had managed to capture it all. I'd still like to know more about HOBY, and how a young Hugh O'Brian went from being inspired by Albert Schweitzer to transforming young lives in seventy countries, not simply to capture some of that inspiration for the work in my own part of the world, but to help point us toward a larger vision for healthy human relationships. I do know that Virginia returns to HOBY to participate each summer, moving from assisting roles to greater leadership roles. I have watched how HOBY wisdom drives her life—from her spontaneous "tell me something good that has happened to you today" (whether to a Nigerian cab driver late one night in New York City or to her little brother at home) to her ability to step back in the face of disappointment in some significant adult leadership in her own life, reflect on the experience, and learn from it. I do know that teaching is a major component of leadership development, and when done well, it is challenging. It can be tough. It is energizing. It is an outrageous adventure. And it can be fun.

HOBY, and other youth-oriented programs, are changing lives. They are sure of their purpose and have developed strategies consistent with that purpose. They are *identifying, naming,* and *taking action* regarding hate crimes, bullying, and violence, both passive and aggressive. And we, in the adult world, have not only fallen short of being sure of our purpose, but have failed to recognize and name these same tendencies, which destroy relationships, render vision and creativity meaningless, and cripple productive action in systems from the Church to academia to athletics to corporate America. Whether stymied by institutional blindness, pseudo-politeness, cultural acceptance, or ignorance, we blunder on, wishfully expecting that with the next project or the next council or the next leader, things will change.

In my day-to-day life in the system of the church, and as a consultant in other systems, I *know.* There are many emperors who wear no clothes, and we adults refuse to look, while a child—or a newcomer who knows not where the family secrets and sacred cows are buried—fearlessly says, "The emperor doesn't have on any clothes!" Bullies abound in the board rooms and pews as they do in classrooms and on playgrounds.

Perhaps we have been too polite in this system of ours, our ideals and expectations too high, our fear of greater conflict and loss holding back the life-changing honesty that lives within us, too often unexpressed. This is not a polite book. Neither the church nor I have time for tip-toeing around the issues that limit. As Rabbi Friedman would say, "When you feel like you're walking on eggshells—stomp!" I suspect that those who read this book will recognize characters and situations from their own life in the church, as well as the impact of behaviors—beginning with their own—in their own part of the system.

While speaking to a class in Leadership Development at the University of Kentucky recently, I was asked how I, as a leadership consultant, thought people and situations differ in religious, academic, athletic, not-for-profit, and for-profit systems. "Each system is made up of human beings," I responded. "The rules of the system may differ, but human behaviors are remarkably consistent, regardless of the system." Thus, while the primary audience and examples come out of the system of the Episcopal Church, leaders in all systems will recognize behaviors and resulting situations and possible approaches to improving the health and well-being of the system in order to focus on its mission.

I have chosen the model of phenomenological and heuristic research for this book—qualitative research models that validate the narrative of lived experience, both those of interviewees (phenomenological) and those of the author (heuristic), while following systematic exploration protocols. In these qualitative research models, the key narrative points made by the bishops, priests, deacons, and lay professionals interviewed over a six-month period, June–November 2012, were clustered without personal identification to discover themes and create depictions representing related individual experiences. Direct quotes come from individuals as spoken, but without identification, as they are of significance not because of the individual who spoke the words, but because they are representative of themes whose priority to report is indicated by repetitions of qualities in numerous narratives. Thus, it may be possible for a reader to believe he/she recognizes a particular location or person, while its usage in the book indicates that variations on this event have occurred numerous times, primarily in Episcopal parishes and dioceses, and been incorporated into an example known as a phenomenological depiction. It is of interest to this writer, however, that informal conversations that have taken place since the completion of this manuscript with individuals from other religious, academic, non-profit, and for-profit systems reveal additional narratives that would have easily enhanced each cluster and depiction! While the mission of each system may differ, each system is composed of human beings whose behaviors are unfailingly consistent, regardless of the context!

There are four basic rules in this research model to optimize the chance for discovery which can be tested for validity, reliability, and findings:

1. The research person must be open to new concepts and willing to change his/her preconceptions if the data are not in agreement with them.

2. The topic of research is preliminary and may change during the research process.

3. Data should be collected under the paradigm of structural variation of perspectives to avoid one-sidedness.

4. The analysis is directed toward the discovery of similarities.[8]

The mandate for honesty with self and others is deeply imbedded in our faith: In the General Confession, Rite II, we acknowledge that we have not been all that we are called to be both in what "we have done and left undone" (BCP, p. 360). Perhaps the words of the 1928 Book of Common Prayer would call us to more honest reflection: "we have erred and strayed from thy ways like lost sheep" (BCP 1928, p. 30). The mandate for honesty within the community was given us in Matthew 18:15–17:

> "If another member of the church sins against you, go and point out the fault when the two of you are alone. If the member listens to you, you have regained that one. But if you are not listened to, take one or two others along with you, so that every word may be confirmed by the evidence of two or three witnesses. If the member refuses to listen to them, tell it to the church, and if the offender refuses to listen to them, let such a one be to you as a Gentile and a tax collector."

Always, always our goal is to stay in relationship and work toward reconciliation and transformation without being held hostage. For those raised on "Gentle Jesus, meek and mild," it may be a radical departure from their understanding of what it means to be Christian. Staying in relationship has meant, to most, no confrontation. When we truly engage the scriptures, Jesus offers a further model.

In John 18, Jesus does not back down from confrontation with Pilate as to whether or not he is King of the Jews. He stays in dialogue. He hangs in there. He is direct, strong, holding to his position, without screaming or yelling. This is the Jesus who will walk with us as we learn together

---

8. I am grateful to the process of qualitative research which encouraged my original idea for writing about transition ministries to evolve to a larger research question. I am grateful to those individuals across the country who entrusted their stories and varying perspectives to this process, and to the process of phenomenology and heuristics which allow the discovery of similarities and give intellectual and academic credence to the systematic examination of lived experience as supporting and greatly elucidating quantitative data and personal opinion.

what it means to call our communities to behaviors that move us toward a Kingdom life.

We have gateway opportunities in our systems in a time of reformation. No more "failure of nerve." It's time to stand up and be counted. To model, teach, and expect the ways that human beings who were created as unique individuals with unique and differing life experiences and perspectives can live and work together as normative practice at every level of our system. Then, and only then, can we truly be the counter-cultural and transformative church that we were called to be.

Let us begin.

Kay Collier McLaughlin

CHAPTER ONE

Parading Pachyderms— Or Naming and the Truth about Christian Behavior

Honesty is the
first chapter of the
book of wisdom.

THOMAS JEFFERSON

The finalists in St. Christopher's search for a new rector were due in town in two days. The church, grounds, and parish house were in readiness; the staff and Nominating Committee busy with last-minute preparations for hospitality and transportation. The monthly vestry meeting was underway.

"We have an issue here," Joe, the senior warden, began. "A member of the Nominating Committee is not eligible to serve—he is not a regular giver—so this is an invalid process."

A stunned silence held the group for a few seconds. Then a young woman rose. Facing the warden, she spoke firmly, with an energy that filled the room. "You," she said clearly, "do not get to sabotage this process."

It was not an unfamiliar scene to those gathered around the table. Some might call the senior warden "outspoken." Others might call him "controlling." Both remarks would take place in private conversation *about* the individual. And about his father before him. Then someone would say, "But he's a really good man." "He means well." "He loves this church." "He's a big giver." "Oh, that's just Joe." And with a sigh, "He's only got another year and a half to go on the vestry. . . ."

The words linger, unspoken. We can survive this behavior. Who knows what might happen if we confront it?

But tonight, the firm voice names it. Sabotage. With the goal in sight, the process is declared invalid. Thoughts raced through the minds of the men and women seated around the table. How would the congregation survive if such a thing happened? What would the candidates think? Would the parish have to start over? What about the member being accused? What could possibly be the senior warden's intent in bringing this up? Why had he gone to the trouble to explore this possibility?

Across the table, a long-time member stood in support. He had sat through this kind of thing from both the current senior warden and his father before, and had often groaned inwardly . . . "One more time. When is it going to stop?" . . . but never challenged the behavior. "That's just Joe. The way Joe is. No telling what he'll do if someone tries to stop him. He probably won't do anything—just needs to know that he's still in charge here." But not this time. The card has been laid on the table.

SABOTAGE: A deliberate action aimed at stopping, obstructing, disrupting, or destroying a course of action.

It's a strong word. But there you have the unvarnished truth.

"Joe, you don't get to do this. We're in a good place, and we're moving on. You can go with us, or not. But you're not ruining this process."

It was the beginning of a new day and a new way for St. Christopher's.

Unfortunately, Joe and the vestry of St. Christopher's exist in far too many places. And those who are weary of their behavior—although they may not have named the impact on their life and the mission and ministry of their church—struggle on, laboring under the myth that, as Christians, they must simply accept this and other destructive behaviors, because "it's the Christian thing to do."

Human beings behave as human beings have learned to behave in the families in which they grow up. Each of us inherits behaviors from our families of origin, as surely as we inherit physical characteristics. Our behaviors are reflexive, for the most part—we are simply not aware of them, much less how they impact others.

Naming the truth is not about hitting people over the head, without regard for the bigger picture or the possibility of raising greater anxiety. Naming the truth requires an awareness of the total situation, the patterns of the organization, and, always, a nuanced understanding of what is worth fighting for, and when. Sometimes getting the cards on the table for everyone to see is enough, and the group itself will do the assessment and monitoring. At other times, it is important for leaders to take charge of the effort, starting now (though yesterday would have been better).

One of the most important things we can do as we look at the issue of honesty in our faith communities is to turn to scripture. For many people, any experience they have had of naming the truth has meant engaging in unpleasant confrontation, conflict, and loss of relationship. In scripture, we read many examples of Jesus speaking the truth boldly, clearly, strongly—

modeling the way to speak the truth *and* to remain in relationship, even pointing us to what being in relationship really means.

In John 18:33–37, Jesus is in dialogue with Pilate, who has asked if he is King of the Jews. At no time does Jesus back down from the truth. Indeed, he stresses that "I came into the world, to testify to the truth." In Matthew 16:23, Jesus speaks strongly to Peter saying, "Get behind me, Satan," making clear that in this situation he was experiencing Peter as an adversary, a stumbling block. And in Matthew, Mark, and Luke, Jesus is confrontational with the money-changers in the temple, stating that they have made his Father's house a "den of thieves," In Matthew 18:15–16, Jesus states quite clearly, "If another member of the church sins against you, go and point out the fault when the two of you are alone. If the member listens to you, you have regained that one. But if you are not listened to, take one or two others along with you, so that every word may be confirmed by the evidence of the two or three witnesses."

In scripture we are not only provided models for truth-telling, but a mandate. There are many individual and collective reasons that both the model and the mandate are difficult for us—reasons that we will consider in this chapter. It is important to frame the considerations with the reminder that truth-telling is what we have been called to do.

In the Diocese of Lexington, an important part of the training of vestries and nominating committees in preparation for the call of a new rector is dealing honestly with the history of the parish, discerning patterns, and processing them. A newsprint timeline invites the participation of all members at the first Holy Conversation or interactive data-gathering session: When did they come? What was happening in the culture? In the church? In their lives?

During the Formation Retreat that the diocese holds for its parish nominating committees, there is a session entitled "Ghosties and Ghoulies and Long-Legged Beasties, and Things That Go Bump in the Night." It is the time to deal with "family secrets"—to get all of the cards on the table.

Too many transition officers, nominating committees, and vestries have been caught off-guard by the presentation of people with the wrong set of skills or presenting persona *because a family secret of alcoholism, pedophilia, sexual misconduct, financial problems—the list goes on and on—has been carefully safeguarded by a few. The damage can be the same, even if the family secret is no longer consciously known by anyone.* The mismatch that results, the stumbling of rectors over issues that have been shoved under the rug, are a major part of what keeps the church distracted from mission and ministry. The issue is not limited to transitions, however. Behaviors that derail the ongoing life of the church are allowed to go ruthlessly on their unnamed and unchecked way, all in the name of "being Christian."

Naming requires, first of all, honesty with ourselves. Parker Palmer, writing in the introduction to *Leading from Within* says, "It is indeed cruel, and the root of all cruelty, to 'know what occurs but not recognize the fact.' Think about those moments when we refuse to know what we know—that someone close to us drinks too much, or that our personal lifestyle diminishes the life-chances of others, or that the corporation's accounting is as crooked as a corkscrew, or that war always breeds more war. To know such a thing, and yet refuse to credit what we know, let alone act on it—that is surely a root cause of cruelty, one that leaders best understand."[9]

Palmer references a poem by William Stafford, who offers a description of elephants on parade. It is an image that is immediately recognizable to anyone who has ever seen the mammoth beasts and their babies parading around a big top or down main street, linked trunk to tail—following each other wherever the elephant who happens to be in front might be headed—whether or not he knows the way, is completely off course, has convinced everyone else his way is the right way—or as the poem says, "the parade of our mutual life might get lost in the dark." For Palmer, that image is a reminder "how easy it is, once we have fooled ourselves, to try to fool each other," leading others sadly off course. If we do not understand the imagery, Palmer says, "in this disastrous opening decade of the twenty-first century, the darkness around us is even deeper than William Stafford imagined."[10] Truth, he concludes, is how we will find our way.

Truth is light. The truth will set us free. It is part of what we teach and say that we believe. And still we shy away from it.

Nothing is ever the same once we face what we know and have the courage to name it. Transformation cannot begin without honesty.

Looking at the story of St. Christopher's and Joe, the senior warden, it is important to note that the recognition and the naming were of *specific behaviors*. No one pointed a finger at Joe and said, "You are a bad person." No one said, "You did a terrible thing." An individual who recognized a behavior as destructive to the community and had a name for that behavior, put that behavior on the table where others could recognize it as well. It is not about personalities. It's about behaviors.

Throughout this book there will be examples of "naming" used to underscore other parts of the process of empowering leadership that can trans-

---

9. Parker Palmer, "Introduction," *Leading from Within: Poetry that Sustains the Courage to Lead*. Sam M. Intrator and Megan Scribner, eds. (San Francisco: Jossey-Bass, 2007), xxxiii.

10. William Stafford, "A Ritual to Read to Each Other," quoted in Palmer, "Introduction," *Leading from Within*, xxxii.

form our church. Each will open the door to people "knowing what they know." To give them permission to redefine what "Christian behavior" and "Christian response" are and are not.

If naming and honesty are so critical to our ability to be the most effective we can be, what prevents such honesty?

First, it is important to delineate between personal, individual honesty and corporate honesty. It takes both to bring health to a system. Both require reflective practice, which includes honest feedback, received without defense or denial. Both require intention, training in "how to," and practice. An individual who not only practices honesty, and is intentional about honesty as a way of living life, and for whom honesty is a core part of their being can feel personally and professionally conflicted when they find themselves in a system where the corporate norm is secrecy or lack of intention around honesty and naming.

What Prevents Honesty in the System?

It's Not Christian Behavior

Underlying all the other reasons for lack of honesty in the system is the concern that honesty itself, or, perhaps more accurately, the potential for confrontation when one is honest, are not "Christian behaviors." The phrase often used to point to inappropriate Christian response is that "if anyone strikes you on the right cheek, turn the other also" (Matthew 5:39), a quotation from the Sermon on the Mount. This phrase is often interpreted to be an indication that Christians must accept any behavior toward them, in the guise of "loving one another." Look away and ignore the behavior. Deeper exegesis of the passage shows that far from being "doormats," Jesus and his disciples were strong in their positions, and while advocating non-violence, "turn the other cheek" actually encourages subversive behavior. Jesus suggests a non-violent response, but not a passive one. Indeed, in that time and culture, the turning of the cheek could lead to further abuse. Without fighting back or responding submissively, Jesus and his followers will stand tall in the face of the abuse. Christian behavior does not mean accepting the unacceptable, the inappropriate, or the dysfunctional. It does mean learning to respond to those behaviors in a fair and appropriate way. Untangling ourselves from the images of "gentle Jesus, meek and mild" with which many Christians were raised, and delving into a deeper understanding of Christian behavior could well be a topic for another book.

Suffice it to say, as we begin to consider other reasons that honesty is not a priority in the church system, the fear that the behaviors connected with being honest might not fly with Jesus is foundational.

The Power of Habit; The Standard of Mediocrity

We have become accustomed to avoiding the truth in order to live with the standard of mediocrity, which the system rewards. Disconnecting behaviors in various parts of the system is one of the habits that allow us to avoid honesty. How might habitual shortfalls on diocesan assessments be connected with dioceses seeing themselves as too important or too busy to be a part of the larger church system? When the habit within the system is to allow certain people, places, or parts of a system to be "untouchable," the brokenness of the system can be denied and avoided.

Anyone who has ever tried to break a habit knows how difficult it can be to get out of the loop of old behaviors. If we don't make connections between the numerous types of unhealthy behavior that suck life out of the system, it is easier to rationalize that it's "only" this one small area where things might be awry. To break the habit of not seeing truth requires that we break the habits of avoidance or denial and give up the familiar reward of the same old mediocrity.

No Mechanism for Accountability in the System

Both lay and ordained leaders point to the fact that there is no mechanism or expectation for accountability on a church-wide, regional, or local level. "Mutual ministry reviews" would never pass muster in a successful business, say several bishops. Indeed, confusion over "business-like practices" and "ministry" seems to keep the church system in a quandary over how to operate what is, like it or not, a huge organization, involving the lives of thousands of people. We claim to be in the people business, and yet we have no mechanism for teaching, supporting, or sustaining the levels of social competency that are needed in both community and outreach We claim to follow a loving God and adhere to commandments that show respect in all relationships, while those who observe the behaviors of people who call themselves Christians from outside our sanctuaries are quick to point out that they see more respectful behaviors, more self- and other-awareness in secular systems. How would we know? We have no mechanism for evaluating or measuring effectiveness, except the numbers that reflect butts in the pews on a given Sunday, gains and losses in attendance and giving in a year. We have no mechanism for holding people accountable, for accomplishments at tasks or relationships. After all, someone always says, "It is the church." "You have no control over volunteers." "They mean well."

A System Designed to Serve a Time and Culture that No Longer Exist

Perhaps it's the biggest elephant in the room: the one we've been walking around at all levels of the church, while in more private pockets of our life, bishops, their clergy, and some lay leaders are saying it to each other in louder and louder voices. We've got to be honest about our struggle to make do with a system that was designed to serve a time and a culture that no longer exist. Once we were the settled church, the incumbents, if you will. A timeless institution with a fixed place in the universe and society. It is simply not true anymore. Technical fixes, or attempts to solve the problems we understand with solutions that we know, just won't work anymore. We're just beginning to face the terrifying truth. "We have evidence," says a bishop, "that things are just not working. We can't figure out why. We feel guilty; we feel like failures. We're not prepared to make adaptive changes (exploring issues we don't understand and don't have solutions for), so we bluster along, serving up helping after helping of baloney because we don't know what to do."

"The world has changed," says another, "and we've not adapted to it. Too many of us are boomers, and the experiences of our formative years are still directing us in what we should do. We resist the truth that the world around us is moving on, with or without us. That's not a threat. It's just the way it is."

Hard truths to name—and there they are.

Fear of Personal and Corporate Consequences

At every level of the church, both lay and ordained, fear came first. Fear of exposure. Fear of inadequacy. Fear of being hurt, and of being hurt again. Fear that drives the creation of a persona considered "acceptable." Fear, backed by the experience of consequences. Staff members or other lay leaders suddenly "not notified" of meetings after they have had the courage to express a minority or difficult opinion. Clergy who have experienced "the people voting with their purses and their feet." Ordained and lay leaders who have lost relationships with friends and family members or coveted social positions due to stands taken on controversial matters. Congregations who fear that the perfect priest they want to call is only interested in the "perfect" parish they've described in a glossy, Chamber of Commerce-type parish profile bearing little resemblance to reality.

Lack of Self-Awareness

Again and again, clergy and laity pointed to lack of individual and corporate self-awareness. Resistance to the self-reflection, openness to feedback, and increasing self-awareness that are foundational to all leadership exists at every level of any organization. It also exists for the community or institution itself. We are doing just fine, thank you. Everyone (within a certain zip code, country club, university alumni group, etc.) is happy with the way things are. It is navel-gazing to study ourselves. Let's get on with it!

At higher levels of power within any organization, leaders can begin to believe their own PR. After all, says one person, they have beat the competition in an election and achieved a level of power. There is propensity to be self-referential: the big "I AM." Asking for feedback requires first an awareness that one needs to know how one is being perceived, and second, an openness to hearing both the good and the not-so-good about oneself. The same is true of congregations.

Best Practices for Establishing a Norm of Self-Reflection and Feedback:

- Begin with groups that recognize the value of self-reflection and feedback, and practice them: Education for Ministry, divorce recovery, Alcoholics Anonymous. Invite those who are participants in these and other groups to gather for discussion on the value of these practices. Solicit their assistance in carrying the norm in an intentional way into other groups in which they participate. (Care must be taken, of course, with those who are members of AA or other twelve-step programs in order to honor their commitment to anonymity.)

- Build the norm into vestry and diocesan bodies over which bishop and rector preside.

- Practice, practice, practice!

Ego

Both clergy and laity identified inflated egos as detrimental to achieving a practice of honesty, either in speaking one's truth, or in hearing the truth from others. Charming, charismatic personalities, in particular, when combined with the perceived authority of ordination, are often able to push their agendas through the system on the power of that charisma, without questions being raised or honest thoughts expressed. Strong lay leaders who carry the aura of personal power and authority through wealth or position, especially those who are also gifted speakers with powers of persuasion, may fall in this category.

In several dioceses, these characteristics, combined with strategic work from a small group of outsiders, have led clergy to believe that they were going to be able to lead their congregations out of the Episcopal Church. The voices of dissenting laity, determined not to leave the church, have surprised clergy with their honesty and strength of resistance when the truth was finally on the table.

Economic Investment in the System

"I am a clergy person invested in the system in terms of my long-term economic well-being," said one priest. "As passionate as I am about honesty, every now and then I am reminded that I do have a stake in whether or not we maintain certain aspects of our communal life. I don't want to tear it all down; I want to build up a system that works."

This priest is not alone in "not biting the hand that feeds you." Numerous clergy expressed hesitation at speaking truth for fear of jeopardizing their families' security. It's a fear bound up in a combination of realities that might endanger a clergy position, including the knowledge that far too many "hire-fire" situations exist across the church, and a clergy pension system that ties compensation to "best years" of service. It is a complex reality—and one that makes it a difficult choice to speak the truth in certain situations.

"We have never dealt with understanding the role of money in our lives," said another priest. "It's different from talking about stewardship. We live out of a scarcity model, with a lack of vision. But it keeps us so afraid."

Accepted Norm of "Talking About" Rather than "Talking With"

Talking about someone rather than talking with him/her directly is so pervasive a pattern that it is generally accepted as normative behavior. Many people do not recognize that there is any problem with this behavior. Often when experiencing the "Behavior-Impact" exercise (Appendix M), individuals will recognize for the first time some of the effects this behavior has on others, and thus begin to identify both the behavior and its dysfunction. It is one of the most common behaviors in both church and culture—and requires lots of practice and support to establish a new norm.

Best Practices for Bringing a Norm of "Talking With"
Rather than "Talking About":

• Recognize fear factors involved

• Model "talking with"

Turn any opportunity for talking about someone into an opportunity to teach the practice of talking with: "I believe it would be helpful if you would talk to _____ about that." If the person is unwilling, and persists in trying to talk to you about the other person, try, "If you are not comfortable talking to them alone, I will be glad to go with you."

Lack of Training in How to Be Honest

"Bull in a china shop—that's what being honest means," Priscilla, a savvy leader, said in response to the question about what prevents honesty in the system. "I've learned to dodge the bullets when I hear someone say 'let me be honest with you.'"

"Feedback? Don't get me started!" said Joe, a priest for 17 years. "That's a signal that criticism is on the way—just a nicer name."

"I am grateful that I learned that honesty doesn't have to be brutal or impolite," said Fred. "I learned how to ask someone if they wanted feedback, and not to offer it too soon, or without an invitation or permission. I also learned that I could ask for feedback myself, and it is invaluable. It was hard to learn, but now it's second nature. 'When you said _____, I felt _____.' Without someone teaching me, I was totally unaware that if I was trying to get that across to someone, I would have started with 'You did _____,' which was really finger-pointing and immediately put someone else on the defensive, ending any possibility of dialogue. It could easily make someone feel shamed" (Appendix A).

"One of the things that has to get transmitted through training is that honesty from self-differentiated leadership holds two things in tension: being *separate from—seeing the emotional process at work and remaining separate from it—and staying connected to others.* It is a hard line to hold, and I can only do that when I am constantly aware that I, too, can be sucked into old and unhealthy behaviors, regardless of what I know in my head."

Training is essential if good practices of honesty are to be built.

Best Practices in Training for Honest Dialogue:

- Training lay and clergy leaders in the art of dialogue, and making them available to teach such practices as "I" messages and respectful listening to others

- Building a culture of "holy conversations," with trained facilitators who can assist a parish, organization, or individuals in having difficult conversations

- Making the expectation known in all levels of parish and diocesan life, and holding people to it

- Continuing training opportunities throughout the diocese which allow practice of honest conversation, modeling through guided holy conversations discussions of hurts and disappointments, so that individuals have an experience of talking through emotional issues without feeling a loss of control

Lack of Modeling from the Top

Across the church, there is a stated need for modeling honesty as a top priority. When such modeling takes place, it can be an expectation of others, becoming part of the cultural norm. When leaders need to be beloved, placating, rather than truth-telling, rules. A person who needs to be liked will tell each individual with whom he/she comes in contact what that particular person wants to hear, rather than the truth.

"If we are going to create safe spaces and encourage people to be honest, which implies a level of trust and vulnerability," says a priest, "leadership has to risk being vulnerable. When a leader is not willing to be a model of honesty, transparency, and vulnerability, there is a problem—a 'do what I say, not as I do,' or simply not valuing honesty enough to teach others its importance."

It's a bit of a dicey problem, with boundaries to be maintained, and clergy not expecting to get their emotional needs met in the parish. If one is aware, however, of the difference between *openness* and *personalness,* and teaches and models from this awareness, boundaries are maintained and relationships built and strengthened—a giant step toward honesty in the system.

In the participant handbook from the Center for Emotional Intelligence and Human Relations, Helene Oswald offers critical definitions to differentiate the two: OPENNESS, she says, is revealing how you perceive and react to the present situation, sharing what you are feeling, thinking, or wanting at that moment, and telling another person how his or her behavior is impacting you. PERSONALNESS is the revealing of intimate, personal details of your private life.

Oswald emphasizes that some people mistake being personal for being open, attempting to get emotionally close by making highly personal confessions about their lives. "Sharing information about one's past may lead to a temporary feeling of intimacy, but a relationship is built by disclosing your reactions to events you both experience, or to what the other person says or does. A person comes to know you, not through your past history, but through encountering you in what you do and say in the present."[11]

Openness requires a willingness for rejection—and also offers the potential for being recognized as authentic, for gaining respect, and for establishing a norm of integrity in relationship. Personalness is actually more about trying, perhaps desperately, to avoid rejection.

---

11. Helene Oswald, in *Participant Handbook, Emotional Intelligence and Human Relations Skill Training,* Center for Emotional Intelligence and Human Relations, October 2012.

22   **Becoming the Transformative Church**

›› ››

Best Practices for Establishing a Norm of Honesty:

- It can be difficult for adjudicatory heads to have a safe place to practice this behavior and obtain feedback. Organizations such as the Center for Emotional Intelligence and Human Relations offer sessions for adjudicatory heads that are interdenominational, offering peer participation and support where bishops and other leaders can feel safe to practice.

- Creating a norm of practice with trusted leadership. The good news is that from around the country, there are reports of living under the authority of a bishop where staff and clergy are given the latitude to be honest, to push back as needed. "She looks us in the eye and expects us to be honest," a priest stated, admiringly. "She not only encourages the norm, she models it, and is not going to allow elephants to sit in the middle of the room, even if everyone does not support her—yet."

- "Being honest is hard work," a deacon said. "Authentic relationships are hard work. It's easier to grin and bear and move on. But the culture change when we do the hard work is more than worth it."

Lack of a Safe Space and Environment to Tell the Truth

When training for being honest becomes an intentionally created norm, the next step is to create a safe space for speaking honestly, building toward an environment where that kind of space and process is expected and can be trusted.

Best Practices for Establishing a Safe Place and Environment for Telling the Truth:

- Build on the practice of Holy Conversation. When we gather to talk as a community, or a part of God's body, it is a sacred time, and the way we talk should reflect that. This doesn't mean being pious or sounding religious in what we say, using "stained glass voices" or staying in prayer, but in being civil and respectful in the way we speak and the way we listen, taking as many opportunities to speak to this practice as possible.

- Establish a norm of confidentiality around difficult issues—the conversation stays in the room.

While an official summary might be provided, "he said" and "she said" is not a part of that summary. Each individual has the right to take out of the room what they said; they do not have the right to take out of the room what anyone else said and report it elsewhere. This norm will allow people to feel more comfortable about being honest.

Sacred Cows

Every family and organization has them: those subjects that are absolutely taboo. Everyone is complicit. It's simply safer not to talk about dad's drinking problem, the affair between office colleagues, or the repeated bad rector calls in the cardinal parish. Then along comes a new set of eyes and ears, new eagerness to become involved, and not only are people walking across the graves, but intending to dig those bovines up and deal with them! The audacity!

The list of sacred cows gets especially long during transitions, as prospective candidates will ask questions. When the truth has not been faced within the congregation, the experience ranges from tension in interview sessions and the potential dismissal of a candidate who comes too close to the truth to congregational resistance, to engaging in honest data-gathering that could challenge those very cows.

Sacred cows might include: an individual who wields particular power and prestige in the congregation; the ministry or program that cannot be questioned; a particular part of the building, piece of art, or item of furnishing; the building itself; or an endowment and its use.

All too often, the "sacred cow" represents an attitude or practice that, to fresh eyes, is in direct opposition to stated values or purpose of the parish. A new rector enthusiastically joined her vestry in their stated goal of being a more welcoming and hospitable church. An additional goal was to invite and incorporate young families into the life of the congregation. The rector and vestry walked the large and beautiful facilities, and, noting that the coffee hour was located on a different level than the nave, the rector inquired about the possibility of moving it to the largest space on the sanctuary level—a light-filled reception room. There was an uncomfortable silence among the vestry members. One mumbled, "unsuitable." Another, "it just wouldn't work."

The rector decided to let the matter rest, and suggested they all spend time considering what they had just experienced on their tour and how the consideration of a new space for coffee hour fit with their goals and challenges. They could talk about it at the next meeting. In the meantime, she made a few inquiries about the reception space, discovering that it was considered "adult space," where children were not welcome as "little hands might damage the furnishings."

For the wise rector, the encounter with the "sacred cow" of the building led to a teachable moment about clarity in setting goals that were honest and consistent with each other and the parish's values, as well as with the gospel imperatives. "You just can't have it both ways," she said. "Welcoming and incorporating young families means little hands and little feet are welcome, too. And that fits Jesus' commandment to let the little children come to him."

Code of Silence

The code of silence is often around some person or incident where conflict, tragedy, or shame occurred, or a matter considered impolite or embarrassing or too difficult for public information or conversation.

There can be a code of silence around financial issues, such as endowments or special bequests. Over time, such a code of silence results in "family secrets," which take on a power of their own, particularly the power to repeat unrecognized and unaddressed patterns. Of course, we humans have a greater capacity for hearing the truth than we sometimes give ourselves credit for. It's the secrets that will do us in.

A code of silence often occurs around issues of alcohol in a congregation, whether it is clergy or staff who have problems with alcohol or a congregation where alcohol is a central part of its fellowship. A combination of financial issue and embarrassment, the matter of embezzlement can fall under the code of silence. At a dinner party, a discussion about embezzlement in a parish centered on whether or not the amount was "over $10,000." "If it was under $10,000," said a man, "it should just be handled discreetly, let the person go and move on. . . ."

Sexual issues fell under the code of silence until the Church Insurance Company and "Safeguarding God's Children" intervened.

Best Practices around "Sacred Cows" and "Codes of Silence":

- As safe environments for honesty are created and people are taught how to be honest, there will be a gradual shift to more openness around difficult issues. There will always be a need to gently but firmly introduce the norm, and to continue to practice it. This pattern does not change overnight, but gradually, through practice at every level of the system.

- Don't buy into the sacred cow or code of silence. Be the new eyes or ears that bring up the topic.

- There will always be a need for "safeguarding God's children"—and for "safe church" practices. All too often vestry members and adult volunteers do all in their power to avoid these trainings, which should remain mandatory, with or without stipulation from the Church Insurance Company. There are still predators and boundary violators out there. If we don't recognize it, we can't name or correct it!

- There will always be a need for creating transparent financial practices within a parish—and that includes the people in the pews taking the time and making the effort to read financial statements, ask questions, and insist upon answers.

- Every parish in every diocese, and every church-sponsored/owned entity, location, and function should be sure that the alcohol serving and consumption policy is clearly posted for all to see, clearly understood by everyone. Parish policies should be, at a minimum, as strong as the national policy.

Assumptions

An assumption is something we take for granted. Usually it is something we have learned early and do not question. It is often taken for granted that "since I know this particular thing, others must also know it." Assumptions are a part of our belief systems. We assume that what we believe is true, and then base our interpretation of the world and events around us on those assumptions. When we assume something to be true in a general sense, we often do not check it out factually, and therefore we both give and receive information that is based more on assumption than on fact. "I assumed you understood that this is how we do. . . ." "I assumed that you knew about the change in time of that meeting. . . ." "I assumed we were all in agreement, since no one said anything to the contrary." All are familiar phrases that prevent directness and honesty in any organization or system.

Lack of Clarity in Stating Expectations

Both laity and clergy point to a lack of clarity throughout the system. Lack of clarity about Episcopal polity and practices for members. Lack of clarity about Episcopal polity and practices on the part of those clergy not trained in Episcopal seminaries. Lack of clarity about the real life of ordained ministry. Lack of clarity about what is expected of a member of a congregation, a member of a vestry or other parish or diocesan body.

"We are so afraid of scaring people off that we fail to set out expectations up front," says a priest.

Some Emerging Best Practices for Setting Clear Expectations at All Levels of the System:

- When a person inquires about transferring membership or joining the parish, a letter is sent from the rector with a packet that includes a pledge card, information about the new member's orientation class, and guidelines about membership in good standing.

- Prior to standing as a candidate for election to the vestry, individuals must meet with the rector and wardens to talk about the vocation of vestry membership, and its duties and responsibilities, including regular attendance.

- When an interim rector begins his/her tenure, a letter from the bishop is read to the congregation, delineating the duties and responsibilities of the interim, and expressing support from the bishop's office. A signed covenantal agreement among the interim, the wardens, and the bishop supports this shared understanding.

- A "Hippocratic Oath" for clergy signed when a priest enters the diocese

- Congregational covenants with the clergy and bishop

- Behavioral covenants that guide all parish and diocesan groups and events

- Training in boundary setting and issues of safety and appropriate behavior should be a part of training for all persons in leadership, and be particularly emphasized with those working with youth.

- Shared parish goals framed by expectations of discipleship, outreach, and stewardship. These goals can also provide a check-in guide for each visit the bishop makes to that congregation.

Lack of Integrated Guidance for Parishes in Transition

Perhaps the resource most under-utilized in understanding lack of honesty on the corporate level is the set of experiences and insights of professional transition specialists, or rectors-in-the-interim. The majority of bishops and ordained persons are familiar with transition processes as a candidate on their own particular trajectory. They leave a cure prior to the activity of the transition period. Transition officers, while hopefully trained to guide such a process, bring a different perspective but are less likely to be on the scene. Trained interim specialists have walked with numerous congregations in transition periods, and offer a wealth of information about patterns consistent in parishes of all sizes and across dioceses.

Best Practices and Important Insights Regarding Integrated Guidance for Parishes in Transition:

- Integration among the roles of interim, vestry, nominating committee, consultant, and/or representative of bishop's office rather than "siloing" provides for a more natural flow of information and support. For example, the lack of resolution in the development tasks critical to the interim period will make themselves known within a nominating committee if that work has begun too soon. If wardens, nominating convenor, consultant, and interim are in regular communication about *process,* the matter can be dealt with efficiently and effectively, *in support of the work of both the interim period and the nominating com-*

mittee. If the groups are working in isolation, holding to an old norm, such issues can fester and be problematic in both areas (Appendix B).

- Expectation that the stated diocesan process will be followed, with firm guidance from a person trained to see that process is maintained. Issues that result from this lack of guidance begin with a rush to call without time for honesty in four major areas (Appendices C, C1, C2):
  - —Training and honest reflection on the part of the vestry in anticipation of the selection of the nominating committee (Appendices D, D1, D2)
  - —Honest reflection on parish patterns prior to data gathering (Appendix E)
  - —Honest in-depth process of data-gathering (Appendices F, G, H, I, J, J1)
  - —Honest analysis of data to develop a list of realistic and candid goals and challenges (Appendix K)

Corrective Measures in Several Dioceses Include:

- Clearly stated guidelines for the integrated work of the rector-in-the-interim, wardens and vestry, nominating committee, consultant, and bishop's representative. These include regular times for checking in based on an understanding of the developmental tasks of the interim period, clearly defined and understood roles, and clearly stated diocesan process

- Meeting with wardens, bishop, and transition officer to discuss transition options, including an honest disclosure of costs of processes and financial ability of the parish

- Vestry meetings at the beginning of the interim period at which the developmental tasks of the interim period and signs of resolution are discussed, followed by regular attention to the tasks and resolution until both vestry and rector-in-the-interim agree that they are at an appropriate level of resolution to request a meeting with the bishop

- Wardens and interim meet with the bishop and transition officer to go over resolution of tasks and state their readiness to begin the process of selection of search/nominating committee, under the guidance of a diocesan trained consultant, who holds them to that process

- Full-day training of vestry and search/nominating committee (see Appendix D) which includes honesty in team building, looking at patterns of past rectors and the story of parish, uncovering of family secrets, and training in a competency-based diocesan process

- Use of interactive data gathering and data analysis (see Appendix K) to achieve honest input from congregation and develop honest goals and challenges which are then approved by the vestry and bishop before publication. Questions to be answered: Do these goals and challenges reflect what was heard in the interactive Holy Conversations? Are they congruent with the stated mission of the parish? The gospel imperatives?

- The development of a "Living Portfolio," which shows current lived information about (Appendix G) what is actually taking place in the parish rather than a Chamber of Commerce–type glossy brochure

- The adoption of the rules and guidelines for an episcopal election in a diocese that are consistent with the process that has been used by parishes within the diocese, supplemented by necessary information and support from the national transition office

These steps enable parishes, and subsequently a diocese, to be more honest in all areas of their common life.

Profound Societal and Cultural Issues

"Even bigger than some of the things we've already talked about," said a bishop, "is the matter of profound societal and cultural issues. We've got more ways of communicating than ever before in our culture, and we are talking with each other less. People are marketing positions, not sharing with each other. There is simply not enough intimacy or trust to allow people to be real with each other, so we trot out the tried-and-true mechanism of the persona."

The cultural reality is that the ways in which people were formed in community have radically changed. No longer do children grow up working in their family and village, spending time together, in settings that allow conversations to develop and people to be known over many years. Parents, who were once the "experts" in developing values and attitude in their offspring, gradually sharing that influence with other adult mentors and peers as teen years approached, are now without the skill sets that are most respected by the emerging generation. Virtual interfaces are more important and involve more time than face-to-face encounters.

"My son is in college now—and he may be beginning to understand some of my skill sets," said one father. It would be easy to weep and wail about the changes and hold up the good old days, which simply leads to the kind of entrenchment we'd like to counteract. The bigger question is: how do we use this larger awareness and do something about it for this new time? "We have to step back and look at ourselves," say several bishops, suggesting that, in effect, we set ourselves up in the system to play into the problems identified, not to solve them. Most agree that the most vital and healthy parts of the church are experienced where there are small groups engaged in the "long, slow effort to build relationships and disciples."

"Jesus lavished his time on a group of twelve losers," says one. "Strategists would have told him to get in front of big crowds more often. But he knew better. He knew that the slow, relentless work together made it all possible; that kept them walking, kept them risking, even when they no longer had him physically present."

"Monastic communities were built on stability," a bishop stated, "and we are trying to lead our church with a norm of mobility. Short-term ministry is killing us. We make our clergy less skilled, and we decimate relationships, by putting people in three- to five-year situations throughout their careers, where they simply repeat the same bag of tricks over and over again—hoping that if it worked in one context it will work again—rather than the continuing development demanded in more stable situations."

And we wonder why we are not open and honest with each other?

The glimmer of hope may lie in the model a bishop referred to as "reverse Tootsie Roll—sticky on the outside and solid on the inside."

This model is based on small groups of deeply dedicated men and women who hold a solid core of faith, and from whom the church expects a great deal. They have "sticky edges," to which more peripheral seekers and attenders can "stick on," and begin a migration to the core, if provided with the resources and support for migration, which might be the work of the church, with a purpose of resurrection.

"On the inside of such a group is a kernel of faith that will not be rocked," the bishop said. "It may be assaulted, set on fire. But it retains a good sense of humor, an appreciation of the absurd, and, despite how ridiculous this whole enterprise might look to the world, is still having fun doing this thing called ministry."

Another bishop speaks: "It's fundamentally a spiritual issue, this honesty thing. We're all really committed to the vision we've been raised with, and have a hard time imagining church any other way. We're afraid of change— and if we are honest, we're going to have to not only begin to imagine a new thing, but to actually change. Because we have such a limited vision, and can't imagine what would happen if we move out of our sanctuaries and settled parishes, we limit God's vision, and can't trust that God has something in mind. We don't really believe that God does. If we can't imagine it—how can God? We're afraid to step out, because we don't trust that God will meet us when we do."

Fundamentally a spiritual issue.

A spiritual journey.

A hopeful journey for a changed time in a post-Christian wilderness.

30   **Becoming the Transformative Church**

$\gg \gg \gg \gg \gg \gg \gg \gg \gg \gg \gg \gg \gg \gg \gg \gg \gg \gg \gg \gg \gg \gg \gg \gg \gg \gg \gg \gg \gg \gg \gg \gg \gg \gg \gg \gg \gg \gg \gg \gg \gg \gg \gg \gg \gg \gg \gg \gg$

REFLECTION: Luke 15:11–32, The Prodigal Son

He came to himself . . .

1. What do these words mean in light of this chapter?

2. SELF-AWARENESS: How well am I practicing honesty with and about myself? Do I have a place where it is safe to tell the truth, to name things as I see them?

3. OTHER-AWARENESS: How much is honesty valued in my community? Is a safe environment and instruction on being honest provided?

4. PRACTICE: What one thing can I choose to do to make a difference in the area of honesty in my own life? In the life of my community?

CHAPTER TWO

Shifting the Focus from Problem to Potential: Empowerment

*The task of **leadership** is to get people from where they are to where they have not been.*

HENRY KISSINGER

The "squeaky wheel syndrome" is well known in every human system—from families to corporations. The drama king or queen in the family whose histrionics have put a damper on every vacation and holiday. The know-it-all who terrorizes every committee meeting with an over-abundance of often irrelevant facts that make her feel important. The chronically late or absent. The malcontent. The negative just-because. The crisis-of-the-day. The depressed. The might-be-crazy. Fill in the blank with your own squeaky wheel.

From family to boardroom, the squeaky wheel has demanded the attention of their particular groups in a way that sidetracks mission and re-focuses energy on the squeaky wheel. Particularly in faith-based groups, there is the sense, sometimes even verbalized, that dealing directly with the *impact* of the behavior of the squeaky wheel is a less-than-Christian thing to do.

Again, we remind ourselves that all four gospels relate the story of Jesus and his disciples traveling to Jerusalem for the Passover, where he expels the money changers from the temple, accusing them of turning "my father's house" into a "den of thieves." And in Matthew, we experience Jesus sternly saying to Peter, "Get thee behind me, Satan! You are an offence to me. . . ." In both cases, Jesus experienced behaviors that he did not find acceptable, and set about addressing them. These are important images to hold in mind as we journey forward.

Intent

One of the ways we trip over our own feet is by focusing on what people *intend* when they behave in a certain way. In church circles, the benefit of the doubt goes something like: "I know she meant well—she's such a good person. . . ." "He would never intentionally do anything to hurt anyone, and certainly not to hurt this parish. Think of all the time and money he gives to it. . . ."

Without asking a person directly what they *intended* when they engaged in a certain action or said a certain thing, those who are speaking are engaging in a guessing game at best, seasoned with a bit of projection and some wishful thinking. The sub-text runs something like this: *This is a church. Good people come here. I can't believe that anyone who is a member would intentionally act in a way that would be hurtful to other people, or to the church itself, so there has to have been good intention that just ended up accidentally being hurtful. . . .*

Throughout this book, there will be a difference in the use of the words *intent* and *intentionality*. As used in this context, *intent* is most often considered after the fact, action, or incident, to explain why something was not well received or was received differently than expected. This kind of intent, from this practitioner's perspective, is not generally planned with forethought, self- or other-awareness. *Intentionality*, on the other hand, has to do with moving into a plan or action deliberately, with both self- and other-awareness.

One of the first steps toward health in the church is setting aside the matter of intent. *Intent does not matter. What matters is* **impact**—by which I mean *the objective effect on the whole.*

Impact

Every action that is taken by an individual, every word that is spoken, every behavior has potential *impact* on a system and the persons who make up that system. In other words, there is an action—and it has an objective effect on the entirety of the system. It is important here to separate the objective effect on the whole to individual feelings about that effect, which are generally irrelevant. Point of clarification—loud and clear. I did *not* say that feelings *in general* are irrelevant. I said that the objective effect of an action on the system exists regardless of the subjective assessment of it through feelings about that impact.

A young man was facing his first major post-college decision. He had been offered a job by a firm whose executives were considered archenemies of his family over generations. It was an extraordinary entry-level opportunity with one of the top firms in his field. The young man turned to his priest for advice. "No one in my family even knows this generation of the owners," he said. "I might never get another opportunity like this. I can't believe anyone would expect me to turn it down. . . ."

"You have every right to make what you think is the best decision for yourself," said the priest wisely. "However, you have to remember that what you decide has an impact on other people, whether you understand it or not, whether it makes sense to you or not. So you have to be prepared to accept the consequences for the impact your behavior has on others."

In this situation, the young man had an inkling that the decision he was about to make would cause a reaction in his family. The priest's words clarified for him that while he had control over his own decision and action, he had no control over the *impact* it would make on others. Nor did his rational assessment of the issues involved soften the potential of the impact.

Sometimes a niggling feeling in the pit of the stomach or the back of the brain as one heads pell-mell toward an action signals that there might be a less-than-positive impact ahead. Far too often, however, there are no warning signals, or if they exist, they are ignored.

The indicators that signal impact are not necessarily deterrents. Sometimes, no matter how fairly or kindly a decision is made or an action taken, feelings get hurt. The ability to state one's position and stay in relationship *despite* the hurt feelings adds a positive impact to a situation. *Impact* counts. In any system, reflection after an event takes into account both positive and negative impact. In the case of the young man, the negative *impact* was hurt feelings. The positive impact was his ability to state his position clearly, stay with his position, and stay in relationship with his family. His conversation with the priest shows the thinking that went into the decision. In his early discussion, he is building a case for the decision he wants to make, as if good rationale will sway his family to his way of thinking and perhaps override the emotional response he senses will follow his announcement if he takes this job. The priest is helpful in clarifying for him that he has every right to make the decision he needs to make but must be aware that he cannot control the impact of his decision on someone else. It is a different way of thinking that has to be practiced.

All too often, we in the Church are asked to make feeling-based decisions. *There is a distinct difference in being objectively aware of the impact behavior has on a system and being held hostage by the emotions of individuals at the table.* Hearing and respecting emotions, being aware of the emotional climate does not mean basing decision making and actions on responding to those emotions. It's a significant difference.

Looking For Strength in the System

David Cooperrider, the founder of Appreciative Inquiry, points us toward the importance of looking for strength in the system. As a business consultant, he relates, he was often flying into different cities, being met at the airport by a representative of the entity with whom he was called to work. On the way from airport to hotel, he reported, he often heard engaging stories about the company; energy and enthusiasm were high. When the group gathered in corporate headquarters at breakfast the next morning, the dynamics had changed. As the problems facing the institution were listed, spirits dragged; energy rapidly disappeared. His awareness of this phenomenon was instrumental in the formulation of the process known as Appreciative Inquiry.[12] A similar shift can happen when that approach is applied to leadership within a system. A parish had been struggling for several years, apparently stuck in some sort of rut, with negativity bouncing from one place within the structure to another. As soon as toxic personalities rotated off the vestry, another would pop up in the Episcopal Church Women, or the altar guild or choir. "We seem to always be dealing with negative personalities," the rector sighed.

"What might happen if, instead of focusing on the negative, you looked for pockets of strength or potential for strength?" a parish consultant suggested. "But these people are pretty powerful," the rector said. "There is power in strength, whether it carries a title or not," the consultant observed.

"Let's look at the parish list, and see where you think there might be untapped potential." He encouraged the rector to think of characteristics that might represent strengths—fresh eyes and insight; more responsive than reactive; firm in their values and beliefs without being polarized; able to think reflectively; self-aware. After a list had been developed, individuals were invited to attend the first of a series of educational sessions about effective leadership behaviors.

The first place to notice change was the ECW. A struggle had been simmering over old hurts, complete with parking lot conversations, divisive e-mails gone viral, and newer members staying away from the unpleasant tensions.

Pat, who had attended the training session for leaders, was approached after one ECW meeting by Gail, who wanted to complain about Susie. That's triangulation, Pat thought to herself. "You need to talk to Susie about your concerns," she said. "Oh, I couldn't do that," Gail responded. "I might hurt her feelings, and I know she doesn't mean anything bad. But you could . . ." "No," Pat said firmly. "You need to go to her directly and tell her that when such-and-such happens, it makes you feel a certain way."

---

12. David Cooperrider and Suresh Srivastva of Case Western Reserve University are credited with being the "parents" of a process whose thesis is that an organization can be recreated by its conversations, or story-telling, in a life-giving way when the conversations are shaped by appreciative questions that allow the identification of what is valued in the life of the organization.

Gail continued to protest, asking Pat to do the work for her. "You need to talk with her directly," Pat maintained. "If you are uncomfortable doing it alone, I will go with you. But you need to set it up."

The appointment was made, and after a bit of coaching on Pat's part, the two met with Susie. Gail was uncertain—the bravado of the parking lot dissipating face-to-face with her nemesis. Pat's presence provided a reassurance. "Susie, when you made a choice to invite some members of our ECW to go with you to the museum on the same day my psychologist daughter-in-law was speaking about "What is a family?" and told people that you didn't need to hear that liberal stuff because you know what a real family is, I felt really hurt personally, and I felt bad for my daughter-in-law that someone I consider a friend was not only attempting to pull members away from a guest speaker's program, but also disparaging her professional expertise." Gail's voice had picked up volume and strength as she spoke, and now she paused for a breath. Susie looked down at the floor, and then at Gail. "I wasn't thinking about your daughter-in-law or you," she said in a strained voice. "I just hate hearing all of these things that go against everything I've been taught or believed all of my life. It's scary!" "I wish you had said that to me and to the group when we planned the program," Gail said. "There might be other people who felt that way and my daughter-in-law could have planned a discussion around it."

A new process had been initiated.

The process was taken a step further when the rector recognized that there were both subtle and not-so-subtle bullying tactics keeping the vestry stuck during its meetings. Some of the bullying was passive-aggressive and more easily spotted. The less easily recognized bullying came in the form of aggrandizing behavior that intimidated others; rather than speaking out in meetings, they took their concerns into post-meeting e-mails and parking lot conversations. The "bullying" took the form of impressive-sounding opinions, often backed by professional articles (little of which might actually be relevant to the subject at hand) and references to conversations with influential people in the community and diocese. These were often accompanied by non-verbal gestures of impatience when clarifying questions were asked, as if to say "Any dummy would know that!"

The more aggressive bullying came in blatant attempts by the senior warden to railroad items in meetings: going around the rector, attempting to take the chair without being asked to do so, withholding information, openly criticizing, staying away from meetings.

A bishop discovered a practice in his new diocese of giving annual $10,000 grants to a list of parishes that were "barely making it." Early in his tenure, the bishop announced that he was cutting off those grants and opening the grant application process to anyone who was interested. The parishes that had their funding cut believed that it was the worst thing that had ever happened to them.

Two years after the change in granting procedures, one of the parishes asked to speak to the annual diocesan convention. "What we thought was the worst thing that ever happened to us turned out to be the best thing," the deputies said. "It was the only way we would ever have grown up. We were on life support. To continue on that path would have broken us completely, and broken the system down. We were told to go do it—and we did. And we're stronger than ever today."

Refusal to play to weakness; building up potential strength in the system.

Best Practices in Empowering Strength in the System:

- The rector planned a series of educational sessions, inviting hand-picked potential leaders to attend. A diocesan consultant led the participants in exercises that enabled them to identify and define anxiety behaviors, the impacts of those behaviors, and options for changing behaviors for securing different impact.

- The rector modeled for the parish by focusing on the tasks at hand and the developing healthy leadership, rather than getting dragged into confrontation with the bullies. When necessary, the rector set firm boundaries. For example, a member of the congregation who was known to all as whiny and negative continually approached the rector following a service with a complaint. One Sunday, after hearing this week's tirade, the weary rector said, "Sarah, do you ever have anything positive to say about anything?" "NO!" the woman snapped. "When you have something positive to say, I'll look forward to talking to you," the rector said, turning his attention to the next person in line. (He is still waiting, by the way!)

- The rector works with leaders of all groups in the parish to help them identify potential leadership—specifying characteristics rather than prestige or influence.

- The bishop holds a firm line regarding assistance to potential, rather than in support of weakness.

REFLECTION: Matthew 7:24

"Therefore everyone who hears these words and puts them into practice is like a wise man who builds his house on a rock."

1. How does this passage connect with the chapter?

2. FOR SELF-AWARENESS: How am I building on my strength and potential? Where have I been focusing on the squeaky wheels?

3. FOR OTHER-AWARENESS: How is my community building on strength and potential? Where is it focusing on or rewarding squeaky wheels?

4. PRACTICE: What one step can I take to build on strength and potential? What one step can my community take to build on strength and potential?

CHAPTER THREE

Gateways to Transformation

*The **growth** and **development** of people is the highest calling of leadership.*

HARVEY FIRESTONE

"By the time we get to deployment, it's too late!"

"If they're sweet and they say that they love Jesus, we put a collar on them and then wonder where the differentiated leaders are!"

The words named a growing awareness that two ends of the church continuum might not be in the regular conversation that would inform their respective tasks. At one end of the continuum, transition officers—about the work formerly known as "deployment"—labor to ensure that congregations, whatever their size, have full-time, part-time, or bi-vocational clergy who not only perform their sacramental duties, but also have the competencies that "match" the goals and challenges of the respective parish. At the other end of the continuum, discernment committees and Commissions on Ministry have the equally challenging and potentially life-changing task of joining with candidates who perceive they have a call to ordained ministry, to determine if the community of the church affirms that call. What happens at the latter end, in large part, determines whether or not the folks at the front end of the continuum will be able to fulfill their tasks successfully. And, of course, all of this work is occurring during a time when congregational life itself is undergoing radical change. All too often, survival is the name of the game.

Cover the congregation for worship, and for the pastoral necessities—such as hospital visitations, baptisms, and burials, with hopefully a wedding here and there. Pay the diocesan assessment. Calm whatever troubled waters are stirred up. And, increasingly, discover how, with Pew Forum data showing more folks who respond "none" to questions about church membership than do those who consider themselves to be Protestant, to provide ordained leadership of any kind. Congregations within the Episcopal Church find themselves with dwindling financial and human resources and demanding physical facilities. They are not alone. The median attendance in Episcopal parishes according to the FACT Overview 2011 congregational research report from C. Kirk Hadaway of the Episcopal Church was 66. Patheos online religion sources report 177,000 churches of all denominations (excluding Roman Catholic and Orthodox) report median attendance of 7–99, 105,000 with median attendance of 100–499.

The two most obvious gateways for becoming the transformative church—the two ends of the continuum: where the call to ministry and leadership, lay or ordained, begins and where ordained leadership is called to minister. Attached to those two ends of the continuum are a myriad of transformative gateways.

On the Parish Level:

- Vestries—elected lay leadership who appoint bodies, such as discernment committees and nominating committees, and make financial and policy decisions for the congregation
- Nominating Committees—appointed lay leaders who conduct parish self-studies, set goals, and name challenges that are approved by the vestry and the bishop, conduct the search for a rector, and make a recommendation to the vestry
- Deputies to annual convention, who vote on issues that impact the larger community
- Parish staff
- Committee chairs and members
- People in the pews
- Opportunities for common prayer

On the Diocesan Level:

- The Bishop—whose vision, modeling, and intention set the tone for the work of the diocese during that Bishop's tenure
- Standing Committee—second in ecclesiastical authority to the Bishop, make policy decisions and serve as council of advice to the Bishop; final approval on ordinations
- Diocesan Council—conduct the business of the Diocese between annual conventions
- Committee and commission heads and members—carry out the mission and ministry in various areas
- Diocesan staff—support the work and vision of the bishop and the diocese
- People of the diocese

The Importance of a Common Foundation and Language

In a hierarchal system, with a Book of Common Prayer, canons that guide our common life, and a shared structure, it is easy to believe that there is a common understanding of the polity and normative practices of the church. In a denomination that has long prided itself on "respecting the worth and dignity of every human being," it has been even easier to believe that behaviors of the people reflect the words we say in the baptismal covenant.

Reflecting on experience, however, it is clear that there are gaps in understanding what we believe and how we live out what we say we believe. Part of the gap can be explained by the demographics of any congregation—the mixture of life-long Episcopalians, who are assumed to have absorbed the teachings of the church by osmosis, if not by teaching and intention, and converts or escapees from other traditions, who are assumed to have taken in, understood, and integrated all aspects of the teaching they received prior to the day that they were confirmed or received in the church. Mix in those folks who "just want to sit in the pew and worship and not get involved beyond that," toss in an issue of physical plant, social issues that touch people's lives, or calling a new rector, and the result is likely to be confusion: chaos.

A transition officer was working with a vestry as they faced calling a new rector following the retirement of a rector who had served the congregation for nearly three decades. The conversation had moved past the grief of the loss to the needs in the future.

"I just want someone who will be here to baptize my children, bury my parents, marry my children, bury me . . ." the voice trailed off, and another chimed in in agreement. "What *is* a priest?" the transition officer asked.

The vestry members looked at each other skeptically. "You mean . . . ?"

"That's right—what is a priest to you? Give me a definition."

"He'll stay a long time—not just a short time." "He'll be great with children." "A great teacher—makes it all interesting." "A real pastor . . . visits people at home and in the hospital." "A really fine preacher." "Good at Bible study."

"Ok—those are all things that a priest *does*. What *is* a priest—to you?"

The room was silent. After a few minutes, someone said to the transition officer, "What's a priest to you?"

"The person God has put into my life at this time to guide me in discovering what God is calling me to do to bring his Kingdom on earth here and now."

There was silence again. It was clear that for most of these elected leaders, the role of a priest was about *doing for them*. They, the congregants, were the passive receivers of the rector's actions.

Understanding the role of the ordained leader is part and parcel of foundational teaching for church members. In the Catechism (BCP, p. 856) we learn that "the ministry of a priest is to represent Christ and His church, particularly as a pastor to the people; to share with the bishop in the overseeing of the Church; to proclaim the Gospel, to administer the sacraments and to bless and declare pardon in the name of God." The ministry of a deacon is to "represent Christ and his Church particularly as a servant to those in need; and to assist bishops and priests in the proclamation of the Gospel and the administration of the sacraments." Section 5 of Canon 111.9.4 of the *Constitution and Canons of the Episcopal Church* is quite specific in delineating the duties of the rector or priest-in-charge of a congregation, from the conduct of worship to the control of the buildings and property of the church to education for Christian stewardship, Christian formation, and keeping people of the congregation informed of pastoral letters and position papers from the diocesan Bishop and Presiding Bishop, and participation in the work and ministry of the diocese or adjudicatory of which the church is a member.

Also fundamental to understanding the role of a rector is the knowledge that a priest is *called* by a parish to this position as spiritual leader, not hired in the secular sense as an employee, and signs a *Letter of Agreement,* which is covenantal in nature. The dissolution of a covenantal pastoral relationship is also governed by canons. Far too many church members have no understanding of the spiritual, relational or legal aspects of this relationship, and bring experiences from the corporate world or Congregationalist backgrounds to life in the Episcopal Church.

Equally clear in the Catechism (BCP 855) is the role of the laity, or members of the church:

Who are the ministers of the Church?
The ministers of the Church are laypersons, bishops, priests, and deacons.

What is the ministry of the laity?
The ministry of lay persons is to represent Christ and his Church; to bear witness to him wherever they may be; and, according to the gifts given them, to carry on Christ's work of reconciliation in the world; and to take their place in the life, worship, and governance of the Church.

The understanding of both roles is foundational to a common language about life in the church.

In one diocese, the transition officer provides a session he entitles "Playing on the Playground of the Episcopal Church"—this is how we get to the playground, these are the rules of the playground. In another diocese, such a session is known as "Episcopal 101." The image of the playground provides almost instantaneous recognition in the eyes of those attending. The playground experience is close to universal. Chloe, a social worker, reported a visceral response to the image during a vestry retreat. "I felt as if for a moment I was about eight years old, and back on a playground in a new school. I knew what the teacher had told us about the rules on the playground. What I didn't know was those informal 'rules' that kids create, and how miserable it felt to stumble over one of them and find myself on the outside of a world that should have been a safe place." Heads around the table nodded in agreement.

"It puts my Episcopal experience into a totally new perspective," said Tom, "and I've been in this church now more years of my life than in any other."

The rules of the "Episcopal Playground" are changing. What does not change is the need for leadership to know and understand what the rules are at any given time. If the elected leadership of a congregation has the *understanding* of the life of the church as consumer driven and its normative *behaviors* those of a dysfunctional, unhealthy system, what is the foundation upon which mission and ministry can be built and move forward?

When the priest is considered an employee and the significance of the full participation of lay members in ministry is not understood, it is too easy to think that the solution to whatever ails a parish is to change leadership.

The good news is, there are foundational theories that undergird and support leadership in all levels of the system, and these theories can be taught and modeled in your parish or diocese. "Gateway" is not an Episcopal term. We do not tend to use it to describe those areas of our program life that are most likely to attract seekers or potential new members. Nor will it be familiar as a descriptor of how we might begin infiltrating our systems with normative practices that build health.

However, within the structure of our church we have the "gateways or means of access" to strengthen the system. We began with the awareness that we are indeed destroying ourselves internally and must stop; we must turn around and live our lives differently or the Episcopal Church will surely die. We must be *intentional,* with a long-term perseverance that will allow the health to become a part of our DNA, passed on from generation to generation, just as dysfunction has been. We must be clear in *identifying and naming* those behaviors that would distract and destroy us, looking at *impact rather than intent,* and making the systemic changes necessary to create constructive impact as our norm. For many organizations, anxiety or some level of discomfort or dysfunction has become so much a part of usual behavior that it seems normal.

Comfortable with being uncomfortable
Uncomfortable with being uncomfortable
Uncomfortable with being comfortable
Comfortable with being comfortable

This little chart describes the progression of an individual or organization from dis-ease to health. Far too many within our institution are comfortable with being uncomfortable—and have come to accept it not only as normative, but also as inevitable.

This is where we need *gateways*—those entrances or means of access to new ways of doing and being in our world. The access point may be different from one congregation to another, from one diocese or adjudicatory to another. The initial gateway might be a strategic choice or it might emerge as a leadership response to a particular situation.

The following examples of both the strategic choice and the situational response gateways are based on the current structure within the system. It is important to note that the process and strategies that undergird the purpose of the organization, the church, are not particular to this structure; rather, they are transferrable as the structure reorganizes over time.

Strategic Choices: Vestries and Nominating Committees in Transition

Readiness for guidance: while there may be various resistances to institutional guidance, the change-point of transition from one leader to another is a time when there is an expectation of guidance from the bishop (or adjudicatory head) and their office. It is important to note that the expectation is gilded with caveats from the parish leadership, who may find themselves caught in the tension of both desiring and resisting that guidance. Both bishop and transition officer have the opportunity to meet together and separately with the vestry, to explain their responsibilities in the interim period, and to explain the diocesan process for filling the vacancy. Each step is an opportunity for teaching, not only normative practice, but also healthy process.

Intentional Vestry Teaching Points:

- Episcopal 101 or "Episcopal Playground"

- Diocesan process for transitions; options for discernment

- Difference in discernment for "call" and corporate "hire"

- Importance of honesty in the process: in the parish's reflection on its history and "family secrets," and in creating the parish profile

- Developmental tasks of the interim period and responsibility of the rector-in-the-interim (Appendix L). It is not unusual for vestries and congregations to see clergy who serve in the interim period as simply supply or "place holders"—someone whose "magic hands" make it possible for them to have the Eucharist on Sunday and other appropriate occasions, someone who will make the necessary pastoral calls. The term "rector-in-the-interim" comes from transitional specialists themselves, who have found that this terminology helps clarify the fact that they are, indeed, the rector during this interim period. A helpful practice in several dioceses is a letter from the bishop, outlining the role of the interim, which is read to the congregation by the senior warden on the interim's first Sunday in the parish.

- Guidelines for selecting a nominating committee (sample application letter)

- History of parish and previous rectors/patterns

- Ongoing communication during process

- Simple instructions regarding anxiety in the system during transition, behaviors to be aware of, responsibility of the vestry

Nominating Committee Teaching Points:

- Episcopal 101 or "Episcopal Playground"

- Importance of knowledge of each other and team building

- Difference in discernment for "call" and corporate "hire"

- History of parish, previous rectors and patterns, family secrets—importance of honesty with self and in parish profile

- Anxiety in system—committee's role

- Diocesan process for transitions

- Particular emphasis on data-gathering interactive process and its role in bringing the parish into process

Member of Parish:

- Introduction to interactive data-gathering process

- Norms and standards during process as managed by Diocesan Leadership Team

- Testing the goals and standards

Approaches to transition vary from locale to locale. Time and personnel can be factors in creating and maintaining an effective transition process.

Reports on diocesan processes range from closely guided processes under diocesan consultants at one end of the spectrum to a paper outlining the process "which we know they won't follow anyway." Regardless of limiting factors, however, one bishop clearly identified his intention when he said "I simply could not sit by and see another mismatch that led to conflict in the parish, and ultimately dissolution, which is spiritually, emotionally, and financially devastating. It was just too costly. Creating a process and requiring that parishes follow it under guidance from my office was just a necessity."

Meeting with a Vestry for Transition Preparation: The Opportunity for Teaching the Vestry to be the Non-Anxious Presence, and the Difference between Discerning a *Call* and Corporate Hiring

Members of the vestry of a corporate-sized parish in a large diocese gathered for a meeting with the bishop and transition officer (who, in this case, was also the Canon to the Ordinary) for information about the transition process. The bishop spoke of the canonical aspects of the transition, including the calling of a rector-in-the-interim, and turned the meeting over to the transition officer, who, he told the vestry, would be guiding the process.

As the explanation of the process went forward, a woman at the table seemed increasingly restless. Finally, she spoke up. "I have been through major transitions in the hiring of a CEO three times in my company. This is ridiculously slow and laborious! There are better and shorter ways to get a good priest to lead this congregation!"

The transition officer smiled. He had heard this line of thinking many times, and was prepared.

"I understand your frustration, Mary," he said congenially. "Let me remind us all that we do not *hire clergy*. They are not our *employees*. In the Episcopal Church, we *call* rectors to lead a congregation, as the spiritual head. That involves a process of mutual spiritual discernment. Obviously, we want to have good business practices in all of our life and work—but you as the vestry have a particular job to do in understanding the difference between a corporate hire and a spiritual call, and in helping others in the congregation understand the difference."

"You know, transition time in any organization can raise lots of anxiety—and it is up to the leadership to try to manage that anxiety by being what is known as a 'non-anxious presence'—or at least, a *less-anxious presence*—the people who don't get sucked into the gossip and the fear, but calmly go about the business of the church, handling the day-to-day matters, calming others' fears, having facts and data available to counteract rumors (which abound in these situations). You can be a real help in that. . . ."

Nominating Committee Formation Retreat: An Opportunity for a Daylong Intensive on Intentionality and Honesty in Church Life and Leadership

When a nominating committee is selected in one particular diocese, applicants for membership must agree to be available for a formation retreat and for interactive data gathering. Interactive data gathering is a series of congregational meetings guided by a team of facilitators from around the diocese who are trained to help people hear each other's experiences and dreams. The face-to-face conversations (interactive) provide a greater opportunity for honest input from members than a paper survey, leading to more honest goals and challenges. There can be grumbling about giving up a Saturday in busy lives. "This is not rocket science," grouched one man. "I could do this with one hand tied behind me."

The formation retreat began with scripture study.

> The Lord answered Moses, "Assemble seventy elders from Israel, men known to you as elders and officers in the community; bring them to me at the Tent of the Presence, and there let them take their stand with you. I will come down and speak with you there. I will take part of that same spirit which has been conferred on you and confer it on them, and they will share with you the burden of taking care for the people, then you will not have to bear it alone. . . ."
>
> Moses came out and told the people what the Lord had said. He assembled seventy men from the elders of the people and stationed them round the tent. Then the Lord spoke to him. He took back part of that same spirit He had conferred on Moses, and conferred it on the seventy elders. *(Numbers 11:16–17, 24–25a)*

Members reflected on ways in which the passage spoke to them and the responsibility they had accepted for the community. Several stated that the most helpful phrase to them as they begin their work is "you will not have to bear it alone."

Team building included sharing spiritual mapping of their own journey from their beginnings in a faith community to this day; a typology continuum, where they experienced their own styles of interacting in relation to the others on the committee; an exercise in spiritual preferences.

They moved on to a consideration of their published parish history, and then, on newsprint, looked at the names of all previous rectors, the dates of their tenures, and what they knew of the strengths and weaknesses of each, after which they looked for patterns in the calls.

"Looks like we alternate between long, fairly staid, and boring tenures and short, dramatic ones," someone said.

Over lunch, the group considered "family secrets." What are the things that you know or suspect are out there in the shadows, known to some, rarely talked about, but still a part of the life of the parish?

There was silence—and then someone said, "There has been in my time here the dismissal or departure of too many lay staff members without any explanation. The parish is just told that it is a "personnel issue" and can't be discussed. But one day, someone who has had a huge impact on people's lives, no matter their personal idiosyncrasies, is here and suddenly they are gone. There might be a token farewell, but then, no one can ever mention them again. There is no time to grieve, even if that person changed your life more than any priest or other person."

Now was the time—and discussion went forward.

At break time, one of the grumblers approached the transition officer. "I had no idea what this was about," he said. "This is some of the most important work I've ever done. This could change the life of our parish!"

"I hope so," responded the transition officer. "*You* can be a leader in that change." (See Appendix J1 for guidelines for a nominating committee formation retreat.)

Situational Response to a Diocesan Council

A diocesan council had been experiencing conflicted behaviors among its members which were distracting the group from its ongoing work. At the annual council retreat, a consultant was asked to provide exercises to bring new members on board. The several members who were exhibiting the most destructive behaviors (intimidating by raised voices and criticisms, negative responses, disrespect, walking out of meetings, etc.) chose not to come for the orientation session, but planned to arrive in time for the actual business session.

The consultant introduced the concepts of Norms and Standards (mutually agreed-upon understandings of how a group operates) for groups, in a generic form, and asked the members to divide up into small groups to adapt the document specifically to their work.

As the small groups reported out, it was clear that they wanted to move beyond the distracting behaviors that had lengthened their meetings and limited their work. The new document reflected attention to process as well as product. One member suggested that they, as a Christian group, were making a *covenant* with each other as to how they would operate. Another said that they were trying to create a "culture of courtesy"—an obvious response to previous disrespectful behaviors.

"That's it!" a man said. "It's our 'Culture of Courtesy Covenant'!"

The document was passed, published in the diocesan paper, and is offered to all diocesan and parish groups as a model. Each year, after new members are elected, it is one of the first orders of business of the Council to read the document aloud and make any adjustments that are needed.

The Culture of Courtesy Covenant

- Meetings will begin and end on time, with consent and discussion agendas planned to maximize time for effective discussion and decision making.

- A detailed agenda and all documents pertaining to agenda items will be e-mailed to members sufficiently in advance of the meeting date to allow for thorough study. It is the responsibility of each member to familiarize themselves with the materials prior to the meeting.

- Come to the meetings on time and stay the entire time. If I am unable to attend, or must leave before the end of the meeting, I will notify the leader in advance.

- I will use "I" messages when I address the meeting: "I believe . . ."; "I think . . ."; "I want . . ."; etc.

- I will listen to what others have to say respectfully without interrupting. I will not engage in side conversations when another speaker has the floor.

- I will not be an air "hog," "bog," or "frog," speaking to hear myself speak, speaking to a point which has already been made when I have no additional information to impart, repeating myself, or leaping over or ahead of the item under discussion.

- The agenda for the meeting and the content of the meeting take place in the meeting room for the purpose of building up the community. Natural and spontaneous conversation that happens outside of the group as a whole could and should be shared with the whole group. Conversations that take place in secret with intent to exclude the whole group bring down rather than build up the community. I will strive to meet standards of conversational behavior that build up truth within the community.

- I understand that process (how we do things) is as important as product (the content or what we do). I will respect both and endeavor to conduct myself in a manner that respects the worth and dignity of every human being. I understand that either a process observer, the chair or parliamentarian may call the group to consider attention to process during the course of a meeting, and that it is appropriate for any member of the Council to ask that attention be focused on the Culture of Courtesy Covenant.

- As an adult participant, I will take care of personal needs during break time or, when unavoidable, other brief period if necessary. I will not send or receive text or other communications during the meeting, unless for emergency purpose.[13]

Other gateways may present themselves at other times in the life of a parish and/or diocese. However, transition offers a unique opportunity for capturing the interest and energy of leadership who are working toward a shared goal, aware at some level that they need the guidance of the institution to help them through this change.

Framing the Gateways: Commission on Ministry and Transitions

It is important before leaving this introduction to gateways to consider the other side of the frame—the Commission on Ministry and entire process for holy orders (the manner in which a person who believes God is calling them to ordained ministry in the church tests that call within the community), including parish and diocesan discernment committees.

This is, quite possibly, the gateway where real intervention can begin. Patterns repeated across the church show that those who get through the ordination process in any diocese are likely to be considered "pastoral" (empathetic, non-offensive) or "deeply spiritual" (can articulate their call and spiritual journey in a compelling way). Here is the opportunity—from the first conversation a rector has with someone who believes they are being called to ordained ministry through parish- and diocesan-level discernment processes—to uphold standards that begin with personal, mental, emotional, and spiritual health as well as the strength and capacity for leadership. While more specific suggestions will be found in Chapter 5, "Playing It Out Throughout the System," it is important to note here that the two endpoints on the continuum—Commission on Ministry and Transitions—are absolutely key to the development and sustenance of healthy leadership in any Episcopal system; they must be in constant interaction with each other about their experiences.

---

13. *Culture of Courtesy Covenant,* The Diocese of Lexington.

REFLECTION: Exodus 13:18; 14:15–31, The Exodus Story

After four centuries of slavery, the people of Israel cry to the God of Abraham, Isaac, and Jacob for deliverance. God has prepared Moses to be the advocate before Pharaoh for Israel, and commissioned him at the burning bush. However, Pharaoh's heart is hardened against letting Israel go. God reveals himself to Pharaoh through a series of plagues. Israel is redeemed through the plague by means of the Passover lamb, and their faith in God becomes the basis for their redemption, God guides them out of Egypt by a pillar of fire and smoke, and miraculously saves them from the pursuing Egyptian army by the parting of the Red Sea. He protects and sustains them in their journey.

1. Change takes place for several reasons in Scripture. The Exodus story is an example of the present situation becoming so unbearable that it is more painful to stay (uncomfortable with being uncomfortable) than to change. Consider the Exodus story from this perspective.

2. SELF-AWARENESS: Where have I become comfortable being uncomfortable with my own behaviors and those of others in my life? Where have there been times in my life when the present has been so unbearable that change was a better option?

3. OTHER-AWARENESS: Where has my community become comfortable with the discomfort of inappropriate or dysfunctional behaviors? What has the impact been?

4. PRACTICE: What one step might I take when I experience behaviors that cause extreme discomfort or distraction? What one step might my community take?

CHAPTER FOUR

The Heart of the Matter: How Does My Behavior Impact My Relationships?

*What if we **discover** that our present way of life is irreconcilable with our vocation to become fully human?*

PAULO FREIRE

Every level of any system is composed of individuals who interact with each other.

In all human relationships—from family to friendships to organizations—there is one thing that matters: how one person's behavior impacts another.

When all of the foundational theories and all of the advice books are culled down to the most basic issue, it has to do with how we treat each other. Not how we *think* we treat each other. Not how we *mean* to treat each other. But how the other party experiences our behavior. This is not about subjective emotional response to behavior. It is about the fact that objective behavior will impact both individuals and the system.

In truth, most of us perceive ourselves to do pretty well in that department. Whether working with couples and families as a therapist in private practice or in my role as consultant and trainer working with groups and organizations, when it comes to assessing our own behavior and how it impacts others, it is much easier to point the finger at the other person than it is to assess our own behavior, recognizing when the impact has been less than desirable.

Coming from the Jungian typology perspective, I might ask a couple to look at the "shadow" sides of their behaviors—those times when the words that have come out of their mouth were not at all what they would have chosen when they were on their "best behavior." There is always a little flinching when we talk about the ingredients in the "shadow bag"— those lesser-known parts of ourselves that we don't want to acknowledge, but which trip us up now and then. When we talk about tendencies of violence, hate, and other such strong words, the usual response is to say,

"I would never do anything like *that!*"—and yet, our disagreements with others, at home and at work, are often peppered with emotionally volatile responses, our criticisms of others leaning seriously toward hatred of an individual or group.

No matter the "hat," the goal for these professionals is the same: to help people be aware enough of self that they can choose differently when the impact of their behavior is less than positive, or repeatedly different than was intended.

As one bishop states: "Most failed leadership is self-inflicted. Lack of knowledge about our own selves, how we are perceived, the responsibility we take (or not) for our behavioral choices, and the impact those choices have on others make so many step in serious do-do. We are hamstrung by being ineffective in leadership." Imagine what might happen to families, to organizations, to world peace if we were to engage in human interactions that were life-giving?

Recognizing and Owning Behavior and Impact

A consultant was leading a congregational data-gathering session for an episcopal election. Regardless of the topic up for discussion, there seemed to be side conversations, some non-verbal disrespect for each other, and a general dis-ease in the room. A side comment about "someone said" was the consultant's cue (see Appendix M).

Across the newsprint, the consultant listed these categories:

BEHAVIOR/DEFINITION	SEE?	SUCKED INTO?	IMPACT?	ALTERNATIVE?[14]
Triangling				
Over-functioning				
Under-functioning				
Distancing				
Conflict				
Sabotage				
Cut-off				
Bullying				

"This transition between bishops is a time of anxiety for all of us," the consultant said. "As a matter of fact, we all live with anxiety most of the time. Sometimes it's like a low-grade fever that just always seems to be

14. Kay Collier McLaughlin, *Behavior-Impact Model: Leadership Development Notebook* (Lexington, KY: The Diocese of Lexington, 2013).

with us. Other times, it's brought on by a particular situation. But anxiety is contagious and cumulative. It runs through a family or an organization like a virus."

"There are some behaviors that grow out of anxiety. I've put them up here. I'd like to ask you to help define them." The group set to work.

Triangulating: not talking directly to someone; involving a third party in a conversation that should take place between two people

Over-functioning: trying to do it all, all by yourself. Not trusting anyone else to get the job done

Under-functioning: doing nothing

Distancing: moving away from people; stopping engagement

Conflict: fighting; strong disagreement

Sabotage: deliberately trying to stop something from happening

Cut-off: completely ending a relationship or any possibility of one

Bullying: criticizing, over-powering, passively or aggressively dumping on another

With the definitions they had written posted on the wall in front of them, the congregation broke into small groups to answer the next two questions:

Have you experienced these behaviors in this church?

Have you ever gotten sucked into these behaviors in this church?

After twenty minutes of small-group sharing, the leaders reported out. Yes, everyone said, they had experienced these behaviors—in this church. A few claimed they had never been sucked into participating in such behavior, but the majority freely admitted they had. Stories were shared around both questions. Rumors abounded through parking lot conversations and e-mails *about* someone or something. Didn't know it had a *name*. Triangulating. People disappearing, just dropping off: so that's *distancing*. Done that a few times myself.

The hardest to name and own were sabotage and bullying. "Those are really strong words" was heard again and again. Words like "strong-minded" and "super-aggressive" were interjected into the discussion. And always, there was a tendency to think about how well intended people were when they tried to control situations through some of these behaviors.

Next came the question: When you experienced these behaviors, what was the impact on the church?

The list beside each behavior filled up quickly.

Triangulating: rumors; untruths; alienation; hurt feelings; anger; division

Over-functioning: worn out, burned out, no one else tries; martyr-complex; loss of potential talent; no delegation

Under-functioning: job not get done; leads to someone over-functioning

Distancing: sense of abandonment; rejection; confusion

Conflict: division; anger; hurt; distraction from ministry

Sabotage: lost opportunity; distrust; anger; confusion

Cut-off: no opportunity for reconciliation

Bullying: hurt, distrust, withdrawal, nothing gets done

The room was silent as the impact sunk in.

"As adults, when we can recognize and name behaviors, becoming aware of the impact of those behaviors, we have a choice. We can choose to continue the behavior, knowing what impact it is going to have, or we can look for alternative behaviors to achieve a better impact. Shall we brainstorm some alternatives?"

Energy buzzed through the room as the men and women worked.

What's the alternative to triangulating? Collapse the triangle. Refuse to get drawn into it. If someone tries to talk with you about another person, direct him/her back to that individual. And, if they seem unwilling, say, "If you don't want to go alone, I'll be glad to go with you."

What's the alternative to over-functioning? Push for delegation, for appointing others to help . . . for under-functioning?

An Eye-Opener for Every Part of the System

The behavior-impact exercise is a major example of how integrated foundational theories can birth an experiential exercise that not only meets the needs of the moment, but also has implications for extended usage. In this particular exercise, systems theory met with experiential laboratory learning concepts to create an activity that would engage the participants—both those whose non-verbal distractions were decreasing the effectiveness of the session and those who were trying to engage for a common purpose. The group facilitators were all trained in the same basic theoretical constructs and could follow the flow of the change easily. The priest marks this session as a dramatic "turnaround" in behaviors for her congregation.

Following are three additional samplings of how this exercise can be utilized with (1) a vestry or small leadership group, (2) conflicted individuals, and (3) a large group of leaders.

It is particularly effective for:

Empowering groups of individuals to stop sabotage
or bullying within a system

A congregation was struggling in almost every area of its life, with leadership and decisions controlled by a small group of individuals. The rector, in effect, served as "chaplain" to this group and others who called themselves members. A financial issue brought some information to the surface that had been withheld from both the rector and the vestry. A newcomer to the parish (too new to fear stumbling over sacred cows or angering the wrong person) became concerned enough about the rumblings in her new church to question why everyone was allowing this to happen. With her encouragement, the rector reached out to the diocese and asked for help.

A small group gathered with the consultant (a neighboring priest) and the rector and went through the behavior-impact model. Definitions of the terms flowed easily; it was more painful to identify the behaviors they had been experiencing with the terms. After the exercise was completed, there was silence around the circle.

"What now?" asked one of the men.

"What do you think?"

"Well, now I see clearly what I hadn't allowed myself to see before. So I think we'll have to do something when these behaviors come up again—and that feels a little scary."

"Awareness is important," the consultant said. "It's the first step to moving toward healthy leadership practices for all in the congregation. What does that mean to you?"

The discussion continued with the group practicing ways they might address the behaviors when they arose, newly aware of the potential for being complicit by their silence.

"It's not an overnight fix," the consultant reminded them, "but you have taken the first steps. And we'll be there to support you all the way."

Helping individuals and groups to internalize their knowledge
and ability to use theories effectively

The behavior-impact model is a good example of experiential education, where a group is offered an experience followed by an explanation, which allows them to internalize a theory. After people have had such an experience, some may then be interested in hearing more about supporting theories, reading books or articles, etc. When the approach begins with head knowledge, a smaller number of people own the concept or buy in to what is being offered them.

A diocesan leadership day welcomed 75 people to an-all day training on Christian Behaviors, which included the behavior-impact model. Working in both large and small groups, men and women enthusiastically participated in defining and identifying the behaviors. The session on alternatives was high energy, and the practice groups for trying on the new behaviors equally so. Said a leader, "Every time we use this, I see the lights come on— real 'ah-ha's'—people 'get it' and remember it."

Giving people practical applications that show good results in a short time

While in-depth understanding will take further training and usage, the behavior-impact model offers a practical application that people *recognize* before they understand the theory—and practical steps to work with immediately.

A vestry had been experiencing extreme division around issues. Behaviors toward each other were so disrespectful that people were beginning to stay away from meetings and talk about resigning their positions.

The rector asked a diocesan leader to take them through the behavior-impact model. It was easy to see the "ah-ha's" in the room as the work progressed, as people recognized themselves and owned their part in the dysfunction.

The evening concluded with each declaring a behavior that they wished to work on, and a covenant that they would each practice and report back to the next meeting. As one vestry member said the next month, "I feel like no one has to 'report'—we *are* our reports in the way we are treating each other."

One of the significant behaviors that people have claimed in the behavior-impact exercise across numerous parts of the Church is over-functioning: the failure to delegate, which leads to burn out, resentment, martyrdom; failure to realize that it is time for a particular ministry to end, which may be why no one else is participating

"The Church as I see it is in the business of transformation," said a priest, "the transformation of us as individuals on our journeys, and the transformation of the world. There are lots of problems along the way as people act out their fears of change and of losing what is precious to them. These are spiritual issues that all come up on a spiritual journey."

"When we're challenged to see things in a new light, there might be inspiration, but there is also a sense of dislocation, a need to adjust and accommodate. How do we hold the truth of the vision of a new heaven and a new earth *and* the sense of dislocation as we consider what in the practice of our tradition is essential and what is not?"

The Church has a powerful opportunity to step into the place where religion, applied behavioral science, and psychology meet and deal with those questions with intention and compassion as companions on this journey, "especially," said one individual, "when I am stupid—and I will be."

REFLECTION: John 11:43-44

He (Jesus) cried with a loud voice, "Lazarus, come out!" And he who had died came out, losing his grave clothes. . . .

1. One impetus for change revealed in scripture is death and resurrection. How does the story of Lazarus' death and Jesus' calling him forth connect with the material in this chapter on impact of behavior, awareness of impact, and alternatives?

2. SELF-AWARENESS: What grave clothes of behavior have bound me? What part of my behavior do I want to die in order that I might live more fully?

3. OTHER-AWARENESS: What grave clothes of behavior are binding my community? What part of our behaviors might we want to die to free us to be disciples?

4. PRACTICE: What one step do I want to take to practice a new behavior to achieve a different impact? What one step might my community take to practice a new behavior to achieve a different impact?

CHAPTER FIVE

Playing It Out Throughout the System

*In times of **change**, learners inherit the Earth, while the learned find themselves beautifully equipped to deal with a world that no longer exists.*

ERIC HOFFER

"I wonder . . ."

I wonder what might happen if we got ourselves together and decided that we were going to be a church where, at every level of our system, we were going to try to be the counter-cultural entity that we were called to be.

I wonder what might happen if every single bishop decided to focus first of all on their own emotional well-being, their anxiety triggers and management, and think about the impact of their behavior when they are playing in those big sandboxes of theirs, deciding to remain aware of the emotional processes swirling around them without getting sucked into them? I wonder what might happen if every priest were expected to be a grown-up, not dependent on their congregation for meeting their emotional needs and expecting the same of their parish leadership? I wonder what might happen if we truly did value the worth and dignity of every human being instead of just saying it—and were as attentive to that value with the people we serve with every day as we try to be with people we don't know on the other side of the world?

I wonder what might happen if all of the energy we expend on in-fighting were available to use in mission and ministry?

I wonder . . .

I wonder what it would look like to do this work at every level throughout our system.

For starters, it doesn't require a new office, a new officer, or a staff. And it doesn't matter if we are working within the structure we know today or structures yet to come. Behavior and impact are consistent across time and tenure.

It requires *intentionality*. It requires *commitment*. And it requires *perseverance—beginning with individuals who are willing to sign on for a lifelong process of personal accountability*.

It can't be a fad that passes quickly. It can't be forgotten in a transition between bishops or rectors. We've tried all that, and you know what? It doesn't work!

My father was a football coach and teacher. He had a saying that students and players remember more than twenty years after his death: "You can accomplish anything you want so long as you do not care who gets the credit." Bishops, clergy, and lay leaders will come and go, as they always have. Each tenure will bring its own vision, its own passions. But the one thing that cannot change if we are going to survive, much less thrive, is our ongoing commitment to becoming the transformative church. We must be committed to moving beyond posturing, territorialism, agendas, and the philosophies of the day or week or month or year to caring more about how we live and work together than we do about individual legacies or credit. Because that's the real bottom line.

It has been noted that crises—earthquakes, tsunamis, hurricanes, floods, fires—bring out the best in people, offering a real understanding of the importance of working for the common good.

Crisis togetherness, however noble and noteworthy, all too often fades as the crisis passes and real-life resumes. In her book *Turning to One Another, Simple Conversations to Restore Hope to the Future*, author Margaret Wheatley reminds us that it shouldn't take a crisis or disaster to meet another in ways that make differences, status, and traditional power relationships meaningless. Such situations focus attention on what is truly important: "working intensely together, inventing solutions as needed, we take all kinds of risks, we communicate instantly." Crisis togetherness, however, has a dark side. Togetherness, particularly togetherness as strong as that born by crisis, pushes people into the "forces of togetherness" at the expense of individuality and self-differentiation. It can work against the well-differentiated thinking that we actually need most in times of crisis. The trick is to capture that spirit and energy as guiding forces every day, so it becomes the standard. Wheatley writes, "We would stop tolerating work and lives that gradually dissolve our belief in each other. We might begin to insist on the conditions that bring out our best, if we stopped accepting the deadening quality of 'the real world.' If we raised our expectations, then it wouldn't take a crisis for us to experience the satisfaction of working together, the joy of doing work that serves other human beings."[15]

---

15. Margaret Wheatley, *Turning to One Another: Conversations to Restore Hope to the Future* (San Francisco: Berrett-Koehler, 2002), 126–27.

The old church—the church that many of us grew up with—is gone. It's been gone a long time, although no one has wanted to acknowledge that reality. The church of today is going to be gone, too. We don't really know what will come to take its place. We are in the midst of a reformation. If we are intentional about taking part in it, it can be our opportunity. If we are not intentional, it will still happen, and the church may or may not be alive when it is done.

The thing we *do* know is that the situation will demand from us that we are intentional in expecting and practicing behaviors that build, support, empower, and strengthen people, mission, and ministry.

How Do We Get It?

Start at the top . . . in the middle . . . and at the bottom . . . in terms of implementation—providing a web-like approach that sees all levels of the system as being of importance. The articulation of the vision must be clearly heard from the top—again and again—with ongoing actions to support the statement.

At every level of the system, bishops, priests, and lay leaders identify the single most glaring and recurring deficit in the church is something akin to EQ (Emotional Intelligence): self-awareness, how one is perceived in the world, the impact that one is making on other people. "Whatever you call it, this lack has caused problems for many people," said one bishop. "While it might not lead to a Title III or Title IV violation (of the canons of the church), it has hamstrung more than one person being more effective in leadership." This commitment to supporting self-awareness must begin with our bishops if we are to be the transformative church.

How it plays out in each diocese will vary, as size and resources, both human and financial, vary. The following suggestions:

- Each bishop makes a serious commitment to work with a coach on his/her own anxiety/reactivity on an ongoing basis.

- Each bishop looks for the strength within his/her diocese: who are the 10 or 15 men and women who:
  —are firm in their faith,
  —responsive rather than reactive,
  —open to new ideas and non-polarized in their stances,
  —have a good knowledge of the polity of the Church,
  —are good listeners,
  —exhibit imagination and wonder, and
  —have a sense of humor.

- Each bishop works with a peer coach/consultant to find a plan that works for his/her diocese and shares it in a compelling way.

- Each bishop agrees to share his/her work with at least one other bishop and the rectors in his/her dioceses.

Look for Resources to Incorporate Training into Your Diocese

There are already dioceses where resource incorporation is going on, including:

- Diocesan norms for covenantal relationships between congregation, clergy, and bishop when a new cleric arrives in the diocese

- A contract with an organizational behavior center to work with the bishop and canon to the ordinary on a regular basis, and to meet monthly with the diocesan staff to insure accountability

- A "'Hippocratic oath" covenant for clergy

- An invitation to work in the areas of emotional intelligence, conflict management, and peer coaching for all clergy and key lay leaders

- A consistent and ongoing leadership training program for lay leadership

- Opportunities for internships and certification in coaching.[16] This type of local immersion, which might initially be led either by a consultant trainer in the diocese (if available) or an external consultant trainer, is most effective in involving numbers of people on the local level immediately. There are also opportunities to send teams of individuals for training outside the diocese, to return and encourage others, which, while effective, is a slower process of incorporation.

Work to Identify Limiting Patterns Within the System

One of the most important practices that can be incorporated into any system is that of identifying patterns within that system. A pattern is a behavior/impact that has been repeated over and over again in a system, through

---

16. Author's caveat: As one who has worked for many years in the field of consulting, and observed the multiple uses of the term, and the emergence of the title and/or descriptor of "coach," I believe that, like the term "consultant," the title "coach" is often used without sufficient training and experience in the area. It is extremely important to connect with resources whose credentials and references show a standard of practice that includes training in the utilization of the foundational methodologies listed here, in order to support the work in a congruent way. Intentionality about training leaders to work with clergy and lay leaders on Emotional Intelligence and other significant areas of leadership basics requires careful vetting or appropriate resources.

several generations. Some examples of family patterns include alcoholism, which appears in several generations; divorce; and death after a particular life-cycle event. One of the most effective ways of mapping patterns is through a genogram. The genogram is more in-depth than a family tree in that it allows the visualization of hereditary patterns and psychological and behavioral factors, as well as medical history and family relationships. It is advisable to work with a trained consultant or counselor when creating a genogram, both to learn how to do it and how to read it when it is complete. A more informal and less in-depth approach would be to list three generations of family and begin to look for patterns that repeat in the generations. Once familiar with the concept for a family, the next step is to adopt the model for an organization such as a church or diocese.

An organized way of tracing patterns in a system offers objective and consistent information that allows an appropriate intervention when a pattern of dysfunction is discovered, and encourages appropriate planning for future directions. For example, the parish described elsewhere in this book that discovered they had "never had a good goodbye" brought real intentionality to a "good goodbye" for a departing rector, allowing them to be better prepared to say a "good hello" to the next rector; the parish that discovered they had a pattern of moving between rectors with long, boring tenures to short, dramatic, charismatic tenures approached their nominating process with a much greater awareness and intentionality; a parish whose vestry recognized their pattern of nominating the most wealthy and influential in the congregation for leadership positions became intentional in recruiting a more inclusive sample from their congregation.

SPEAK UP! Have Your Own "Covenantal" Agreements and Stick by Them

Covenantal agreements, such as the "Culture of Courtesy Covenant," meet a growing desire to make tangible the intentional expectation of appropriate behaviors and mutual accountability, while holding in balance a call that has been mutually discerned and the development of good business practices. Like most aspects of walking a tightrope, this will take careful consideration and will be as effective as the people who sign it, and those who stand behind them. The encouraging factor is the recognition that such documents are needed and could be helpful in the quest for more effective relationships.

Training Young People to Recognize Anxiety Behaviors

It is never too early to begin identifying behaviors. Most of us do it with children when they are learning the basics of socialization, and later, when safety and well-being are involved. If we have not learned to identify anxiety behaviors ourselves, understand their impact, and look at alternatives, we will not pass that skill on to our young people.

My granddaughter Virginia and her HOBY cohorts, as high school juniors, were learning to recognize behaviors that are destructive to human relationships and reflecting on what this learning meant to them. This is an important part of the formation of young people in their faith tradition, and can be incorporated in both Christian Formation and youth activities. One of the great benefits of experiential laboratory learning is that its interactive nature engages the energy of young people, who will undoubtedly add their own creative elements to the teaching. The intentionality in making it part of the curriculum, however, must come from the adults.

Commission on Ministry

The Commission on Ministry and related groups, such as parish, convocational, or diocesan discernment committees, are one of the most important of all gateways, as the work they do literally provides some of the human material for leadership in the church. All too often the focus is upon either accepting or rejecting a person for ordained ministry. Much work needs to be done on broader discernment for ministry. If, as has been observed, "being sweet and loving Jesus" is the only prerequisite for ordained ministry, without regard to necessary competencies, we are, indeed, a system in trouble! Seminary will prepare people in the *tradition*, but seminary does not change character or behavior or aptitude; it does not teach students how to be a differentiated leader in a parish.

Several dioceses have initiated changes in their discernment processes, beginning with qualifications that must be met before a person is referred to the Commission on Ministry. Bishops and transition officers are becoming more and more concerned about recruiting self-differentiated individuals to become clergy. "People think because they have attended Cursillo that the next step is ordination, and that has got to stop," says another. "People don't understand what the role of an ordained person really is. I think it is important at the discernment stage to ask people if they should be in this circle. Are they already seen as a person with a vocation, which is ready to be refined? I don't think you can teach vocation, and that's precisely what we keep trying to do. It all depends on having the raw material to refine—and that begins with setting high expectations for clergy from the very beginning."

The Diocese of Georgia has taken two steps in particular that point the way to effective gateway behaviors that can lead to health within the system:

First is the compilation of a list of ten qualities, which they believe rectors must observe in an individual's life and work prior to sending them into the discernment process. Second, they have moved from utilizing parish discernment committees to a model of Convocational Discernment Committees (CDCs), which recommend to the Commission on Ministry. They believe this enables more "positively objective" discernment regarding the competency of the individual for ordained ministry.

The Diocese of Georgia's "Qualities for Ordained Ministry," from their *Requirements for Holy Orders, Discernment Handbook* (at *www. EpiscopalGeorgia.anglican.org*), include:

1. Should have a living, growing, and healthy faith relationship with God, knowing and experiencing through a commitment to and relationship with Jesus Christ as Lord and Saviour.

2. Should have leadership ability. This is the ability to get others to move; to listen and respond to one another, to the needs and opportunities, to God; political common sense; to occupy that role in a parish's life in such a way that the parish is moved toward greater health and faithfulness, capable of exercising leadership and independence while maintaining a healthy accountability to the community and its structures of authority.

3. Have emotional maturity. This includes awareness of your own emotions; accepting responsibility for how you are acting on your own emotions; an understanding of the impact of your behavior on others; self-confidence; self-control; the ability to stay with something while being flexible; the capacity to negotiate with others; the ability to be a part of the group as well as stand apart from the group.

4. Have spiritual maturity. This means being a person of Apostolic faith. Including maintaining a spiritual discipline that includes a Rule of Life.

5. Have competency in many of the skills related to effective ordained ministry. This includes leading liturgy, preaching, spiritual and pastoral guidance, Christian formation, etc. In each there are skills related to design as well as implementation.

6. Loyalty to the Episcopal Church while at the same time able to be reflective and constructively critical.

7. Have a healthy passion for the mission of the church embracing the whole gospel in its liturgical, evangelical, social, pastoral, and prophetic dimensions.

8. Ordained persons are called to be "wholesome examples to the flock of Christ." Applicants for ordained ministry must exhibit the teaching and virtues of the Gospel of Jesus Christ in their personal lives. Family

life must be characterized by faithfulness, monogamy, life-long commitment, mutual caring, and affection.

The Diocese of Olympia's five expectations for ordained clergy, as listed in their *Manual for Discernment and Expectations* (at www. Ecww.org under Commission on Ministry, *Resources*), include:

1. Are spiritually grounded and Christ centered

We ask persons who have a practiced life of prayer, can articulate their faith in a way that draws others into "The Story," and who find strength in the Christian community and their own personal spiritual journey. We seek persons who are culturally aware and have a deep appreciation and experience with diversity. We seek persons who have a rule of life and experience in receiving spiritual direction and are willing to continue this path throughout their lives.

2. Have a proven gift of gathering and developing a community

We desire ordained leaders who have an entrepreneurial spirit and can articulate a proven history of connecting, inspiring, and unleashing the gathered body as well as the capacity for developing that body toward greater health and faithfulness over time. They demonstrate an ability to effectively articulate their faith verbally and in writing in a way that forms those to whom their words are addressed. We seek persons who have a deep love for the Church and a missionary heart, and are grounded in congregational life.

3. Practice Christian stewardship

We seek persons who can articulate clearly their stewardship journey as it relates to money, resources, and relationships, and who personally practice the tithe and are willing to be a living witness to it in their communities.

4. Demonstrate emotional maturity

We seek clergy who are aware of who they are and their impact on others in their personal relationships, in their role as leaders in congregations, and in any role they play in the work of the diocese or the broader Church.

5. Understand authority

Our clergy have a clear ability to be in touch with their own authority and respect the role of authority that is unique to our Anglican/Episcopal identity. They have a firm understanding of the polity of the Episcopal Church.

Particular emphasis should be made here on the word "competency" in all of these areas. In order for the "raw material" to be refined into the differentiated leadership sought by transition/search processes, those entering the discernment process must possess basic competencies in these areas. If individuals with such competencies are not on the ordination track, it will be impossible to find them at the deployment or calling stage.

Emphasis should also be given to the canonical expectation that rectors should "identify and select" individuals who are candidates for ordained ministry. All involved in the discernment and transition process need to rid themselves of the fallacy that "God has already chosen your next rector: all you have to do is find him or her." Magical thinking has no place in this process. Several bishops report conversations in their dioceses around new processes for discernment to better meet the changing times. "We cannot continue to send people out into the field who are not equipped, have no desire to be equipped *in what is needed*—and feel called to a church that no longer exists. It is not fair to anyone!"

The makeup of Commissions on Ministry is also critical. Far too many COM's see themselves as guard dogs to the faith, holding tenaciously to the church of the past without anticipation or imagination about what qualities and competencies are needed for the church of today and tomorrow. (Bishops, on the other hand, actually take a vow to *be* the guardians of the faith—a vow that is a serious part of their conversations about the church of the future.) On some commissions, there is a "payback" streak—"they made it really hard on me to get through the process and I'm going to be just as tough on the next group of aspirants"—rather than a "pay it forward" mentality with new thinking about a new church for a new time. One bishop reported sadly, "It has taken me half of my time as Bishop to realize that I was not appointing the right people to the COM for the task of helping prepare for the church we have and the church we have to anticipate, not the church that once was."

Diocesan Council and Standing Committee

Offer groups the opportunity to create their own Culture of Courtesy Covenant (it may have another name) that outlines expected behaviors and holds members accountable. "Clarity at the beginning—how we operate here," is what one trained interim hopes to see further developed, after serving in several provinces of the Church. "From expectations of parish membership, to the vocation of all leaders, the role of interims, and appropriate behaviors on diocesan bodies—where congregations and dioceses lay out their high expectations up front is where I experience the greatest health. People soft-pedal because they're scared of scaring people off. Actually, it's just the opposite, in my experience. Modeling high standards and clear expectations at the level of diocesan councils and Standing Committees has a ripple effect as leaders return to their congregations and other groups within the system and pass on the norms of behavior.

Parish and Diocesan Youth, College, and Young Adult Ministries

As secular youth leadership training activities such as the Hugh O'Brian Youth Leadership (HOBY) training indicate, youth are more than open to education about living and working together effectively. Elementary school teachers have noted and made organized efforts to deal honestly with cruelty in the classroom as early as kindergarten. Just as effort has gone into developing curriculum such as "Protecting God's Children" to address issues of abuse by adults, so could time, energy, and the expertise of gifted teachers be brought together to develop curriculum on healthy behaviors, with a variety of age-appropriate resources. Excellent examples already exist; again, intention at all levels and consistency with the work across changing tenures is crucial.

In one diocese, the leadership team has created a design to present to the Youth Commission and Camps and Conferences Committee that would offer leadership training for young people congruent with the models used throughout the diocese. A bishop states, "The most vital ministries in my diocese are the youth and college ministries, where there is openness to ideas, real concern about life in community and treating others with respect—that's when we need to offer the skills to support their passion."

Language, Ministry, and Worship

Across the Anglican Communion, groups and individuals are about the business of a new way of being church. They are looking for new words for a new time—words as well as actions that will assist in what is to come.

While the need presents itself in the way we worship, the way we speak of our faith, and the way we do ministry, the underlying area of concern is far larger and has to do with how people of faith express themselves, welcome others, and do the work of God in a post-Christian, consumer-driven era. The liturgy has, in the past, been a major gateway into religious life. Different styles of worship speak to different types of people. Increasingly, however, worship must speak to people of all ages who do not know *the* Story, do not understand Biblical references or images, and who do not "get" even the more modern language of the 1979 Book of Common Prayer or the New Revised Standard Version of the Bible. Sunday morning is no longer the only time and form to gather the community. Ministry itself, in terms of outreach and service, attract those who want an active faith.

Clergy and lay leaders alike refer to the difficulty in imagining beyond what we know. "We talk about doing new and different ministries, but they end up being different in specifics, but not in kind," said one. "We talk about jazz masses and new ways of doing worship, but we're still focusing on 10:00 on Sunday morning, in our building. What's really new about that?"

Gateways in language, ministry, and worship call us to consider what it means to encounter people where they are, whether at Starbucks, the health club, or at "Ashes to Go" on street corners. To listen to the stories, and be prepared when we have touched something in someone's life to follow it up.

REFLECTION: Matthew 16:28-17:7

And when the disciples heard it, they fell on their faces, and were greatly afraid. But Jesus came and touched them and said, "Arise—do not be afraid."

1. While scripture points us to change through crucifixion and death, it also points us to change that happens unexpectedly, through pure grace. Peter, James, and John were never the same after experiencing the fleeting moment of transfiguration. How does this story connect with the concerns raised in this chapter?

2. SELF-AWARENESS: Is there an experience of unexpected awareness for me about opportunities in my roles, in what God is calling me to do?

3. OTHER-AWARENESS: Is there an experience of unexpected awareness for my community about what God might be calling it to do?

CHAPTER SIX

Foundational Theories That Undergird the Work of Transformation

*"These **ideas** speak with a simple clarity to the issues of effective leadership. . . .*

They recall to us the power of simple governing principles, guiding visions, sincere values, organizational beliefs. The leader's task is first to embody these principles and then to help the organization become the standard it has declared for itself." MARGARET WHEATLEY

"I don't think we understand the potential we have to be transformative," the bishop said, "if we were really serious about working to build leadership at all levels of the church, in every diocese; if training for leaders became so normative that it was simply understood as what we do in this church. But there is no ongoing effort to do this work. . . ."

The bishop's words raise three important questions:

1. What is "this work"?

2. Why is there no across-the-board effort that is "what we do" to develop healthy leadership in the Church?

3. What can we do about it?

My fifteen-year-old granddaughter Virginia and her HOBY leadership colleagues introduced us to the concept of developing leaders through laboratory learning (experiences) in foundational theories, as we consider core ingredients for leadership training for the transformative church. As in all laboratories, the experiment is performed and then analyzed. In experiential learning, an activity takes place and the group reflects on their learnings from it.

"It's just normal for me to speak up in a group, to take the lead," Virginia said. "I realized that some of the other people in the group didn't talk very much. They hung back. I wondered what might happen in the group if I didn't talk right away, if I wasn't the one to take the lead. So, I decided that I would try it and see. And other people *did* speak up—not always as fast as I would have, or in the same way. But I could see them get stronger and more confident. It was pretty neat."

Virginia had just described one of the most important concepts in leadership development, in bringing health to all levels of a system: self-awareness and other-awareness. This awareness led her to deliberately experiment in the group setting with a different behavior, to see if there might be different results. In leadership lingo, it's called the "provisional try." Try it on and see if it works.

Daniel Goleman, author of *Working with Emotional Intelligence,* defines self-awareness as "an ongoing sense of one's internal state. In this reflective experience," he says, "mind observes and investigates experience itself, including the emotions."[17] Other-awareness builds on self-awareness. The more open we are to our own emotional process, the more skilled we are in reading the feelings of others. That capacity, says Goleman, comes into play in a vast array of life areas, from sales and management to romance and parenting, to compassion and political action. It is, indeed, the foundation undergirding the skills needed in leadership, at any level, in any field.

The foundational theories that undergird the suggestion of change at all levels of the institution include:

- Human interaction—small-group reflective process, design skills, and group development
- Emotional intelligence
- Appreciative inquiry
- Family systems
- Boundaries
- Typology; awareness wheel, spiritual quadrants
- Tutu truth and reconciliation; bereavement theory
- Transparency: tell the truth, tell the truth, tell the truth

A Bit of History on Theory and Church Practice

The concept of laboratory learning and experiential leadership training has been used in the United States for over 75 years. Many of the training models are, at least in part, based on the works of English psychiatrist Wil-

---

17. Daniel Goleman, *Working with Emotional Intelligence* (New York: Random House, 2000), 126–27.

fred Ruprecht Bion (1897–1979) and Kurt Lewin (1890–1947) along with second- and third-generation adaptations of their work. Lewin, a social psychologist, made major contributions in the study of how inner resources and human potential develop, experiential learnings, group dynamics, and action research, and founded the Research Center for Group Dynamics at MIT. Bion made extensive studies of group processes. During the war, he worked in a hospital for officers who had experienced breakdowns during their service. He designed and led groups that enabled the officers to recover their self-esteem and willingness to fight. After the war, he was involved with groups at the Tavistock Clinic in London. Many of his articles on group processes were published in a volume entitled *Experiences in Groups*. During the 1960s and the 1970s, this work and its derivatives profoundly influenced a wide variety of human resources, management, and training programs that made laboratory and experiential learning mandatory experiences.

In much of current culture, *prescriptive techniques* for management of human systems have come to be recognized as "leadership development." Books containing such prescriptions are popular for a year or so, with their vocabularies and specifics becoming catch-phrases in certain circles, until they are replaced with the next prescription. Sooner or later, the latest prescription always fades, and is replaced—for the problem with prescriptions is that when the prescribed techniques have all been tried and there is still need for something else to happen, *there is no ingrained understanding of underlying theories from which a leader can adjust to the demands of the moment.*

Theory, Not Prescription, Leads to Major Ah-Ha

A diocesan trainer and leadership team facilitators were visiting a small parish to assist in data gathering for an episcopal election. Aware that parking lot conversations and e-mail exchanges both began and perpetuated the rumors that were swirling around the congregation in a disturbing way, repeated particularly passive-aggressive comments from one small group alerted the trainer that what was brewing below the surface of the evening's agenda was likely to sabotage the process.

The leader did, indeed, turn on a dime, creating an experiential exercise that not only informed this parish, but also has become an invaluable tool across the diocese. While the action—an interactive teaching session on anxiety behaviors and their impact—was immediate and spontaneous, it came from a well-trained trainer who had a reservoir from which to draw— a foundation of solid theories, each serving as the ground on which an exercise could be built to fit the current situation.

Thought Processes and Time Warp

If the leader's thought process could be run in slow motion like an NFL instant replay, it would show:

- The group needs to be aware of the destructive behaviors that are constantly going on around here.

- It needs to happen without embarrassing anyone.

- The group needs to own it.

- They don't need theory—eyes will glaze over. They need action.

- They also need something they can practice beyond tonight, or they will revert to old patterns as soon as everyone leaves.

Like a picture instantly compressed for the web page, this chain of thoughts was embraced in a responsive reaction.

The concept of Laboratory Learning and Experiential Leadership training provides a ground or foundation that gives a common theoretical and experiential base of understanding and a common language to leaders, regardless of content or constituency, and allows leaders to reach into their reservoir of skills at any given moment to respond to a situation.

The Episcopal Church, the Presbyterian Church, and the United Church of Christ in particular were instrumental in working to establish models and organizations utilizing the principles that were understood to be theologically and philosophically compatible with the belief systems of the Church and the model offered in the life of Jesus. It was the hope of those who worked in this field that such training would not only provide leaders to carry on the work of the Kingdom, but also further enable the living out of the baptismal covenant to "respect the worth and dignity of every human being."

It was a heady environment, with funding available from denominational headquarters to provide regional training networks, encouraging the use of methodologies across content. In the larger Episcopal community, there were also field officers who went out from the Church Center to work in dioceses across the country. These training networks were founded by Episcopal, UCC, Presbyterian, and Lutheran clergy and laity who saw the work "at the cusp of applied behavioral science, psychology, and religion, offering three-phase training, conflict resolution, and training of trainers," as Dr. Pearl B. Rutledge told me. There were spin-offs of the training entities and trainers who took their experiences in organizational development to the founding of such now well-known church institutions as the Shalem Institute and Roslyn Retreat Center. In the secular world, National Training

Laboratories in Bethel, Maine led the way, while on the west coast, Esalen Institute at Big Sur was immortalized in the movies, doing no favors to the human potential/human relations movement. In Seattle, the Leadership Institute of Seattle (LIOS) was born, offering a Master's Degree in Applied Behavioral Science in both counseling and organizational development tracks. Bennett Sims, the retired Bishop of Atlanta founded the Institute for Servant Leadership, with both religious and corporate tracks. In Washington, DC, laity and clergy came together to create the Association for Creative Change. The Alban Institute, a training and consulting entity for churches, Cornerstone Project for Clergy Development, Education for Ministry, Disciples of Christ in Community (DOCC), and others were designed and pioneered by individuals who came out of this system of leadership training.

The core ingredients of this training include:

- Self-insight
- Better understanding of other persons and awareness of one's impact on them
- Better understanding of group processes and increased skill in achieving group effectiveness
- Increased recognition of the characteristics of a larger social system
- Greater awareness of the dynamics of change
- Greater awareness of how conflict can be managed and utilized
- Greater skills in discovering the needs of a community, and skills for planning and administering experiences that meet those needs

What Happened to the Church-Wide Initiative in Leadership Training?

Dollars for church-sponsored training dried up around the same time that the focus shifted from Christian Education to other priorities, and "field officers" who took the training and mission into the dioceses were no longer utilized. No discernible effort was made to ask, "What was valuable from the last experience? What did we learn from it? What would be helpful to take forward into the future? What would we like to leave behind?"

There was also a level of fear that this out-of-the-box approach was dangerous. Instead of didactic teacher-to-student classroom interaction, experiential education was interactive, put a high premium on visceral as well as cognitive response, and encouraged intimacy and truth-seeking. The fear was not only perpetuated by movies on the human potential movement, such as "Bob and Carol and Ted and Alice," but by the very real fallout from within the movement itself.

Where Did It Go?

The Episcopal Church and related organizations today are full of evidence of the importance of the original human relations/human potential theories and practices for religious life. We see evidence in Education for Ministry (EfM), the four-year program of theological education for laity, based at the School of Theology at the University of the South, Sewanee. The founders were Flower Ross and Charlie Winter, both human relations trainers. EfM's reflective process, called "Theological Reflection," is but one example of the experiential learning methodology employed by these designers. The Alban Institute, a training and consulting entity for churches, the Center for Emotional Intelligence and Human Interaction, and the Church Development Institute continue the work of these significant ways of learning and understanding.

Why Did It Experience a Resurgence?

In the early 1980s, a number of bishops were elected who had been a part of the human relations/human potential work in the Episcopal Church. Once in office, they began looking around for leaders in their jurisdictions. Where, they wondered, had all of the leaders gone? They were concerned enough about the absence of well-trained leaders in the church that they called a meeting at Kanuga Conference Center in North Carolina to brainstorm what needed to be done. How could they address the mistakes that had been made in the past and build for the needs of the present and future? They were convinced that there were foundational models in the curriculum they had known, as well as new and complimentary theories that needed to be added to the mix to strengthen leadership in the church.

New Wineskins Needed

An ongoing conversation between two former trainers endeavored to determine what essential ingredients of training needed to be transmitted to a new generation. The old system was predicated on a repetitive cycle of exercises over a five-day residential period, which allowed for the beginning of an integration of the work into an individual's personal system. It was clear that this process worked, and worked well, providing a foundation for the deepening of the work over time.

But the five-day residential experience is not always possible. The new norm appears to be intensive weekends. Is it possible to provide a training that could be truly internalized by the participants in an intensive weekend setting?

One Model . . .[18]

A bishop and canon to the ordinary had been working with a conflicted parish and were ready for a step that would move the process out of the vestry and into the congregation. A design consultant/trainer was asked if it was possible to create a design to facilitate this process with the goal of some healing of old wounds and a values-based step forward.

Behind the draft design was:

- The need to establish a safe environment for conversation—a space where the values of the Culture of Courtesy Covenant would be respected.

- Underneath the current polarization was unresolved grief manifesting itself as anger. There was need to name and validate hurts and disappointments, and have an experience of healing and reconciliation.

- There were various myths about "the good old days"—stories that had taken on the veneer of "fact" over the years and were still institutional "truth," despite the differing truths of institutional documents.

- The group was resistant to change.

- There was a need to turn toward a future, identifying wishes, hopes, and dreams.

- There was a need to learn a new way of listening and speaking to each other.

Time was short to accomplish the work. The model that was presented to the bishop included:

- Up-front presentation/facilitation from a script that offered theological and scriptural background

- Small assigned groups where couples, families, and cliques were separated to allow for individual response

- Small group leaders from parishes across the diocese who were known to have specialized training in group process through EfM mentor training, pastoral care team training, and/or other process work or professional training

The meetings were named "Holy Conversations"—an indicator that the meetings would be a safe and sacred space, with special intention for respectful listening.

---

18. *Holy Conversations*, Transition Manual of the Diocese of Lexington, Kentucky.

Session #1, "Things We Value," would utilize concepts of Appreciative Inquiry, to mine values held by the parish and reveal in their stories those times when they had been most engaged and excited in their church.

Session #2, "Hurts and Disappointments," would utilize concepts of Bishop Tutu's Truth and Reconciliation work in South Africa and bereavement theories, to discover what behaviors have caused the hurts and disappointments of the past, validate the storyteller's truth, and incorporate a liturgy of healing and reconciliation.

Session #3, "When My Safe Place Changes," would look at concepts of change and attitudes toward change.

Sessions #4, "Wishes, Hopes, and Dreams," would look at spiritual preferences in the congregation, and wishes, hopes, and dreams for their future.

Results:

- While the congregation was initially skeptical, attendance increased at each session.

- A parish geographically distant from the diocesan office, with emotional emphasis on distance, experienced the concern of the diocese through the attention of the bishop and Canon to the Ordinary and through the facilitators who came from six parishes across the diocese.

- Participants experienced a new way of listening to each other and speaking to each other.

- Participants had new information that allowed for new perspective.

- The majority attended the Liturgy of Healing and Reconciliation; there was clear identification of the group who did not attend the service.

- Potential new leaders were identified among the participants.

What If . . . ? The Creation of the
Diocesan Leadership Team

Bishop Stacy Sauls, now COO of the Episcopal Church, was the Bishop of Lexington who requested the intervention in the story above. He recalls the movement from that intervention to the development of the Diocesan Leadership Team, and then to the application of the work to transition ministries: "We had a parish situation that appeared intractable and approached this particular intervention outside of 'normal' conflict intervention modes. We knew we had to get accurate information out there, which we researched in diocesan files, and then to create a design that allowed the maximum number of people to tell their truths and get the ghosts out of the closet. That meant small-group conversation, which meant trained facilitators. We were looking for where the strength was in the system, and wanted to try to strengthen and encourage what we found. The team was intended to facilitate that, and they did well. Unintended (from my perspective) benefits of the team are that they were healthy demonstrations of effective communication and non-anxious presence, and they came from literally across the diocese, putting a real face of caring for each other as part of the diocesan family. We then realized that if this approach was useful in a conflicted congregation, it could be even more useful in strong, healthy congregations—and we just took off from there, concentrating on how to develop and deploy resources toward strength in our congregations—and all of our leadership areas."

Vision

The vision was for a team of trained leaders who could be of assistance in interactive work for many purposes, including transitions, long-range planning, and conflict resolution. Those who wished to pursue further training could also work with designs in response to special needs, be trained as parish consultants, or do mutual ministry reviews or other special tasks as requested.

Implementation

Invitations were extended to persons who were identified as having the necessary skills and attributes to be trained for facilitation and were perceived to be life-long learners, always open to new things. Each would agree to attend an intensive weekend. The trainers for the weekend were long experienced in the old five-day format and had identified the essential ingredients for the shorter training:

- Yon Competency/Commitment Model (Appendix N)
- "View from the Pew" small group for self- and other-awareness (Appendix O)
- Reflective Process—there is no learning from unprocessed experience
- Culture of Courtesy Covenant (Norms and Standards)
- Group Development
- Boundaries
- Inclusion, Control, Affection
- Confidentiality
- Systems Theory
- Iceberg Theory

The trainers were aware that the shorter format prevented the all-important cycles of repetition. Plans called for supplemental continuing education weekends and day-long intensives, while using each team's de-briefing time as an opportunity to reflect on where they saw the theories in play in a parish and how they were utilizing their skills.

What They Learned

Benjamin "Bungee" Bynum was 29 years old and serving on the diocesan staff when he attended the first training for the Leadership Team. He states: "The leadership development skills I learned in this weekend training have been transformational for my understanding of the organizational culture of the Episcopal Church. They've put data and science behind perspectives of leadership I once thought were common sense until I realized that not everyone shared my viewpoint. These theories have helped me understand why things work the way they do—wonderfully or more frustratingly—what my contribution is, what others' contributions are, and how many events are systemic to the culture of the church."

Bynum received his Master's in Applied Behavioral Science from the Leadership Institute of Seattle in June of 2012—and hopes for a career furthering the development of leadership skills and transition ministries in the church.

The Rev. Timothy Fleck was no stranger to leadership or management, coming into the ordained ministry after a career heading an architectural firm. As part of the Network for Pastoral Leadership and Sustaining Healthy Congregations, he was expected to take part in the leadership training. Fleck recalls: "When I was invited to be a part of the leadership team tasked with facilitating healthy conversations around transitions and crisis, it frankly sounded like dark, heavy work, and I went into the initial training with a pretty negative attitude. I was bowled over by the loving, positive, honest spirit in the training groups, and I have been amazed at the transformation and reconciliation that I have experienced among participants in the Holy Conversation process."

Fleck, who has served as both table facilitator and up-front presenter/team leader, continues: "Make no mistake, it is hard work and a big commitment for the leaders and the participants, but it is joyful, organic, growing work that yields an abundant harvest of truth, mutual understanding, and shared vision. Again and again, I have heard from participants that they were dreading Holy Conversations, dreading what they feared would be lots of talk and lots of whining. Again and again, I have heard these same people speak with astonishment at how energized for mission they feel at the end of the process. When was the last time you heard participants in a transition process say, "We need to do this every year'?"

REFLECTION: Matthew 9:16-17

"No one sews a piece of unshrunk cloth on an old cloak, for the patch pulls away from the cloak and a worse tear is made. Neither is new wine put into old wineskins; otherwise, the skins burst and the wine is spilled, and the skins are destroyed; but new wine is put into fresh wineskins, and so both are preserved."

1. How does this passage connect with the chapter?

2. FOR SELF-AWARENESS: In what ways am I trying to "fix things" with technical fixes (ways that I already know or believe that have worked before)? How do I rely upon the familiar and known instead of doing the hard work of being open to and seeking new answers (adaptive change)?

3. FOR OTHER-AWARENESS: How is my community trying to fix itself with old solutions? What kind of "worse tears" are being made? Have there been adaptive challenges identified? Is the community open to, resistant to, or oblivious to these challenges?

4. PRACTICE: How will you encourage others to identify their "old wineskins" of practice and be open to new ones?

CHAPTER SEVEN

Deep in the DNA: Integrating Complementary Theories of Human Behavior

Behaviors don't change just by announcing new values. We move only gradually into being able to act congruently with these values. . . .

To do this we have to develop much greater self-awareness of how we're acting; become more self-reflective than normal. And we have to help one another notice when we fall back into old behaviors." MARGARET WHEATLEY

When the church decides to make leadership training a priority, the investment must go beyond lip service. Leadership training that becomes integral to individuals, parishes, and dioceses must be practiced with consistency, intentionally maintaining good practices in the periods between tenures of bishops and rectors, and undergirding all particular missions and action plans. When the practices are embedded in a system, ready to be handed down, generation to generation, they are beyond automatic.

When a practice has become internalized by an individual, it has become integral to whom they are and what they do. A simple example is the act of riding a bicycle.

Knowledge level. This is a bicycle. It takes a combination of balance and speed for it to stand upright, and requires my legs to pump the pedals to make it move. Someone may push me on the bicycle now.

Ability level. I no longer need assistance to balance the bike and can maneuver it by myself. I need to concentrate on what I am doing and remind myself of the separate skills I need to keep riding. I might sometimes wobble, but I have a new ability.

Mastery level. Riding my bike is something I do without thinking. It is beyond automatic. If I went years without riding, I could immediately ride again at any time. I can talk to someone else while I am riding. I might even be able to pedal without my hands on the handlebars!

When theoretical constructs are first learned, they are at the *knowledge* level. We know *about* them. I might be able to choose a particular theory to use in a particular situation. More than likely, I would find myself brushing up on it before using it or attempting to teach it to someone else.

A student teacher was observing a class, taking copious notes on everything the teacher was doing. The teacher was creative, innovative. The student teacher was excited about the new approaches to learning and enthusiastically taking it all in. One day the teacher was ill, and the director of the school asked the young man if he would like to take the class for the day. "Yes!" he replied eagerly, going to his notes to see what would apply.

At the end of the first hour of his teaching day, the young man turned to the director in frustration. "I've already used every idea in my notes and it's not even 10 o'clock!" The director listened and then replied: "You were watching a master teacher at work—someone who has a reservoir of ways to help students ingrain an idea. Those notes you've taken represent many weeks of teaching. I bet you didn't write them all down in one day—and they aren't gimmicks intended to entertain or be used in one day."

The student teacher nodded.

"Today, you used all of those ideas as a list to run through, gimmicks to keep the students' interest perhaps, instead of allowing them to surface inside of you as just the thing you need at a particular time, or for a particular student, to emphasize a certain point. You were checking your notes constantly to see if you'd left anything out. One of these days, those ideas— and others that you invent as you need them—will be yours. They will live somewhere deep inside of you, connected not only to the theory that helped birth them, but to the many students they've helped. You might use one or two in a day . . . but they will be a part of you that doesn't even think—it just responds to the needs of the moment."

Experiential leadership training strives to do just what the wise director described to the student teacher—to turn theory into an experience that lives deep inside a person, both undergirding every aspect of their work and surfacing when the time and situation call for it.

A vestry was on retreat. Things had not been going well for this congregation. Spirits were low; giving was down. There had been some notable departures from the parish. There were tensions between the rector and some staff members, and between the rector and various individuals in the parish. The triangles of rumor and discontent were everywhere; nothing seemed to work. The rector had requested an agenda based on a book that he believed would inspire the leadership to think about parish growth. Despite all efforts to spark some enthusiasm through creative exercises, the inspiration was clearly not happening. During a break in the activities, the retreat leader overheard a muttered comment from one of the vestry members: "Who wants to come to a dead church?"

As the group reassembled, the leader set aside the planned agenda and introduced an exercise that included the congregational life cycle and a timeline. Initial foot-dragging gave way to participation as the leader encouraged full disclosure of experiences. At a pivotal point in the conversation about the congregation's life cycle, vestry members who were long-time parishioners identified a crisis in the life of a previous rector, which had led not only to his departure, but also to deep division within the congregation, never fully addressed.

"Tell me more," the leader urged. "Was there a good goodbye?"

"We've never had a good good-bye—whatever that might be," someone said. "Everyone who has left has left under some sort of cloud—and they're just here one day and gone the next."

"Tell me about the work of the interim period," the leader encouraged. There were exclamations of disgust from several vestry members. "Don't even say the word interim around here. That is a dirty word. Charged too much money and did nothing . . . we should have just gotten another priest right away." After more complaints were aired and listed on newsprint, the leader introduced the developmental tasks of the interim period, with their signs of non-resolution and resolution. There was silence in the room.

Finally the rector spoke. "It looks like I've been the interim," he said. "Only no one told me I was."

Heads nodded in agreement.

The ability to respond as the situation demands reveals new and important information and shifts the retreat for the good, offering new direction for follow-up.

The assistant priest, officers, and council members charged with the ministry with single adults in a large congregation had invited a consultant to work with them on long-range planning. The congenial group was happily settled into a beautiful beach home for the weekend. Things were moving along as planned when the tone of the meeting turned dark and tense.

Apparently continuing with the agenda, the consultant quickly reflected on what had taken place prior to the change of mood. The congregation was a little over a year into the tenure of a new rector. The group had been discussing the role of the clergy in this particular ministry area. At the first pause, the consultant named the shift in atmosphere that she had experienced and asked if anyone else had experienced it as well. There was silence—and then, a few heads nodded in agreement.

"We have a choice to make at this moment," the consultant said. "Obviously there is a story here that some of you—possibly all of you—know and

I do not. Only you can say if this part of your story is of enough significance that it is now interfering with your ability to make plans together for the future of the ministry or if it is not and will not.

So I believe the choice is this: you can choose to name what is on your minds, so that we have the whole story on the table—or you can hold that as a family secret and try to plan around it. Does anyone have a thought about what the choice should be?"

Silence. Then a woman spoke. "It is a pretty big issue for some people—and it is causing a real problem. But I think it would be pretty painful to talk about, because there are several different perspectives on it."

"Any other thoughts?" the consultant asked. No one spoke. "How many of you are in agreement with Ann, that this would be a tough conversation?" Hands went up.

"What is your greatest fear if this is talked about?" Suddenly the room was alive with comments. "I'll lose a friend who doesn't see it the way I do." "R— (the assistant to the rector) will quit being our staff person." "C— (the rector) will find out and we'll be disbanded, or he will just be disgusted with us and not want anything to do with us." "People will be critical of S— (the former rector)."

When the room was quiet again, the consultant asked, "How many of you would be willing to work on ground rules for this conversation, and pledge your willingness to be a respectful listener as well as speaking your truth?" Hands went up. For the next hour, the group worked earnestly on ground rules for a respectful conversation, signing the final document. Then, gathered in a circle, they each told their truth about their individual and corporate experience of the relationship of the previous rector to the ministry, and the relationship of the new rector to the ministry. The unresolved grief at the loss of an old friend who had enjoyed partying with the singles on Friday night was named, and an opportunity given to honor what had been. Those who had not found the relationship helpful were encouraged to speak their truth and were respectfully heard. The issue of not yet being able to establish a relationship with the new rector, and wondering what shape it might eventually take was named. Members spoke of the expectations they had of the new rector, and looked at what reasonable and unreasonable expectations might be. They brainstormed ways in which they could find opportunities to develop a relationship with their new rector.

Experiential Laboratory Learning

In a laboratory, we perform experiments and analyze the results. In experiential laboratory learning, we have a life together that we put under a behavioral microscope to see how we interact as we work. Process time, when we look at what we have been doing and how it has impacted us and others in the group, is an essential aspect of leadership development. In experiential laboratory learning, every aspect of our life together is an *experience* that we will *reflect on* in order to learn from it and make choices about future behavior. Process here is both a noun and a verb: We have a *process (n.),* a systematic set of actions by which we do our work and through which we reflect, and a *process (v.)* by which we come to an understanding of what we have experienced.

Of equal importance to Experiential Laboratory training is the foundational work of *Systems Theory.* There are numerous books written on the subject of family systems theory which offer substantial in-depth thinking on the subject (see bibliography). This overview is intended to point the uninitiated reader to a fuller study of the subject.

Dr. Murray Bowen was one of five individuals who independently and simultaneously "discovered" family systems as a holistic approach to psychotherapy in the 1970s and early 1980s. The other four include Paul Watzlawick, a communicational therapist from the Mental Health Institute in California; Jay Haley, one of the Strategic therapists; Carl Whitaker, an existential therapist; and Salvador Minuchin, the structural family therapist. Family systems theories suggest that individuals cannot be understood in isolation from each other, rather as a part of their family, as the family is the basic emotional unit. Families are systems of interconnected and interdependent individuals, none of whom can be understood in isolation. The "family" may be a nuclear family unit, or it may be a larger organization. Certain behavioral patterns develop within a given system as individuals play out their roles. Roles and patterns may lead to either balance or dysfunction in the family constellation. As one bishop says, "as a matter of theology, we say that the diocese is the basic unit in our system. However, the congregations, or families within the congregation, may be the basic emotional unit. The traditional understanding of the diocese as the basic unit is an intellectual approach, when the behaviors and issues we're dealing with are emotional issues. We also have to consider the interlocking system of systems—families in a congregation, congregations into a diocese. This bears further thought."

There are eight interlocking concepts in Dr. Bowen's theory, according to Dr. Roberta Gilbert of the Center for the Study of Human Systems:

1. Triangles: the smallest stable relationship system. When a twosome is in conflict, they will bring in a third to stabilize the relationship. Diads are inherently unstable. Triads are naturally more stable, and probably are, in truth, the basic emotional unit.

2. Differentiation of self: The variance in individuals is their susceptibility to depend on others for acceptance and approval. A well-differentiated leader is someone who has clarity about his/her own life goals and is therefore less likely to become lost in the anxious emotional process that swirls around every system. The differentiated leader is separate while remaining connected, able to maintain a modifying and non-anxious presence with sometimes challenging nuclear family emotional systems.

3. The four relationship patterns where problems may develop in a family include marital conflict, dysfunction of one spouse, impairment of one or more children, and emotional distance.

4. Family projection process: the transmission of emotional problems from a parent to a child, or from the organizational parent to the organizational child.

5. Multigenerational transmission process: the transmission of similar levels of differentiation between parents and their children.

6. Emotional cutoff: the act of reducing or cutting off emotional contact with the family or organizational entity as a way of managing unresolved emotional issues.

7. Sibling position: the impact of sibling position on development and behavior.

8. Societal emotional process: the emotional system that governs behavior on a societal level, promoting both progressive and regressive periods in a society.[19]

Rabbi Edwin Friedman, a family systems therapist who brought the insights of the modality to religious systems, explored the organic nature of human colonization, and posited that leadership in both families and organizations was rooted in processes that could be found in all colonized life. Friedman's revolutionary approach to leadership training focused on supporting strengths in the system rather than pathology, emphasizing the self-differentiation of the leader rather than focusing on method and technique. He also stressed that before any technique or data could be effective, leaders had to be willing to face and work on themselves.

Emotional intelligence is the ability to perceive, control, and evaluate emotions. Peter Salovey and John Mayer, leading EI researchers since 1990,

---

19. Roberta M. Gilbert, *The Eight Concepts of Bowen Theory* (Falls Church, VA: Leading Systems Press, 2004), 4.

say that Emotional Intelligence is a subset of social intelligence that involves the ability to monitor one's own and others' feelings and emotions, to discriminate among them, and to use this information to guide one's thinking and actions. In his book *Working with Emotional Intelligence*, author Daniel Goleman lists the five factors of Emotional Intelligence as:[20]

1. Self-awareness

2. Self-regulation

3. Motivation (how we manage ourselves)

4. Empathy

5. Social Skills (how we manage relationships)

It is believed that emotional intelligence can be developed and strengthened as needed.

Supporting these three primary foundational theories are:

Yon Competency and Commitment: Inspiration and motivation are important to the leader of any organization, and often a consideration as organizations offer trainings of various sorts. To what is each person being inspired? For what are they being motivated?

The majority of leaders can recall returning from a workshop or training inspired and motivated, only to have the new energy fade as weeks and months go by. Others have sent employees for training, or brought a particularly fine speaker into the organization to inspire and motivate, but been disappointed in terms of lasting results.

Trainer Bill Yon emphasizes that it is important to understand (1) the interface between competency and commitment, (2) oneself in relation to one's own competencies and commitments as a basis for understanding and relating to others' competencies and commitments, and (3) the practice of behaviors and models that are sustainable over time, and evolve in an organic manner, rather than providing short-term techniques or gimmicks.

The grid to the right shows the interface between competency (skill building and training) and commitment (inspiration or revival experiences):

	Lo	Hi	
COMPETENCY Skill Building Training	Goof Offs	Producers	Hi
	Do Nothings	Goof Ups	Lo

COMMITMENT
Revival Experiences

---

20. Goleman, *Working with Emotional Intelligence*, 26–27.

>> >>

Low competency and high commitment = Goof offs
Low competency and low commitment = Do nothings
High competency and low commitment = Goof ups
High competency and high commitment = Producers

Group Development: There are predictable stages in the life of any group. There are two definitive descriptions of the stages, developed by Richard Weber and Scott Peck. Weber aligns the stages of group development with the stages of human development: infancy or forming, adolescence (storming), norming and performing, and transforming. Peck's stages (see Appendix P) parallel Weber's—carrying the names *pseudo-community, chaos, emptiness,* and *true community.* Both define the stages that move a group from its inception where everyone is polite and "nice," through the predictable chaos (and who does not recognize this stage as adolescence?) when issues of control are being addressed, to the working stage of "norming and performing" (creating norms and performing tasks), to the final stage which may, in an open-ended group, repeat its cycle or may lead the group through a re-birth (Appendix P).

ICA (Inclusion, Control, Affection): Psychologist and author William Schutz developed the concept of ICA (Inclusion, Control, and Affection or Openness) to help people consider and become aware of their own and others' needs to be a part of the group (included), to control the group (control), and how affectionate (open) with others they are willing to be (see Appendix Q).

Boundaries: These can be defined as the intangible lines that mark where one person begins and ends. A boundary is like a fence with gates, which an individual can choose to open or close as needed in a particular situation or relationship. Physical boundaries are most easily recognized and defended, but individuals also have mental, emotional, and spiritual boundaries. A society that values enmeshment and lack of privacy often does not respect boundaries. Individuals need to be taught the basics of understanding and using boundaries. It is critical to all leadership to understand healthy and unhealthy boundaries, and not violate those boundaries (see Appendix R).

Confidentiality: Current cultural norms show little respect for privacy, nor understanding of confidentiality. Confidentiality is different than secrecy. To be confidential is to hold information that is entrusted to one and not reveal it to any other person. It has been said that there is no such thing as confidentiality; if a second person holds the information, they, too, may choose to pass it on to one more "trusted" person—and suddenly the confidential information is no longer confidential. While it is assumed that conversations with clergy and spiritual directors are confidential, it is sadly true that confidences have been violated enough times that it is difficult for people to trust that even clergy will hold things in confidence.

A basic rule of confidentiality in any group of people is that I have the right to take out of the group what I said; I do not have the right to take out of the group what anyone else said, nor do they have the right to take out of the group what I said.

Another way of explaining the difference between confidentiality and secrecy is that confidences are something we keep to protect another; secrets are something we keep to protect ourselves. Confidences are other-focused. Secrets are self-focused or selfish.

Norms and Standards: These list how a group functions regarding attendance, timeliness, breaks, confidentiality, and other concerns. At the beginning of a group's life, it is important for the members to help create the norms and standards and agree to them. The norms and standards provide clear, upfront expectations for the life and behavior within any group. The functioning of any group can be improved dramatically by an up-front agreement, with "buy-in" by all members as to how the group chooses to behave and monitor the behavior.

Post-Meeting Response: A post-meeting response exercise—written, experiential, or both—enables the designers and facilitators to know what worked and what didn't, and gives a voice about the experience to participants. The post-meeting response is directly related to reflective process, calling individuals to identify what was most helpful and least helpful to them, and to make comments and suggestions. So, the purpose of the PMR is really two-fold: to assist the planners/facilitators in determining how effective the work was, discerning what changes might need to be made in the future, and of equal importance, helping participants begin to reflect on their experience in an analytical way. An interactive end-of-meeting exercise, where participants move along a continuum answering such questions as "On a scale of 1–10, how would you relate your learning today?" "Would you recommend this training to others?" "Did you find this training applicable to experiences in your life and work?" provides an energizing opportunity for immediate reflection, while the written format allows for more in-depth consideration.

Many times, mistakes are made both in terminology (using the word "evaluation" rather than "post-meeting response") and in asking too many questions. The most effective PMRs get at three basic questions: What was most helpful and why? What was least helpful and why? What suggestions would you make for the future?

Tutu Truth and Reconciliation

Bishop Desmond Tutu provided perhaps the most important model of dealing with individual and corporate grief in the Truth and Reconciliation work following apartheid. Most of us will never have to deal with the atrocities experienced by the people of South Africa. However, our lives, and our life in the church, have their own losses and resultant grief. This model aids healing by encouraging individuals to hear the truth of other people's loss and grief without the need to correct, interrupt, or defend. It is this respectful listening that honors grief, assisting in long-term healing.

Again, the integration of all these skills requires repetition and intentionality. That intention is seen in planning ongoing opportunities, in making the work and practice normative, and in resourcing these efforts with adequate financing and staffing. Intentional local efforts are at work in pockets of the church. In the dioceses of Georgia and Olympia, outside trainers in Emotional Intelligence and Human Relations are helping prepare local leaders to be certified in the work of Emotional Intelligence, a certification required of all clergy. In the Diocese of Lexington, the training of diocesan leaders continues through the Diocesan Leadership Team. Each year, individuals who have been identified by clergy, leadership team members, or diocesan staff as potential members for the team are invited to attend a Friday night/all-day Saturday training in one of three geographic regions of the diocese. After the initial training, they are invited to work with an experienced team in facilitation of Holy Conversations. Opportunities for further training and practice working with the Deputy for Leadership Development in design, vestry training, presenting mutual ministry reviews, and other areas which assist in building and maintaining healthy patterns of behavior as well as healthy transitions across a diocese extend the work throughout diocesan and parish systems. Other dioceses are paying attention and asking questions about these resources.

The use of outside experts who can help us see and understand ourselves is critical to these models. "We have for too long tried to 'fix' ourselves from inside, so we keep repeating old ways and wondering why nothing changes. We have to avail ourselves of resources outside our system who can help us see ourselves honestly, and see ourselves as others see us," say several bishops.

In one diocese, this means a two-phase process where, under the leadership of outside consultants, the diocese looks at who they say they are. Phase two takes the conversation into public places—libraries, bars, health clubs—and asks the question, "What does the world say about us?" "We are interested in what the gap is, between who we say we are and how we are being experienced by those outside," says the bishop. "We need people able to take a non-defensive look at this, without critiquing the process or trying to rationalize the results. It's hard to see from inside."

In the Diocese of Lexington, a letter to vestries and nominating committees prior to Holy Conversations asks leadership to step back from their role as planners and implementers of the vision and allow themselves to respond as members, while listening to the experiences of those who are more on the periphery of the life of the congregation. The perspective is quite different from the outer circles—and there is much to be learned!

REFLECTION: 1 Corinthians 3:10-13

"By the grace God has given me, I laid a foundation as an expert builder, and someone else is building on it."

1. How does this verse connect with the chapter you have just read regarding foundational leadership theories?

2. SELF-AWARENESS: What are the foundational theories that undergird my leadership? Which do I need to develop/develop further? How am I passing this foundation on that others might build on it?

3. OTHER-AWARENESS: What are the foundational theories that support my community? What needs to be further developed? How might that happen? How are we passing a strong foundation on so that others might build on it in the future?

4. PRACTICE: What is one step I can take personally to strengthen my foundation? What is one step my community might take?

CHAPTER EIGHT

Why Do We Really Do Things "The Way We've Always Done It"—Bold Challenges to Accepted Norms

*The dynamic **tension** between the message and the culture is not about what Jesus once said, but what Jesus is saying. . . .*

The intersection is not simply between an ancient message and a contemporary context, but between an eternal God and this moment in history." ERWIN RAPHAEL MCMANUS

When I became the transition officer for my diocese, the bishop and I sat down together and made a list. There were four columns, all referring to the work of the transition time:

ESSENTIAL INGREDIENT	RATIONALE	LIVED EXPERIENCE	BASED ON LIVED EXPERIENCE RECOMMEND

It's a pretty good list. Along the way, I've discovered that many of the things on it have to do with much more than the transition periods in the life of the Episcopal Church. And that it's a good idea to figure out what norms need to be challenged, in many areas of our corporate life. Sometimes we find that it's a lot like the woman who was cutting off the end of the ham before she put it in the roasting pan.

"Why do you cut that off, Mom?" her daughter asked.

The woman paused. "I don't know, honey," she responded. "I guess because my mom did, and that's what I learned. I'll have to ask her."

"MM-m, good question," the grandmother responded. "My mother did it that way, and so I did, too—and I'm pretty sure it was because she had to fit the ham in a smaller roasting pan!"

It's time to see if many of the things we have considered normative actions and behaviors in our church fit who we are and what we say we believe, or if we're automatically repeating an old pattern, not even aware that the old "roasting pan" is long gone, and we have other options.

This chapter is a list. The items on it came from bishops, parish priests, transition officers, canons to the ordinary, church communication professionals, commission on ministry members, diocesan council members, standing committee members, people in the pews.

It is a beginning.

The **blank pages at the end of the list** offer a space for you to continue . . .

- We need to challenge the norm of nineteenth-century decision making, spending time on resolutions no one is going to pay any attention to.

- We need to stop preparing to fight the last war by preparing clergy for a church that used to be.

- We need to challenge the norm of the "new" Prayer Book; the 1979 BCP only went part way and is still perceived as too formal and distant from most people, not connecting to real life in the twenty-first century.

- We need to challenge the norm that only Rite I and Rite II are really used.

- We need to challenge the norm that Rite III is too much time and trouble, finding more ways to use it on more days.

- We need to realize that everyone who is sweet and loves Jesus does not need to be ordained.

- We need to challenge the norm that only clergy can do certain things, like pastoral care.

- We need to challenge the norm that certain groups are just "doing the church's laundry" and others are doing something holy. By meeting regularly with all ministry groups, we have the opportunity to help individuals discover more deeply how participation in a ministry enhances their relationship with Jesus Christ—or to find one that does.

- We have to challenge our unwillingness to confront difficult behaviors in ways that are effective.

- We need to challenge the norm of our current diocesan structures—how many do we need and how do they need to be configured?

- We need to challenge the norm that we are not accountable for our behaviors.

- We need to challenge the norm that longevity is all we need to move up in the church, and acknowledge that appropriate skills and competencies are more important.

- We need to challenge the norm that we can fix ourselves from inside, finding outside expertise to assist us in looking at enormous and critically important areas of our life, such as structure.

- We need to challenge the norm that it is acceptable for issues to become more personalized as we become more desperate.

- We need to challenge the norm of our independent nature and our unwillingness to be interdependent.

- We need to challenge the norm that differentiated leadership can be only clear or only connected and realize that truly differentiated leadership is both clear and stays connected.

- We need to challenge the norm that a new person or leader will get different results—that if we change this one part of the system, the whole machine will be improved or different.

- We need to challenge the norms of worship and community life and our settled notions of Church.

- We need to challenge the norm that every parish needs a building.

- We have to challenge the norms of the perfect parish: the idyllic community that clergy project and the fantasy priest that parishes project.

- We need to find a middle ground between utilizing people's gifts only in ordained ministry or not recognizing them at all.

- We need to challenge the norm that big churches don't need any guidance.

- We need to challenge the norm that people who are elected bishop come to the office already understanding the work.

- We need to challenge the idea that there are a certain number of Episcopalians out there and we just need to find them.

- We need to challenge the idea that as Episcopal Christians we just sit in the pew and wait for people to come.

- We need to challenge the norm that we are the church of the culture—and get out there and train our people like the first-century church in Corinth.

- We need to challenge the norm that Episcopalians don't speak about their faith because they might sound like Southern Baptists, so we can speak about our faith and sound like excited Episcopalians.

94 Becoming the Transformative Church

›› ››

- We need to challenge the norm of being disingenuously polite rather than true and honest.
- We need to challenge the norm of considering rectors as employees.
- We need to challenge the norm of thinking that everyone should know what we stand for.
- We need to challenge the norm of thinking that the church operates just like corporate America.
- We need to challenge the norm that people who speak up with different perspectives and real truth-telling are troublemakers.
- We need to challenge the norm that chaos and conflict are bad things and learn how to live into them as part of a growing, flourishing system.
- We need to challenge the norm that power is manifested in titles.
- We need to challenge the norm that bishops serve forever and the longer a rector's tenure, the better.
- We need to challenge the norm that the only real ministry for the ordained is in a parish church.
- We need to challenge the norm that anyone can call themselves a "consultant" or "coach."
- We need to challenge the norms that there are certain ladders of expectations clergy have to climb.
- We need to challenge the norms of Episcopal polity, how business is conducted in the Episcopal Church, what it means to be an Episcopalian, and what being a missional church really is.
- We need to challenge the norm that relationships and skills can be built in shorter clergy tenures of three to five years, only to move on and repeat the patterns, rather than sustaining relationships over a longer tenure, developing skills from challenges of a longer pastorate.
- We need to challenge the norm of institutional secrecy.
- We need to challenge the norm that trained interims are simply glorified supply priests and give them the support they need to do their work.
- We need to challenge the norm that female clergy are not to be taken seriously.
- We need to challenge the norm that this is a "good old boy" church and the "good old boys" can get away with anything.

- We need to challenge the norm that those with financial know-how can control mission and ministry.

- We need to challenge the norm that benefits are for full-time parish clergy only, and deal with pension and health care concerns for part-time clergy.

- We need to challenge the norm of full-time parish clergy.

- We need to challenge the norm that candidates for a church position won't be interested if transition materials tell the truth.

- We need to challenge the norm of sending ineffective parish priests for interim training.

- We need to challenge the norm that most churches just need a "place-holder" or a sacramentalist during a transition.

- We need to challenge the norm that being "beloved" as a pastoral presence is more important for a bishop or rector than being a differentiated leader.

- We need to challenge the norm that there is one priest out there that God has hand-picked for a congregation and the nominating committee's job is to find them.

- We need to challenge the norm that we still live in Lake Woebegone and recognize our post-Christian context.

- We need to challenge the norm that it takes less skill to be a "one-person show" in a small parish than to minister in a large multi-staff parish, and realize that big systems can often cruise, while there are usually no margins for the smaller ones.

- We need to challenge the norm that Father Tim (of Karon novel fame) is a good model for parish clergy, de-frock him, and move on.

- We need to challenge the norm that being nice is more important than being truthful.

- We need to challenge the norm that conflict is bad and must be avoided or suppressed rather than managed.

- We need to challenge the norm that mediocrity is acceptable.

- We need to challenge the norm that "we're just fine the way we are."

- We need to challenge the norm that we can hide behind "we don't disagree—we're just not ready yet" when the church has long since moved on.

- We need to challenge the norm that constant presence at church equals competency for tasks as we choose suitable leaders, rather than rewarding people for hard work and frequent attendance.

- We need to challenge the norm of using vestry membership as a "carrot" to get people more involved.

- We need to challenge the norm that people of power, wealth, and influence have disproportionate power and authority, learning to act democratically as well as talk it.

- We need to challenge the norm of lack of succession planning in leadership, and recognize that generativity (grooming future leaders) and overlap are important to continuity.

- We need to challenge the norm of possession—"Gladys's altar guild," "Peter's Bible study group," etc.

- We need to challenge the norm that "everybody feels the way I do (how could they not?)."

- We need to challenge the norm that if someone doesn't speak up, it means they agree with what was just said.

- We need to challenge the norm that everyone is Biblically literate.

- We need to challenge the norm that Episcopalians have no interest in the Bible.

- We need to challenge the norm that episcopal elections have no relation to ongoing transitions in the life of the church.

- We need to challenge the norm that computers do it all.

- We need to challenge the norm of secrecy (different from confidentiality).

- We need to challenge the norm that there is a certain external model one must fit to be a rector, and a certain trajectory one must follow.

- We need to challenge the norm that there is only one acceptable style of liturgy and music.

- We need to challenge the norm that ordination is for full-time ministry.

- We need to challenge the norm that priests sit in their office counseling, hearing confessions, and writing sermons, and we need to look instead for differentiation, flexibility, and adaptability.

- We need to challenge the norm that the Church will take care of the priest.

- We need to challenge the norm of a narrow understanding of the episcopate.
- We need to challenge the norm that seminary-trained clergy and a weekly celebration of the Eucharist by such clergy are necessities for all congregations in order to recognize that gathering as the Body of Christ can take many forms.
- We need to challenge the norm that "bigger is better" and realize that 70 percent of Episcopal churches have an average Sunday attendance of 150 or less.
- We need to challenge the norm that clergy get their emotional needs met in their congregations.
- We need to challenge the norm that people primarily experience God in the church on Sunday mornings.
- We need to challenge the norm that small churches have something wrong with them and are less worthy and able to serve God than big churches.
- We need to challenge the norm that real leaders do not show vulnerability.
- We need to challenge the norm of guaranteed tenure for rectors.
- We need to challenge the norm that healthy behaviors and all that goes with them are separate from theology and spirituality.
- We need to challenge the norm that "daddy or mama" knows best and gets whatever they want.
- If we think of it as a norm, it probably ought to be challenged.

- _____
  _____
  _____

- _____
  _____
  _____

- _____
  _____
  _____

- _____
  _____
  _____
  _____

- _____
  _____
  _____
  _____

- _____
  _____
  _____
  _____

- _____
  _____
  _____
  _____

- _____
  _____
  _____
  _____

- _____
  _____
  _____
  _____

- _____
  _____
  _____
  _____

- _____
  _____
  _____
  _____

- _____
  _____
  _____
  _____

- _____
  _____
  _____
  _____

- _____
  _____
  _____
  _____

- _____
  _____
  _____
  _____

- _____
  _____
  _____
  _____

- _____
  _____
  _____
  _____

- _____
  _____
  _____
  _____

- _____
  _____
  _____
  _____

- _____
  _____
  _____
  _____

- _____
  _____
  _____
  _____

- _____
  _____
  _____
  _____

- _____
  _____
  _____
  _____

REFLECTION: Proverbs 2:2–4

Tune your ears to wisdom, and concentrate on understanding. Cry out for insight, and ask for understanding. Search for them as you would for silver; seek them like hidden treasures.

1. The Book of Proverbs offers thoughts on moral discernment and on the development of mental clarity and perception. How does this reading challenge the norms that I have come to accept?

2. SELF-AWARENESS: What feels so "normal" to me that it is hard for me to ask questions about it? What norms is it easy for me to challenge?

3. OTHER-AWARENESS: What are some of the norms that are hard for others in my community to challenge that are different from mine?

4. PRACTICE: What norm am I willing to think about from a different perspective if someone else challenges my presumption? Who can I ask to be in conversation with me about a norm I would like them to consider differently? If we need a third party to join us in conversation, whom might I ask?

CHAPTER NINE

Daring to Find and Become the Transforming Leadership We Need

> *Leadership is best thought of as a behavior, not a role.*
>
> JILL JANOV

"I dare you!" "I double-dog dare you!"

Words from childhood, but they fit.

It is a daring thing to become a leader—and even more daring to become a differentiated leader, to know what a differentiated leader is and does, to support the differentiated leadership around you, and encourage its development throughout the system. Add the cultural context (both locally and in the global community) and leadership is guaranteed to be an outrageous adventure.

The "outrageous adventure" began for me at a training event in human relations in the summer of 1968. In the familiar setting of an Episcopal girls' school in Versailles, Kentucky, my understanding of educational experiences was turned upside down and inside out over a long weekend, working in small groups under the expert facilitation of the Rev. Dr. W. Robert Insko and the Rev. Bill Yon. I know that what kept me on this path, through resistances and changes of focus that dropped training from official radar screens, is the knowledge that I had experienced Christian community in a way that exemplified for me what the Church could be at its best—and that a new call had been born in me with that awareness. Participation in the creation of healthy Christian community through the work of leadership development in training events across the country, the Church, and other systems kept me on track with a continuing conviction that there really *is* a better way to live and be. In 1987, Scott Peck named it in his book, *A Different Drum*, when he said, "Four times I had been in a group of different people who loved each other in a sustained fashion. It might never happen to me again. But I did have a dim sense that it could be a replicable phenomenon. And ever since knowing that a group of very different people loving one another was potentially repeatable, I have never been able to feel totally hopeless about the human condition."[21] The good news was, and is, that men and women who share both the experience and the call to move from hope-less to hope-full are scattered across the world. Some have given up on the Church as woefully unable to live into its call to be the counter-cultural entity desperately needed in this world, taking their leadership to other systems. Thankfully, others have remained convinced that the Church *is* the place for the transformation to begin, even if it has to face its own demons and demise before it sets denial aside and chooses new life. Edwin Friedman was right: our tendency is to eat ourselves alive. We don't need any enemy to do it for us, thank you very much—we do it so well ourselves.

A bishop told me, "The reality is that in previous generations, being an effective leader was not all that important. When our churches were full and we were in a culture of Christendom, we were the beneficiaries of privilege—especially the men. We didn't rely on or need highly competent leaders. Now, however, we need a level of social competency that is not there. We need the equivalent of upper-level management in our parishes and councils. We have never had to name and call out bad behaviors before, and we have no formal system in place to do so, no training, no way to practice."

Daring to find and become the leadership we need begins with the un-derstanding that the only person I can change is me. My work on myself is the most important thing I can do to *become* a healthy leader, to *model* healthy leadership, to remain *accountable*. The same accountability must be present at every level throughout the system.

I must know my own wounds, and my own reactivity which grows out of those wounds. The more I understand my own reactivity, the more I will be aware that other people's reactivity grows out of their wounds. The same must be true on a corporate, community level.

When we transfer this thinking to the parish and the diocesan levels, in the ongoing search for both ordained and lay leadership, professional and volunteer, we need to heed the words of a transition officer: "When they ask me who their parish ought to call, I say, 'the healthiest person you can find; one who is aware of their own anxiety-driven reactivity and works to manage it, understanding that everyone in the system has the potential to be automatically reactive.'"

For those who think of leadership in terms of power and control, the call to and for new leadership is more unsettling than it is exciting. For those who are ready to own that they are in a pioneering, pilgrim paradigm, the call to and for new leadership is exciting.

---

21. Scott Peck,*The Different Drum* (New York: Simon & Schuster, 1998), 52.

When considering change in the system, one bishop utilizes the image of leaving Jerusalem. What is unessential to the journey? What will they leave at the Mount of Olives? A similar imagery recognizes the journey of Abraham and Sarah, leaving behind their homes to "live in tents of perpetual adaptation"—leaving behind all but the essentials.

In larger leadership circles, some of the unessential items that have already been left behind include the use of information as power; traditional hierarchies, structures, and titles; the status quo; limited local thinking; tradition; a "ladder" organizational model; unlimited resources (which few had in the past—and even fewer have today); and problem solving.

In one diocese, such questions are included in the training of vestries and nominating committees in transition. An experiential exercise divides the room into three sections. On half-sheets of newsprint, individuals are invited to write what practices and behaviors they would like to carry forward into the future, what they would like to maintain in the present, and what they would like to leave behind.

Soon the floor is covered with the sheets, each one bearing a behavior or practice written in brightly colored ink. Members are invited to walk among the sheets and study them, making mental or written notes.

Later in the morning, as past rectors are listed and their strengths and weaknesses named, patterns are located. When the notes from the "essentials" exercise are included in the study, a picture begins to emerge of the competencies needed in the parish at this time.

As we consider the qualities essential to lay and ordained leadership in the transformative church, the overlapping and integration of these qualities, as they inform each other and work together for the whole, are a hallmark of this new leadership.

Qualities of Leadership

Holistic vision: To think holistically is to look at a complete system, a larger entity, rather than simply one of its parts. In the Episcopal Church, the local organization, the parish, is a system composed of family systems. Each parish is part of a diocesan system, which is part of the Episcopal Church system, which is a part of the Anglican system, which is a part of the system of Christian denominations, which is a part of the system of faiths in the world. While local vision and action will be sensitive and responsive to local needs, awareness of the whole of the world of believers is more critical than ever before. Research by the Pew Foundation identifies 2012 as the first year that those who list "None" for their religious preference outnumber Protestants. Most of our communities are not the homogeneous communities of our parents and grandparents, often born, raised, and buried in one locale.

The "whole" includes much more than denomination. Our lives and the ways we live out our faith are touched today by poverty, homelessness, abuse, global warming, technology, disease . . . the list, and the need for holistic vision and response, are far-reaching. A vision that limits itself to how we worship in a building on Sunday morning will find itself increasingly out of step with pilgrim people. A vision wide enough to offer a launching pad for response to the real lives of real people is needed if we are to become the transformative church.

Non-anxious presence: While many attributes of leadership may be about *doing,* characteristics of *being* undergird the doing. The majority of this list of characteristics of new leadership are more about presence and attitude than about action, providing a springboard into both reaction (the ability to move quickly and decisively, and then think) and response (acting out of a deliberate plan). The non-anxious presence of leadership is, first of all, how a person handles his/her own anxiety—a subject referred to in discussions of self-awareness throughout this book. In other-awareness, the question is what the leader does with the anxiety that others bring to him/her, individually or as a system.

I believe this is one of the areas where confusion about the self-differentiated leader arises, as this ability to remain calm in the face of others' anxiety can be misinterpreted as cold, uncaring, or unfeeling. Note: while the official term is "non-anxious," in working with our leadership team and other leadership bodies, I spend some time talking about being "less anxious" and working on these capacities, plus having the safe place to process one's own anxieties or frustrations.

Peter Steinke, author of the book *Congregational Leadership in Anxious Times: Being Calm and Courageous No Matter What,* lists the "way of being" of the non-anxious presence as the capacity to:

- Manage our own natural reactions

- Use knowledge to suppress impulses and control automatic reactions

- Keep calm for the purpose of reflection and conversation

- Observe what is happening, especially with oneself

- Tolerate high degrees of uncertainty, frustration, and pain

- Maintain a clear sense of direction[22]

Entrepreneurial spirit: In 1964, organizational writer Peter Drucker defined an entrepreneur as one who "searches for change and responds to

---

22. Peter Steinke, *Congregational Leadership in Anxious Times: Staying Calm and Courageous No Matter What* (Herndon, VA: Alban Institute, 2006), 35.

it. Innovation is a specific tool of an entrepreneur—hence an entrepreneur converts a source into a resource."[23] While the term has been applied largely in the business world, the characteristics most associated with it speak to the spirit: Wikipedia, the online encyclopedia, continues: "Entrepreneurs take initiative, accept risk of failure, and have an internal locus of control" (Albert Shapero, 1976), "the pursuit of opportunity without regard to resources currently controlled" (Howard Stevenson 1976). An interesting term, applicable to the system of the Church, is *intrepreneur*—defined as "a person who started a new business where there was one before" (W. B. Gardner, 1985).[24]

I believe that the critical factor here as we move through reformation to becoming the transformative Church is the entrepreneurial or intrepreneurial *spirit*—whose characteristics are clearly congruent with movement away from the status quo; movement born not of fear, but of a sense of adventure.

A pilgrim heart: A pilgrim is a journeyer seeking a holy place, either specifically or metaphorically. The significance of that seeking is that the pilgrim is traveling with God on a journey that lasts a lifetime. Brett Webb-Mitchell, author, educator, and Presbyterian minister who has led many pilgrimages and workshops on pilgrimages, was the keynoter at a SOLO FLIGHT conference several years ago, and as I was writing the words "a pilgrim heart," I could picture Brett sharing his own experience of being a pilgrim and inviting his listeners to join him on the road with "no one and no other place to call home but God." He was explicit in pointing out the dual emotions of fear and excitement that accompany pilgrims as they travel. My notes from that conference underline two particularly important characteristics: the letting go of expectations so that God's grace has room, and that, as he traveled, Brett would periodically turn around and look back, realizing that the path from which he came no longer made any coherent sense. It was as if, he said, "I had to move ahead."

The sense of becoming a new person seeing the world in a new way is characteristic of those who approach life with a pilgrim heart. The journey to who God is calling us to be is indeed a pilgrimage and requires a pilgrim heart.

Interconnectedness: The quality of interconnectedness goes beyond the connection of people and organizations to the interconnectedness of the life of the system today with the life of the system of yesterday and tomorrow. While this concept may sound contradictory to the shifting of paradigms and the openness to new ideas, I believe that, to the contrary, this larger

---

23. Wikipedia.org/wiki/Entrepreneurship (accesssed 6/11/13).
24. Wikipedia.org/wiki/Intrepreneur (accesssed 6/11/13).

awareness of our interconnectivity with its intentionality and consciousness of impact *is* new thinking.

Certainly each generation and each stage in the life of an institution will have its own language and symbols—and that is as it should be. Where I believe we have been *disconnected* in our history as a system is in the faddishness that has marked our institutional life, wasting valuable resources of people and ideas. Interconnectedness is a concept that goes hand in hand with living a reflective life, becoming aware of patterns in our experiences and benefitting from the knowledge gained in this awareness. Our institutional pattern has been to shed ideas without mining their full value; believing, for instance, that every tenure of a bishop or rector has to have a unique legacy all its own that dares not touch the previous legacy in any way. It's hard to discern patterns when one is disconnected from the ideas of the past—both the good ones and the not-so-good ones.

A candidate in a recent bishop's election said to everyone with whom he came in contact during that process: "Every tenure has in it both very positive things and some which are less than positive. When you think about the episcopate that has just ended, what do you believe is important to carry into this next chapter, and why?" I contrast this with a new CEO in town, whose high-profile position had been under attack. At an interview shortly after he arrived in town, he was asked a question that referenced previous administrations. His answer missed the mark, where interconnectedness is concerned. "I'm not concerned with what has been, just with what's ahead," he stated.

I would refer him to the great question asked by the episcopal candidate—a question too few leaders ask. We are disconnected at our own peril; destined to repeat the mistakes of the past and miss out on the evolution of great ideas in the present and future if we fail to see the interconnectedness of people, resources, and ideas. This interconnectedness requires leaders with enough self-confidence and self-awareness to remain non-anxious and unthreatened by the good ideas and good works of others. When that occurs, along with birthing ideas of their own, leaders will continually feel free to connect what has been with what is and what will be.

As Dr. David Sawyer reminds us in his work on change in systems,[25] as living organisms are transformed, they carry some essential quality of their DNA into the transformed organism. As we move forward into the massive changes that we know must come for our survival, we must consider what those essential elements are. Without interconnectedness and reflection, we cannot know the answer.

---

25. David Sawyer, oral conversation; November 2012.

Stakeholders: Who are the stakeholders in this potential new shared vision? Who are the people in the larger community who have similar values and concerns? Can we have a conversation about what is important to us? Are we open to see where shared values would lead us in recognizing the needs in our community and how we might respond to them most effectively?

A downtown parish in the city has gradually seen a significant number of its members move to the suburbs, leaving both the changing demographics and landscape of the city behind as they invest their time and pledges in more homogeneous outlying congregations. The vestry and congregation of the downtown parish appear bewildered. The new residents of the neighborhood are not the middle- and upper-management folks who once made up the rolls of this parish, and those who are left haven't found a comfortable way to become acquainted with the new neighbors who occasionally come to worship. The property includes a large parish hall and adjacent offices that are not in use. Outside the doors of the church, downtown organizations such as the Urban League and a daycare center for children of workers in nearby factories are seeking venues for their offerings. Artists, musicians, and a local theater group are also seeking space. All of these groups are *stakeholders in downtown.* They may come from different perspectives, but they all have a vested interest in a viable downtown. Thinking in terms of stakeholders could solve issues for at least two organizations, if not more.

Engaging the idea of stakeholders asks us to leave territorialism, ego, and need for credit behind, making recognized needs and shared values a priority. In this economic climate, it is not only philosophically and spiritually a good way to go, but perhaps the only sustainable way to go, as well.

The empty chair at the table: The empty chair at the table symbolizes an organization's continual questions on any issue: What voice is not here that needs to be heard? What eyes might show us something we have not yet seen? What mind would allow us to think about this issue in a different way than we have yet considered?

Openness to new perspectives as a natural part of information gathering and problem solving is a different concept than more tightly structured committees and commissions, and encourages cross-fertilization of ideas. Diverse opinions and ideas are critical elements for all systems.

Global thinking and understanding: As technology becomes increasingly a part of our lives, we like to think of ourselves as people who are more aware of the larger world than ever before. Certainly we are more able to be connected to people anywhere in the world than ever before, whether in a Skype session with a friend in Senegal, ordering a kotatsu mat from a

108   Becoming the Transformative Church

>> >>

department store in Japan with delivery before the week is out, or seeking a solution to a problem from a colleague on the other side of the world. But in truth, despite this global capability, we humans tend to organize in tribes of like-minded people, wherever they are. It's a natural tendency—and not all bad—so long as we are aware that we are, in truth, reaching out to sameness globally, just as we do at home.

Our own American culture offers many possibilities for wider understanding of people and differences. We do not have to travel to Africa or the Middle East or Haiti (although those are fantastic opportunities for any person who can do so!). Creating opportunities for conversations across ethnic, faith, and other lines broadens understanding of the world in which we are called to live and serve.

Another reminder from our twenty-first-century leader (and my granddaughter), Virginia. Speaking to a group of community leaders after her return from the International Hugh O'Brian Leadership Conference, she told them: "When asked to share something of our cultures, no one talked about war, no one talked about politics, no one talked about religion—everyone shared something of the arts and culture of their country." Imagine what might happen to global awareness and understanding if we took the time to make such opportunities?

Creativity and innovation: All too often when people hear the word "creativity," their thoughts go immediately to art or craft or performance. Creativity and innovation are not only possible but necessary when faced with new questions for which there are no obvious answers. Capacities that have lain dormant in people can pop up when opportunities are offered for thinking in new ways.

It is important to note here that for people who view their life as open-ended in terms of conclusions, this type of invitation will be welcomed enthusiastically. For those who enjoy clear-cut decisions on a timeline, it will take some adjustment, and some stretching. Creativity and innovation, however, do not mean working without timelines and parameters; rather, they indicate an attitude and a culture that are open to new ways of approaching questions in the life of any organization.

Risk-taking: Risk-taking is generally thought of in terms of finance—exactly how much risk is one willing to take in the stock market to make a gain? A stockbroker was talking to a newly single midlife woman who was clearly scared about her finances, making it clear to the broker that she was not any sort of a risk taker. "That surprises me," he said. "I see you as a risk taker in terms of ideology and behavior . . . but you don't seem to see yourself that way."

Risk-taking is closely aligned with an attitude of abundance, rather than scarcity. Scarcity says "there might not be enough _____ to go around, so I dare not risk any of it, or I could be the one who ends up without." Abundance says, "I am so blessed by all of the material things in my life— my cup runneth over. Of course I can take a risk."

Good humor and fun: In the Introduction, a young teacher was quoted as saying that he found the whole business of youth leadership development "fun." His remark was followed by that of a bishop who said that if it wasn't fun, he didn't think it was of God. Now clearly, there are times that things aren't fun—but both points are well taken. Good humor and fun are great stress relievers. They also prevent people from taking themselves too seriously, a deadly malady for anyone. Good humor and fun are generally found where work is stimulating and adventuresome, and creative wheels are turning. Good humor and fun mark a people at ease with themselves, each other, and their place in the system. Attention: good humor and fun are *not* the same as sarcasm or jokes at others' expense. The latter can be warning signs of poor leadership or a team in need of some help.

Room for provisional tries, or failures: Living and working on a new frontier means that there are more questions than there are answers, and experimentation—sometimes known as "provisional tries"—must be a part of the life of any organization. Something may not work the first time around. There are no roadmaps on this new frontier, and it is going to take some experimentation. An early effort may need some "tweaking," or it may have no salvageable parts for the particular situation. Creating a culture where experimentation and provisional tries are expected and accepted (as are both the successes and failures that go with them) promotes willingness to create, to suggest, to risk. Our present culture relies on short-term quick fixes utilizing solutions that have worked in the past. New questions demand the opportunity to try and try again.

Willingness to bury the dead: It's hard to let go of things that are familiar and comfortable, even if they've been collecting dust in a symbolic corner of an institution or organization for a long time. The "dead" may be a ministry that once served a great purpose and now has difficulty getting anyone to participate. It might be a particular organizational structure that was effective for a number of years for a particular group of people and their talents, and now lacks energy and vitality. It could be a building itself, or a program. It's important to be willing to pay attention to the heartbeat of an organization. Look and listen for vitality and life-giving energy. Encourage. Nurture. Support. Assess. And when the time has come, honor the contribution and bury the dead.

Integration and collaboration supported by communication: Integration and collaboration are not simply healthy, they are good stewardship of people and resources; they strengthen a sense of shared purpose and the ways in which a vision is carried forward; they build relationships; they support a system in carrying forward the best of what has been to support the new. Communication is essential to integration and collaboration; ironically, it is not easy to come by when everyone is glued to their instruments of communication. We may tweet, Facebook, and e-mail incessantly, but we are not communicating well past our office doors.

Webs, not ladders: The term "web" surfaced in leadership thinking prior to its common usage in reference to the internet. The concept of ladders—hierarchal up-and-down thinking—was still more common in most systems. Today, the concept of the web is a familiar one. It allows us to access resources easily, from formal or informal sources, titled and degreed, famous or unknown. Transferring that image to the arena of leadership and the system of the church, it is about respecting human resources of all sorts—and the web of relationships that allow us access to those resources.

Emotional intelligence: Self- and other-awareness are critical capacities in all organizations today. Some people refer to it as "street smarts." Emotional intelligence is the ability to know oneself, motivate oneself, and manage one's own emotions; to be aware of others as of self; to have both empathy and effective relationships. Emotional intelligence is an intelligence that acknowledges and utilizes both the rational and emotional brains—emotions informing the rational, and rational shaping the responses of the emotional. Unlike IQ, EQ can be strengthened and is measurable. A person can be extremely smart, have a high IQ or intellectual quotient, and not function effectively in everyday life. To move from functioning to effectiveness in any level of any system, from family to corporation to religious system, emotional intelligence must play a significant role. Without developing these capacities, an individual cannot truly achieve their potential as a human being, and certainly not as a leader of other human beings and human systems.

Relational capacity: The relational capacity of the differentiated leader in the transformative system is, as has been noted throughout this book, a different "take" on what being relational means; too often it is misinterpreted as a "warm fuzzy" commodity without boundaries or expectation of accountability. True relational capacity is about staying in communion in the system. That does not mean staying in relationship regardless of unhealthy behaviors. It does mean being willing to expend the energy and the effort to stay in contact with difficult relationships and being intentional about not being triangulated. It means taking on the sometimes painful and difficult job of holding other people responsible for their own actions rather than avoiding that work or refusing to see what needs to be done. It means giving up playing savior, knowing that no one can prevent another person's suffering due to their own behaviors. It means accepting that it may take a long time for others to understand the value of this brand of relational capacity, and adopting a Teflon coating that allows the arrows of misunderstanding and accusation to fall to the ground rather than piercing the heart.

Creative utilization of limited resources; transforming liabilities into opportunities: There have always been "glass half full" and "glass half empty" folk—different perspectives leading to attitudes of abundance and attitudes of scarcity. Human beings have always had the capacity to use whatever resources are available to them in tough economic times, but our luxurious lifestyle in comparison to the majority of the world has led to an expectation that we must have certain commodities to create successful programs, or do certain work.

In truth, we live in a time where resources are and will be more limited than in the last quarter of the previous century. It is time to cast a fresh eye on those parts of our organizations that we have viewed as liabilities, bringing creative, out-of-the-box thinking to bear on what might emerge.

Mining qualities beyond the obvious: In working with congregations and dioceses, I've seen a tendency to use that which we know as reference points. If X ministry has been effective in the past, let's bring X ministry back and we'll recapture the good things we remember about that time period. The experiences that are remembered are what are being referenced and held on to. They are experiences, not qualities.

Reflective process, the ability to mine beyond the obvious, allows stepping back and asking the question, "What are the qualities that you valued in that experience?" or "What were the qualities in that experience that were troubling and you would not like repeated?"

This kind of reflection can produce a list of qualities that connect with patterns of functioning; it can also lead to creativity and innovation. It involves people at the congregational level in naming what they truly value and want to carry over into the future while honoring the stories of the past. At the conclusion of a series of Holy Conversations in preparation for the election of a new bishop, it had become clear to the leadership team that there were experiences that had been valued greatly at a particular time in the life of the diocese which particular interest groups were convinced must be "brought back" for the good of the whole. The awareness had been highlighted during the leadership team "prep" session, and as the evening drew to a close, presenter and facilitators made eye contact during report-outs, which again referenced these specific experiences. Moving to the microphone for the closing narrative, the presenter, supported by team awareness and discussions, non-verbal support from the team, and shared theoretical foundation, left the scripted conclusion and spoke extemporane-ously—thanking the participants for raising up experiences that highlighted qualities they valued and wanted to carry forward, as well as qualities they hoped to leave behind. "It's hard for us to remember today," he said, "but there was a time many years ago when we didn't have a Camp Hope—but we knew we needed a place for our children to gather, and Bishop N— led us to the creation of that center. There was a time earlier in our history when we didn't really know much about spiritual formation, or activities that renewed our sometimes flagging faith—and then Bishop L— came to us, and we learned about activities already available to us and created some of our own. The *qualities* which you value will open the door for our next bishop to help us vision where God is calling us in the future—places yet unknown to us, experiences yet unknown to us—waiting to be named and experienced. Thank you for your openness to all that is to come."

Conflict utilization, mediation, resolution, and reconciliation: Just as training for honesty has not been a part of formation in our system, neither has training for mediation, conflict resolution, or reconciliation. Certainly some leaders have sought such training as they recognized the need for it. However, it has been considered "extra"—something that is needed in critical situations, rather than a normal part of everyday life in a family or organization.

Human beings rub against each other as they go about the business of life. We need a simple mechanism that can manage small irritations before they become large, as well as providing more serious intervention for larger issues. Conflict, at its many levels, is a normal part of life and requires our time and engagement. Living in process with, as the Culture of Courtesy Covenant says, as much attention to how we do things as to the end prod-uct, is about taking the time and making the effort to deal with that conflict.

There are excellent resources for training (see Resources), and there are also several processes that can become a part of any system. Perhaps most important is normalizing conflict and differences of opinion, approaching them with a non-anxious presence, and providing choices in how to ad-dress them.

Effective structure undergirding all: Two important statements have been made about structure of the church: first, that we do not know what structure will come to replace the one we've had—we simply know there

must be a new one; and second, that the rising generation is not interested
in infrastructure—a statement that carries with it questions about the main-
tenance of any new structure that is established.

Perhaps the resistance of the rising generation has to do with a belief that
more effort and resource has gone into structure and administration than
into mission and ministry. There is a desire to reprioritize. Leaders need to
be aware that this is not a time when technical fixes—downsizing or retool-
ing the old familiar structure—is going to be enough. And those who would
call for the reordering of priorities need to be aware that without some form
of infrastructure, the priorities of mission and ministry will not happen in
a sustained way.

It will take time and many different perspectives to find the foundational
support with the flexibility and strength to undergird this rebirthing system.
In searching for a word to describe whatever that new structure will be, I
discarded many of the usual candidates, such as vehicle and mechanism, for
they speak of a time and a structure that is gone. We are not organizational
machines with predictable, unchanging parts. Like new structures that have
been built to withstand the tremors of earthquakes, swaying as the earth
moves, we must search for an image to help us create such a structure for
this time of perpetual change. A foundational structure is still necessary. It's
shape, texture, construction are still unknown.

Preparation for the unknown: One of the hallmarks of a pilgrim life is being
prepared to face the unknown, for surprises appear all along the way. History and
folklore are full of the challenges for pilgrims, whose lives were often in danger
from human enemies, the environment, and predators in the fields and forests.
While their identities might differ today, enemies of the pilgrimage, an untamed environment, and lurking predators are not simply metaphorical aspects of the fable
when stepping out in a time of reformation.

While the words "prepare" and "expect" might seem counterintuitive
in speaking of the unknown, they speak to an important mental, emotional, and spiritual mindset, which, if we are honest, is already true of the
spiritual journey. Deep inside, we know that life is full of surprises, full of
unknowns, while we delude ourselves in thinking we are writing a story in
which we have control of every chapter and can predict the ending. That
delusion leaves us open for perpetual shock—"I didn't see it coming," "I
wasn't prepared."

We may not be able to predict the "it" that is coming. What is predictable is that there are many unknowns on the horizon as we journey, and
surprises are a guarantee. Factoring them in from the beginning, so that
they become part of the data, part of the creative process, is the best prepa-

ration one can make and opens the door to the benefits, as well as possible interruptions that await.

Valuing intuition and measurement and the accountability that grows out of context: While referenced elsewhere, it is important to realize that both decision making and accountability in a system need intuition and data—*and* that it is critically important in this pioneering adventure that we do not rush to adopt measures that do not fit our context. Rather, utilizing good minds within our context, we develop those measures consistent with our context and purpose, so that we are adaptive rather than adoptive, innovative rather than imitative in this very important area.

Awareness of and respect for boundaries and confidentiality: One of the most foundational aspects in creating and maintaining healthy organizations is an awareness of and respect for personal boundaries and confidentiality. While this seems basic to understanding human relationships, with such mechanisms in place as "Safeguarding God's Children" to remind of how easily one can cross a line of safety, I find that repetition of boundary awareness and training is continually important.

Because we are relational people and are dealing with the "stuff" of people's lives, we must be doubly cautious about these two areas. I believe that they are closely related. A leader who maintains his/her own boundaries is also likely, in my experience, to maintain confidentiality. And a person who understands and respects confidentiality is likely to understand, maintain, and respect both their own and others' confidences and boundaries.

Two red flags in this area: Leaders often can find themselves in intimate situations of listening or counseling. Emotions of the moment, the desire to help or comfort, or personal charisma and style can easily lead to a moment of overly long or close hugging, or a posture that can be misinterpreted, causing confusion and pain for all. Every leader needs to be aware that they are on the top side of a power differential, with ordained leadership often seen as the "God-figure" and endowed with special qualities of wisdom. So special responsibility for setting and maintaining boundaries (and an awareness that one's emotional needs are not met through the people one serves) is critically important.

Likewise is the ability to maintain confidences. This is an area where I do not believe sufficient training is given to most leaders, lay or ordained. Confidentiality is absolutely essential to building trust and honesty in relationships. All too often, I am aware of leaders conferring with other leaders, using the phrase "professional confidence." This phrase, which is borrowed from the mental health profession, carries with it an obligation to safeguard the identity of the people involved and should only be used when a person is pursuing advice about an appropriate response. In the mental health area, it would be a form of treatment. Since ordained and lay leaders, unless licensed to do so, are not about the business of treatment, I would suggest that unless one is unsure whether to refer a person on for treatment or needs advice in how to handle a situation, holding that confidence is a sacred trust. Far too many casual stories emerge from what were considered confidential sessions. Beware! Boundaries and confidentiality are sacred trusts in all relationships.

Readiness for a spiritual adventure: When I am working with vestries, I generally begin with thanking them for agreeing to take on the role of becoming part of the spiritual leadership of their community. Inevitably, someone in the group will challenge my statement, often offering to read from the canons to prove their point that they are in charge of the temporal affairs of the parish, while the rector is the spiritual leader. Yes—and yes.

It is my belief that all leadership is a spiritual task, engaging timeless spiritual questions, and taking an individual or group further and further into their own spiritual journey as they work. It is impossible to seriously engage the level of life and relationship involved in such leadership roles as bishop, priest, deacon, active lay leader without having one's own life journey affected. Again and again, individuals who have served on nominating committees, vestries, standing committees, planning groups will say to me, "I had no idea how this would change my life" or "because of what I learned during this time, I decided to. . . ." I believe it is time that we are intentional about naming this part of the leadership adventure, at every step and stage of our life together. As one priest said earlier in this book, "If what you are doing brings you closer to your Lord and Savior Jesus Christ, then by all means, continue. If not, you are just doing the laundry." While he was referring to finding that place one is truly called to serve, the point is well taken. Any position of leadership in the Church is a part of the spiritual journey, both individually and corporately. Whether you begin or end this list of characteristics of leadership for the transformative church with the category of "spiritual adventure," if we are endeavoring to become the transformative church, all qualities can and do fall under this one category. Let's name it, and claim it.

REFLECTION: Genesis 12:1-2

Now the Lord said to Abram: "get out of your country, from your family, and from your Father's house to a land that I will show you. I will make you a great nation; I will bless you and make your name great."

1. How does this scripture connect for me with what I have just read on daring to become a leader?

2. SELF-AWARENESS: What is God calling me to leave behind as a leader? Individual? What is my "tent of perpetual adaptation" like?

3. OTHER-AWARENESS: What might God be calling my community to leave behind?

4. What kind of courage is required to give up your home and all of the possessions that you have acquired and journey without a known destination?

5. What would you be willing to give up if God asked you to backpack into the desert for him?

CHAPTER TEN

How "Change Back Behaviors" Sabotage Differentiated Leadership—and How Differentiated Leaders Say "NO!"

> People don't **resist** change. They resist being changed.
>
> PETER M. SENGE[26]

Hostility in the environment—the urge to rid the system of the differentiated leader—is a sign of growth, according to systems theorists. It is a sure sign that a leader is on the right track. Check with anyone who has attempted to stop drinking or over-eating, or to bring healthy behavior to a dysfunctional relationship, and the truth will be underscored.

Any system, from families to organizations, will automatically attempt to preserve its own organizing principles. It's not a rational, cognitive process, but an emotional reflex to return to the familiar, the known, the comfortable. This concept, known as homeostasis, highlights a unit's resistance to change. It helps explain why systems from families to large businesses will tolerate the "squeaky wheels"—the "trouble-makers"—while the person who attempts to bring new eyes and ears, new insights, new thinking that upsets the familiar balance has to go. It is a form of self-induced sabotage that rears its head when change is on the horizon.

A young woman had come to therapy to end a relationship with a married man. The therapeutic work had been slow and painful, but she had done what she had come to do and was working on rebuilding a life for herself. As she walked into the therapist's office one day, she said, "Remind me why I should be doing this?" The therapist looked at her quizzically, waiting for the line which came as no surprise: "The healthier I get, the more screwed up everyone else is, and the harder they try to screw me up again!"

---

26. www.goodreads.com/author/quotes21072Peter_M_Senge (accessed November 2012).

Reactivity to a systemic move toward healthy functioning comes out of emotion and fear. It is asking people to change—not just their attitudes and behaviors, but their hearts and minds, their habits.

Said a different way, it's about secondary gain.

A man who was struggling with serious weight issues was talking with his doctor. "What do you like best about being fat?" the doctor said, going for the terrible *F* word rather than the less-abrasive euphemism, "heavy."

"Nothing!" said the man, clearly offended.

"How about, if you no longer care whether or not you gain weight, you can eat anything you want—you don't have to make choices . . . to think about it. . . ."

Understanding the secondary gain was a helpful step on the way to correcting the problem. In both the situation of the woman trying to end the destructive affair and the man who said he wanted to lose weight, the primary gain, which was easy to recognize and name, was clear. End the relationship. Lose the weight. So why did they fail again and again? *Secondary gain* is about the more subtle, but powerful thing individuals get to keep if they don't make the change. The woman wants out of the relationship, which her head says is destructive for her, *and* she can remain connected to the good parts as long as she doesn't completely end it. Secondary gain: the good parts of the relationship. The man can continue to eat whatever he wants, whenever he wants, as long as he "can't stay on a diet" or "it doesn't work for me." Secondary gain. As the famous television psychologist would ask, "So, how's that working for you?"

In behavioral change, it is not the change itself that is so hard, but the *loss, real or perceived,* associated with the change. When loss is pressing upon us, the human instinct is to hang on for dear life to what we imagine to be secure, safe, and always glorious. Anger and grief, two intimately related emotions, both emerge. It often looks like anger. It really is grief. In the church, when there are efforts toward healthy, differentiated leadership in the system, some of the *perceived losses* are of long-held beliefs. We may know (at least at a subconscious level) that the *old* church had as a significant part of its mission the protection of sacred knowledge and beliefs, which built in a protection of the status quo and an aversion to change. At an organic level, for any organism to be transformed, some of its essential DNA must be made new. So at an organic level, the role of change-adverse behavior is the overweight patient who asks again and again, "Are we going to totally lose ourselves in all of this? What am I going to be required to give up?"

In his ongoing research on change, the Rev. Dr. David Sawyer, Presbyterian minister and organizational consultant, looks at what he calls the "rubber band" theory, or "change back behaviors," in a system undergoing change. The fear is real, as change indicates loss, and no one knows for sure what the loss will be, so those within the system work to "bring the rubber band back to its original shape." The "change back" behavior is real, says Sawyer. In his book *Hope in Conflict: Discovering Wisdom in Congregational Turmoil,* he lists common symptoms of congregations in conflict:[27]

1. Expression of emotion or presence of pain out of proportion to the issues involved

2. Noticeable or significant over- or under-functioning

3. Blaming one person or group for many of the church's problems, projecting the system's turmoil on an unidentified problem person

4. Physical or emotional impairment in key leaders

"We're not dealing with terrorists," Sawyer explains. "We are dealing with the diversions and resistances that indicate reactivity to change."

Why do the behaviors, whether identified as sabotage, "change back" behaviors, diversions, or resistances, go unnamed? In an effort to avoid the potential confrontation, those of us within church systems can tell ourselves:

• As a Christian, I overlook behaviors because we accept everyone; we turn the other cheek.

• As a Christian, I am sure these people's intentions are good.

• A good leader is empathetic—that's how I know they care about me.

• A good church leader is pastoral—saying what I need to hear, demanding nothing from me.

• Church is about good, warm, safe, secure feelings.

• The Church is to minister to me.

• The Church is stable and unchanging in a world that is changing too fast.

Differentiated leadership will not overlook destructive, dysfunctional behaviors. It names them, models healthy behaviors, and expects those healthy behaviors from others. Differentiated leadership knows that impact on people, not an individual's intent, is what matters. The differentiated leader is aware of the emotions in the system, but will not get sucked into them or make decisions based on those emotions. The differentiated leader

---

27. David Sawyer, *Hope in Conflict: Discovering Wisdom in Congregational Turmoil* (Cleveland, OH: Pilgrim Press, 2007), 82.

calls others to personal responsibility, to grow up into who God created them to be, caring deeply and desiring to stay in relationship, but not held hostage to or tolerating destructive behavior. The differentiated leader is clear and consistent about their own beliefs, and is able to state them and hold to them in the midst of chaos and crisis. The differentiated leader calls the church out of safety to adventure. The differentiated leader is able to tolerate the pain of others, which is often dumped on them.

Above all, the differentiated leader brings both clarity and connection to their system. A bishop suggests that the term "entrepreneurial leader" should stand side by side with "differentiated leader." Entrepreneurial leaders see themselves in the business of development, spiritually and in terms of leadership and "doing church." They, too, are often sabotaged by individuals struggling with change.

An even greater danger is that the system will simply sabotage itself, looking for technical fixes to help do more efficiently what it already does, rather than investing in the transformation of adaptive change. Technical fixes allow for solutions to problems for which some answers are already known. Generally, technical fixes divert the solution to a quicker, more shallow look at the issue at hand in order to achieve simple, easy answers. Adaptive change asks for an in-depth exploration of problems for which solutions are not yet known.

It is always easier to go for the "quick fix" than the longer and more complex process of adaptive change. "Adaptive change stimulates resistance because it challenges people's habits, beliefs, and values. It asks them to take a loss, experience uncertainty, and even express disloyalty to people and cultures. Because adaptive change asks people to question and perhaps refine aspects of their identity, it also challenges their sense of competence. Loss, disloyalty, and feeling incompetent. That's a lot to ask. No wonder people resist!"[28] Dr. Leonard Sweet, author of *SOUL TSUNAMI: Sink or Swim in New Millennium Culture,* says that in the face of such sea-change, the tendencies are to either hunker in the bunker and hope it will pass or to catch the wave.

The Episcopal Church has been waffling between hunkering in the bunker and making some technical fixes. It's time to catch the wave and ride it to whatever God is calling us to. We've been sabotaging ourselves along the way. It's time to call ourselves on those behaviors.

How is the sabotage, "change back" behavior manifested in the church?

---

28. Ronald A. Heifetz and Marty Linksky, *Leadership on the Line: Staying Alive through the Dangers of Leading* (Boston: Harvard Business Review Press, 2002), 26–28.

Emphasis on Quick Results with Resistance to Process as Time Wasted

Transition officers and bishops alike are familiar with the scenario. Aware that a successful search/nominating process is dependent upon self-reflection by the vestry and nominating committee, honest interactive data gathering, honest goals that reflect gospel imperatives, and mutual discernment based on competency rather than charisma, the carefully designed diocesan process is introduced. That process is received by all too many wardens, vestry members, and a variety of others as "too long," "unnecessary," "ridiculous—we can hire a CEO in half that time!" A history of poor relationships with bishops or diocesan representatives can rear its head at this juncture, as can basic misunderstandings of Episcopal polity for the search process. Basic control needs surface here, as wardens adopt a corporate CEO attitude about hiring an employee rather than understanding themselves as being part of a church under authority, where clergy are called through a process of mutual discernment. There is legitimate criticism that congregations are left in transition, without leadership, for too long. It is a conversation that needs to take place between bishops, transition officers, and other good minds to mine what is essential and refine a process with both flexibility and guidance. There are also legitimate complaints that sufficient guidance is not offered, or not offered in a timely manner. This concern highlights the need for attention to the roles of transition officer and trained consultants in the life of a diocese. In the meantime, efforts at sabotage range from stacking the nominating committee to firing a consultant or refusing to acknowledge or follow the guidance of the bishop's representative. "We know how to do it!"

As one trained rector-in-the-interim named the phenomena: "Who made you the boss of me?"

Counteractions:

- Short term: The bishop, Canon to the Ordinary, and/or transition officer work with the group and hold to their position for the good of the congregation.
- Long term: A definitive diocesan process is available online, guided by the work of a trained consultant speaking on behalf of the bishop and with the bishop's full support.

Resistance to the Work of the Qualified Interim and the Developmental Tasks of the Interim Period

Rectors-in-the-interim, bishops, transition officers, Canons to the Ordinary, and wardens are often faced with this variety of "who made you the boss of me?" Unfortunately, the wardens may be the ones asking the question! The sabotage is generally to the work of a strong, well-qualified interim, whose tasks are to ask hard questions regarding current practices, help manage change where needed (including on the staff), and in general prepare a congregation for their next rector. There are given developmental tasks for the period, with guidelines for measuring how a parish is performing. In the most successful interim situations, the following ingredients are present:

1. Thorough assessment of the needs of the particular congregation for the interim period, in terms of prospective length of interim, work to be done, placement

2. Careful recruiting of right competencies for the parish

3. Letter of agreement with the interim, bishop, and parish signed by all parties, and shared with the congregation on the interim's first Sunday, to delineate the role and responsibilities of an interim

4. Ongoing support by the bishop and staff

Sabotage also comes in the form of staff resistance in larger churches. "They couldn't wait for the rector to leave," reported one Transition Officer, about a parish staff member given a voice in the interim-selection process. "The interim hadn't been here two weeks when they started complaining, talking about their former rector as though he were God!"

In several large parishes, ordained staff resistance has been reported: going around the rector-in-the-interim, calling meetings that the rector should attend on his day off, triangulating with other staff members and members of the parish, causing a divisiveness that sabotages not only the interim, but the work of the transition period and the search/nomination process itself.

The term "rector-in-the-interim" was coined by a group of trained interims to make it clear that they were, in fact, the rector during this interim period, and not extended supply, and should be respected as such.

An important caveat: Far too many reports were heard of ineffective clergy sent by bishops for interim ministry training, retired clergy with no training or expertise placed in parishes as interims, and parishes having suffered the ill effects of these situations, now gun-shy of any mention of the term "interim." The emphasis on qualified interims and the process of screening and matching professional interim specialist to congregation cannot be overstated. As with the discernment process itself, the raw material is what counts. A priest who was not an effective rector will not be an effective interim. Effective rectors-in-the-interim are strong, self-differentiated persons who have proven that they lead well. Bishops, dioceses, and parishes have been burned by individuals who did not bring basic competencies to the position and have learned the financial, emotional, and spiritual cost of a poor interim period. "I have to trust my transition officer to do thorough vetting of prospective interims, and I have to take responsibility for seeing that the person is who they claim to be before I allow their name to be passed on to a parish," a bishop states, reflecting the experience of many colleagues in this area.

The church has yet to measure if every parish in transition needs an interim rector, how long an effective transition needs to be, how to determine the length and needs of individual transitions, or whether or not succession planning would be a helpful option. Intuition alone cannot provide the answers, nor can moving reactively from no guided transition to an identical plan for every congregation, or from mandated plan to none.

Counteractions:

- Short term: The bishop provides a letter regarding the work of the rector-in-the-interim and the developmental tasks of the interim period to be read to the parish on the interim's first Sunday and signed by the vestry, interim, and bishop.

- Long term: The diocese provides an online guide for parishes and interims, with regular support for interims.

- Bishops seek strong, effective clergy with particular competencies for becoming transition specialists, and invite them to consider interim ministry work.

- Interim ministry training is included in continuing education work for all clergy to understand the specific gifts and skills required for this ministry.

Attempt to Manipulate the Transition/Nominating Process Through "Stacking" the Nominating Committee (or to Control the Rector Through "Stacking" the Vestry)

One of the strongest efforts at sabotage comes when a parish attempts to avoid the guidance of the transition officer/consultant regarding the timetable for selecting and the training necessary for a nominating committee to discern the next rector for the parish. Efforts include "stacking" the committee with an inner circle of the congregation, bartering to get a particular person on the committee, the vestry appointing a nominating chair or convenor rather than allowing that person to emerge from the training retreat, and allowing the chosen chair to influence those accepted for membership.

Symptoms of this issue include repetition of family names on the vestry rotation, exclusion of newer members or diversity on the vestry, assumption of certain individuals as wardens, etc. This kind of "stacking" of a vestry leads to entrenchment, and often to a less-than-collegial relationship with the rector.

Counteractions:

- A well-thought-out diocesan nominating process, which is required of all congregations

- Following of the protocol for application and selection to a nominating committee (see Appendix B)

- A trained consultant to guide the process (either trained by the diocese to fully understand the diocesan process, or approved by the bishop for this work)

- The approval of the bishop at specific points in the process to proceed to the next step

- Full support by the bishop for transition officers and consultants

- Training sessions for clergy, vestries, and wardens on the roles of each

- Emphasis on responsibilities of vestry membership and nominating processes that bring good balance and spiritual leadership to each parish

- Bishop meeting with vestry during each visitation

Passive-Aggressive Efforts at Sabotage

Perhaps one of the most difficult types of sabotage to detect, and thus name and deal with, is passive aggression. The passive-aggressive saboteur often presents a charming persona in public, while using whatever position, people, or activities under his/her control to undermine a situation.

Fear is often a motivating factor for the saboteur.

In a certain diocese, an external consultant recommended a means of assisting an important ministry of the diocese which had been struggling financially. The bishop happily agreed and participated in the hiring of a project manager with the particular skills needed to bring new life and energy to the ministry. The consultant, project manager, ministry director, and board met together, and while there was some resistance from a few board members about the "outside" approach, it appeared that all agreed that the ultimate goal of saving the ministry was worth giving this recommendation a try.

The project manager's vision and enthusiasm sparked renewed interest in the ministry. New donors and volunteers pitched in with money and time to create fresh contributions to the ministry's home base, offering new opportunities for its use by community groups as well as the congregation and diocese. "There were struggles along the way," the bishop said, "as it's hard to work on a physical plant while the regular activities are going on. I thought that the reports from the project manager and volunteers about the difficulties they were having with the director were due to scheduling, and pretty natural. But I had to look at the pattern when a family of donors came to see the room that they had given in memory of the parents and grandparents. Although it was a weekend, they had called in advance and made arrangements to see the renovated building. When they arrived, having traveled from three states, the room had not been cleaned since it had last been used. Common sense says that if you are the director of a ministry that is struggling financially and you have donors coming in to see the results of their gift, that you bend over backwards to see that it is in tip-top shape—unless, since it was someone else's part of the story and not yours, you want to see it fail. Sad. Sad."

A Canon to the Ordinary reported another type of passive-aggressive sabotage, when one staff member made accusations of impropriety of another staff member in a highly accusatory inter-office memo, without asking for any explanations from the colleague. "In my book, there is no place on any staff for someone who has so few interpersonal skills that they behave in such a manner, regardless of their personal feelings or intent," said the Canon. "When you are a member of a team, or in charge of a part of a team, you go directly to a person and have a conversation with them first, before you begin making accusations. Accountability does not mean running a police state, and detecting passive-aggressive behavior cloaked in the authority of a position or title needs to be detected and dealt with."

Attempt to Unseat Current Leaders

All too often, leaders may find themselves blindsided by a request for their resignation. An individual may assemble a small group of disgruntled parishioners, presuming that secular employer-employee approaches are appropriate for what is instead a covenantal relationship among parish, priest, and bishop. When no Title III or Title IV canonical concerns are involved, this feigned or real misunderstanding of the difference between a call and a hire may be in service to a personal agenda. If that is the case, this is a form of sabotage of leadership.

Strong leadership maintains a less-anxious presence, making such statements as "I'll have to think about this and get back to you." The power of the saboteur, notes a long-term priest/consultant, lies in getting people to react with outrage and anger, or in skewing the truth. In the latter case, the rector might say, "Let's all check out the facts on this situation before we get back together." These same stances are equally important for a bishop who hears such charges against a priest of the diocese.

Counteractions:

- Short term: Leaders should have in their tool kit a selection of non-reactive, non-anxious phrases to utilize when blindsided: "Tell me more about that"; "I will give that some thought and get back to you"; "Can you give me some documentation on your thoughts and process here?"

- Long term: Sessions on "Episcopal Playground" or "Episcopal 101" are part of new member orientation, vestry orientation, and other opportunities for educating members about Episcopal polity and practices. Every vestry and warden should be fully informed of the difference between a "call" and a "hire." Covenantal agreements between clergy, parish, and bishop become normative practice for all.

Attempts to Sabotage Efforts at Transparency and Collaboration

Individuals who feel most secure when they hold the reins of power and control use secrecy and fear as ways to sabotage efforts to share information freely and interact with others. As in cases of spousal abuse, if a vestry or congregation can be kept isolated and subject to a single source of information, that source holds the power and controls the agenda.

In the climate of division pervasive throughout the Episcopal Church in the early 2000s, several clergy reported powerful wardens/leaders raising anxiety in a congregation by reporting that "the bishop is going to take our church and our money," and then pointing out that he, the warden, was protecting them by changing the deed for the parish so that the diocese was not involved. As the tensions of the first part of the new millennium eased, tactics changed from "protecting us against the big bad diocese" to "I will take this church out of the Episcopal Church if I want to because the diocese's name is not on the deed."

A close relationship with the diocesan office, and asking to see the deed can often alleviate fear, and reassure a congregation that their building was given in perpetuity and that the deed is in order. Saboteurs hate facts—they bring the light of day to otherwise secret information!

One of the main dangers inherent in this form of sabotage is isolation. When an individual or organization is isolated from others, whether the isolation is real or perceived, they are more likely to acquiesce to the demands or agenda of that control. The more isolated an individual or entity becomes, the less information they have available to them to make independent decisions; the less confident of their own abilities and more dependent they feel on the person in charge. Books have been written on this topic, including some by people in the Church who have experienced this form of isolationism.

Counteractions:

- Short term: Name the behavior and continue working with whomever from the vestry shows the greatest potential for cooperation with the diocese.

- Long term: Continue to educate the parish regarding Episcopal polity and the role of the diocese; develop relationships with diocesan representatives on other bodies; involve individuals from the parish on diocesan bodies and in diocesan events.

Unwillingness to Give Up Historical Enmities

Far too may clergy, both interim and full time, run into situations of long-term bad blood between a bishop and leader/s in the congregation or a former rector which has been allowed to fester for years. The unwillingness of individuals to move past the old hurt or division for the good of the Kingdom is a heart-breaking reality.

Counteractions:

- Short term: Seek new representation from and for the congregation for working relationally.

- Long term: Provide accurate data where rumor and misinformation have been utilized to continue the alienation; seek participation and representation from newer and more congenial people; maintain civility and stay in relationship.

Sabotage around Financial Issues

Both bishops and priests report passive-aggressive (and outright aggressive) acts of sabotage around financial issues. This is often where anxiety in the system resides. One priest suggests that there is a continuing back story to the common reactivity to such simple acts of transparency as posting parish financials on a bulletin board or offering a summary in a newsletter. These instances are connected with resistance of lay leaders to participate in stewardship campaigns and discomfort with personal finances. "This is not an excuse," he offered, "rather, another way of understanding that most sabotage is from people who have lost something or fear losing something, or have unresolved grief from past situations. It's that 'other-awareness' that I need to respond rather than react."

Lay leaders commented on individuals on vestries and councils who are "financial bullies." "Because they might have more experience with reading financial statements or working with figures than I do—that is definitely not my area of expertise," said one new member of a diocesan body, "I know that someone can easily intimidate me or raise questions for me by the way they focus on a particular line item, or the way something is written. I don't even know what questions to ask. I am learning to say things like, 'I am not clear what you are getting at—maybe for those of us who are more big picture people, someone could offer a narrative explanation of what's going on'—and when I do, everyone cheers. I am not the only one who is tired of being bullied!"

"There can be everything from innuendo to silent, passive-aggressive refusal to promulgating false and disparaging gossip to open rebellion," stated one priest. "Who does these things? People who have lost something or fear losing something important to them—and often, it is power and prestige."

"People complain about miserly giving," said a bishop. "I ask them to think about calculated giving—giving at a level that keeps things from changing. A minimalist approach makes it difficult to do something new."

Counteractions:

- Short term: Provide accurate and transparent information on financial issues; use outside experts to provide objective input.

- Long term: Work toward balancing vestries or committees with persons of stature and expertise to counteract the bully; provide open and transparent records; involve respected diocesan players in working with parish or diocesan entities on these matters.

Cynicism about Change and the State of the Church

Cynicism about change and the state of the church is another form of passive-aggressive sabotage, and one which sucks people in insidiously. The sabotage occurs as the cynical attitude begins to touch others, affecting their attitude and their involvement. Cynicism casts doubt on the worthiness or the viability of a given project or ministry; it can also diminish a project in the eyes of others. Cynicism is a bit like the kind of "creeping crud" that infects people with low-grade infections over the course of a long winter, slowing down bodies and minds, and in general often causing the world to be viewed through a tired, gray haze. It's easy to feel as though the sun will never shine again and that there is little to smile about. The Creeping Crud of cynicism works in much the same way—coloring attitudes with a negative, depressive, and biting kind of knocking down of anything that might possibly smack of hope and the positive.

"I became aware of my own propensity for cynicism at an ecumenical meeting," said one priest, "when a speaker told us that cynical people haven't been able to connect their life purpose with the necessary change."

This self-aware priest was able to recognize his visceral response to the statement he heard at the meeting, and do some further personal reflection to find out what was going on within him to cause a strong reaction to that statement. His self-awareness allowed him to speak up about what was happening in environments where cynicism is considered "cool."

Counteraction:

- Short term: Provide opportunities for discussions where purpose, goals, and challenges are held up and people are encouraged to consider their responses and the decision in light of the purpose.

- Long term: Plans for change involve keeping the membership talking about their personal reactions in relation to their purpose, and looking at the overarching purpose.

Entrenchment

"One of the sabotage behaviors I see is entrenchment," said a priest. "It's the attitude that everything worth doing has been tried, and the current program or way of doing things is the only thing that will possibly work. There is nothing new under the sun." Entrenchment kills creativity and involvement, leading to sabotage of new ideas to enrich a ministry area or congregation. Entrenchment sabotages the saboteur by leading to overfunctioning and martyrdom on the part of an individual or individuals. Without the ongoing evaluation and feedback that leads to new dimensions for any ministry or congregation, entrenchment will eventually lead to death.

"The tradition, and its traditions, are living processes we ossify—and thus miss any real understanding of tradition," a priest observed.

Counteractions:

- Short term: Invitations to be included in what is going forward, without chasing

- Long term: As one bishop stated, "They have been told that if they wish to get on the wagon and go with us, I will make sure that they get equal time, attention, and resources for the things that are important to them as well as to the common mission. If they insist on holding to this position, I will no longer fight for them to have their fair share of resources."

Pushing Personal Agendas

An instrument called "The Awareness Wheel" asks training groups to number 1 through 5 the way they approach information or decisions: thinking, feeling, sensing, wanting, acting. It is one of the only such preferential instruments to acknowledge that "wanting" can be an important factor in any group process. When wanting turns into a personal agenda, however, it can become an instrument of sabotage, with the individual desire taking precedence over all other considerations.

Sometimes personal agendas are well known by others; other times they may be more elusive. The power of the agenda, however, is the strength it gives to an individual to focus solely on what would further the meeting of that need, regardless of how that might negatively impact other aspects.

Self-Sabotage

Examples of self-sabotage range from the inability or refusal to look at one's own patterns of behavior with some regularity, to bishops and priests who rely on their own ministry trajectory experience as the primary guide for staffing and decision making. Without the self-awareness offered by a regular evaluation of one's own behavior, destructive patterns are repeated. Without the other-awareness of the diversity of life experiences, a broader, more fulsome perspective is missing.

A case in point for both bishops and priests is the cycle of farewell (through a new call or retirement), search, and call within the life of an individual parish. After participating in a conversation with her vestry about "good goodbyes," a priest said to the consultant, "I have never experienced what happens to the parish I am leaving after the farewells. From what I'm hearing, it sounds like all clergy should know more about this business of how a congregation is affected by the kind of goodbye they say. It affects both the search for the new rector and the life the new rector experiences in that place. It would certainly make life a little more understandable!"

A bishop confessed to many errors early in his episcopate regarding the interim period, acknowledging that his primary concern had been that the transition officer adequately provided for parishes' worship needs. After several unsuccessful situations with interim rectors who claimed training, yet whose service led to more difficulty than assistance in already-conflicted parishes, the bishop and his transition officer now both understood the work that needed to be done. They began to recruit only the best-qualified rectors-in-the-interim to serve in the diocese.

One trained interim, always in great demand, claims that his "training" included the "school of hard knocks," as well as the years he spent in interim training, listing his time as both a senior warden and chair of a nominating committee prior to seminary as providing a crucial part of his understanding of the work that needs to be done, and helping him build his skill sets.

"Bishops can really benefit from hearing the stories of work they have never experienced themselves," he said. Again and again, we know from bishops, clergy, and laity that sabotage, bullying, and other behaviors that distract from being the transformative church are best counteracted by a bishop with backbone holding to healthy processes. By using his/her authority when and where it is most needed to support honest, mature team players in both ordained and lay leadership throughout the diocese, a bishop can set the standard for the diocese.

"When this happens," said one diocesan staff person, "systems can get healthy. Personnel problems are resolved rather than scapegoating; brains and hearts are fully engaged in being healthy and productive for the work of the Gospel."

Said a bishop, "Dysfunction is always successful for some within the system . . . has gotten them something they wanted, over and over again. We have to interrupt that pattern of dysfunctional or unhealthy behavior. Unhealthy behaviors and manipulation don't work under differentiated leadership."

Many leaders, lay and ordained, spoke forcefully for accountability. "The church is the only organization that will not call its people on bad behavior, and then shoots its wounded."

"'Not acceptable' is a healthy response," said one bishop.

"My job is to help people on their spiritual journey," said one bishop. "The discipline of healthy behaviors is as important to that journey of spiritual development as the discipline of prayer and worship. This is a discipline we all have to keep working on."

Another concluded: "When I call my clergy to the work of healthy behaviors, some might complain that we're asking them to jump through a lot of hoops before they can serve the people here. The simple answer is this: I love my people and I want the best for them. I love my clergy, and I want them all to have as many tools in their tool belt as I can provide."

Counteraction:

Says a bishop, "Where there has been clear vision, clearly articulated, there can be connectivity. There will still be resistance, still be sabotage. I believe that the best way to counteract sabotage is by honoring the people in opposition, by walking with them in their grief, while not changing course."

"It might mean saying to the opposition, 'I know it's hard. I am listening, and I might alter the plan slightly, but there will be no radical changing of the course we are on. I will hold your hand, and we will walk together, but we will push on.' And we push through and learn to live with loss, and embrace the new."

Meanness or Mean-Spiritedness

"No one talks about this. Perhaps we should," a bishop said. Meanness and mean-spiritedness exist in the church just as anywhere else. People simply do not leave their humanity at home when they come to church. It comes with them—and "them" includes both clergy and lay. There does not seem to be an exemption where meanness is concerned. If meanness is a pattern of behavior that has been working for a person for a very long time, behavior that has been allowed without consequence, meanness will take up residence right there in the pew or in the pulpit. We have to take off the rose-colored glasses and call some things by their real names—and meanness and mean-spiritedness are among them. They may manifest themselves in bullying, or appear all by themselves. Meanness appears to have a target and be a sure-shot. You know if you've been hit. We've been guilty of letting meanness go unnamed for far too long.

Lack of Formation as a Baptized Christian

A recurring theme among bishops is a concern about the lack of formation in the basics of what it means to be a baptized Christian, an Episcopalian, and a member of a parish. Efforts to build numbers, responding to a consumer mentality in the culture, and a lack of attention to the importance of formation have together "dumbed down" this work. Without adequate catechesis, signing on for the life of a baptized Christian seems irrelevant at best. "There is little understanding of the depth and gravity of the power of following Jesus Christ," says a bishop. "We've spent too much time trying to be a comfortable Rotary Club or attractive country club instead of talking about the sacrificial walk of the Christian life."

A strong consensus speaks across the ordained and lay leadership of the Church: We should be different from the world, and one of the ways we sabotage ourselves is by not being different. We look the same as the world around us, and we don't form Christians to understand how and why we should be different. We sabotage ourselves by this lack of attention to ongoing formation, and by the "dumbing down" of formation at key teaching points in the life of individual congregants and the corporate life of the congregation.

Lack of Understanding of and Training for Ministry in the Complex System of the Church

One of the ways we sabotage ourselves is by continuing to romanticize the church and the ordained life rather than understanding the complex system that is the church. This understanding begins with self-awareness. Without self- and other-awareness, and an understanding of the complexities of human systems, sabotage will reign.

REFLECTION: Mark 14:10-11

Then Judas Iscariot, one of the twelve, went to the chief priests to betray him to them. When they heard it, they were glad, and promised to give him money. So he sought how he might conveniently betray him.

1. How do I connect this chapter with the familiar Judas story? How do I read the story if I substituted the word "sabotage" for "betrayal"?

2. SELF-AWARENESS: When have I initiated or been a part of the sabotage of someone or something with which I disagreed? What was my "money"—either a recognized or secondary gain for me?

3. OTHER-AWARENESS: Where is sabotage occurring in my community? What is the "reward" or secondary gain?

4. PRACTICE: What one thing might I choose to practice regarding awareness of my intentional or unintentional role in sabotage when I am uncomfortable, fearful, or angry? My community's role?

CHAPTER ELEVEN

Transporting the Outrageous Adventure to the System of the Episcopal Church

*I don't think of it as **working** for world peace, he said I think of it as just trying to **get along** in a really **big strange family.***

BRIAN ANDREAS

Leadership training weekends, workshops, transition periods . . . are all temporary communities with specific goals in mind. Each contains some of the elements that make the sort of "Himalayan adventure" we discussed in the first chapter: a temporary community devoted to a common cause, a place set apart, a major responsibility and goal, a spiritual setting. Surviving and thriving—remembering the ways of healthy community—are intentional parts of these particular adventures, with time spent reflecting on how well the human interaction has gone. But sooner or later, intensive weekends and transition periods end, and it's back to the real, everyday world, where the real work must happen. Every day, forever and ever. As someone once said about developing a new, healthy habit, "But it's so borrrring. It's just like dusting. You do it one day and you have to do it all over again the next if you want to sustain healthy practice."

The question is: is the outrageous adventure truly transportable from the Himalayas to the system of the Episcopal Church and to the ongoing everyday life of the people who make up the Church?

The good news is that the answer is "yes." The harder news is that it takes intentionality, effort, and perseverance to transport the adventure and make it part of the DNA of the culture. Transporting the outrageous adventure means, first of all, acknowledging that this is no longer simply an interesting proposition to discuss, something to put on an agenda for later, or a technical fix that could make the system a little healthier. It is critical to survival. Do or die.

It's time to face the reality, as one bishop said, that there is absolutely no mechanism in the current system for accountability, and without it, neither the current system, nor any structure that is created to take its place has a chance to make it. The over-arching mechanism for transporting the outrageous adventure is a church-wide process for accountability. That process will require an affirmation from across the system: this is the expectation for how we operate, how we treat each other here, and how we hold each other to this standard. It has never been more important than it is today. Such a mechanism and mandate need support for every individual and part of the system embarking on this "do or die" adventure.

Let's look at some things to consider in bringing the adventure into every part of life, from home to office to organization.

Could I Be the One Who's Crazy?

The Ability to Stand Back and Question Oneself

Remember the woman who came to therapy with the goal of ending an affair with a married man, and began to wonder if health was worth the cost, as everyone else seemed so screwed up? "Sometimes I think I'm the one who's crazy!" she said.

"The fact that you can ask the question tells me you're not the one who's crazy," her therapist replied.

As leaders and systems move toward healthy behaviors, it *can be very lonely*, particularly if an individual has embarked on the journey without institutional or personal support. As an individual is intentional in practicing new behaviors, the environment responds by seeming to conspire against them, to force them back into old, familiar behaviors, regardless of how dysfunctional. Personal change in an individual affects all relationships. There is a growing sense of discomfort when familiar patterns change. As the system endeavors to pull an individual back into familiar behaviors, the question raised by the woman is not uncommon.

A certain comfort level exists when mired in old but familiar behaviors (comfortable being uncomfortable). With an increasing awareness of the impact of old behaviors, and the option of choosing new behaviors, comes a discomfort in participating in unhealthy patterns. When the behavior was automatic and not yet recognized as unhealthy, it was not a problem.

Once aware that the behavior has a name, and an unhappy impact, individuals may experience an increased discomfort at being uncomfortable or participating in unhealthy behaviors. At this point, the individual who is trying to change his/her behavior looks around and sees others in the system continuing with old behaviors and feels pressured to return to the familiar old behaviors. The "new eyes" of the newly aware see that change is necessary, but something inside says, "maybe I am the one who's crazy."

One mark of differentiated leadership puts both the difficulty and loneliness in theological and psychological context. One bishop relates her experience of pondering a terribly difficult decision for the diocese. "I was pacing back and forth in my office," she said, "with a final decision in front of me. Although there was another person in the room, I had never felt more alone in my life. It was just me and God. It made me think of those times that Jesus went off to a lonely place, and how I've come to understand the Garden of Gethsemane. I believe the essence of Jesus' prayer there is this: 'maybe I'm the one who's crazy.' And it must have looked that way." The differentiated leader learns to thrive even in the difficulty of such moments.

Develop a Research Culture to Support Intuition-Based Decision Making with Data

A bishop reports that he has been searching for empirical studies that would offer data on what makes a "good leader in the church," a "good rector," a "good bishop." We have plenty of informal narratives that indicate qualities that have been effective in certain situations and those which have not. This anecdotal evidence is not to be discounted. The truth is that we are an intuition-based system, lacking in formal evaluation practices and studies that can name, based on viable data, what effective and dysfunctional behaviors are.

Once that baseline has been established, establishing a mechanism for calling out behaviors that are dysfunctional and destructive becomes possible. Intuition (the ability to acquire knowledge that cannot be reasoned or justified) and data gathering (a formal process for collecting information that is defined and accurate) are two sides of the coin of decision making—and both are important.

After gathering facts and opinions from trusted advisors, numerous studies report that successful CEOs and entrepreneurs use intuition or "hunches" to make a final decision. Dr. Diane Snow, professor of neuroscience at the University of Kentucky, has published "Neural Basis for Intuition," a paper designed to help prospective leaders develop their intuitive skills. Her work builds on that of the late Dr. Paula Raines (1942–2009), developer of a workshop for building and trusting capacity in intuition, and the work of John Allman, PhD, a leader in the field of intuition research, dedicated to the link between emotion and cognition.

The key word in this equation is "and." Neither data nor intuition by themselves is sufficient for good decision making. In some systems, intuitive skills need to be taught and encouraged. In the system of the Episcopal Church, experience would show that intuition has been utilized without the balancing support of data

The use of both intuition and data are critical at this stage of the game. Neither is a perfect tool, of course, but the seeking of both is, in itself, important. Of particular importance is how we create the measure that fits the context of the work we are called to do. It is not a one-size-fits-all kind of measurement, which can borrow from outside its context. The system itself must generate a mechanism that measures appropriate input to produce the needed results in assessments.

Establish a Highly Structured Organization
That Promotes Flexibility and Imagination

Several leaders, lay and ordained, referred to successful organizations as models for a new structure in the church. "We want to be like Google," one said. "And when people say that, they mean they want to be that highly creative, casual dress, adaptable organization that looks so low-key. What they don't understand is that it requires a highly structured organization underneath to achieve that kind of operation."

"When you are structured for legislation," says a bishop, "you are structured to fail." Numerous leaders pointed to "nineteenth-century" structures and processes currently in place. They voiced frustration at a system that seems to center on the time-consuming work of resolutions-based governance, with its posturing and territorial debates, now too cumbersome to engage well with imagination or mission. A new structure must reflect the twenty-first century and be prepared to move beyond it. Nimble. Visionary. Data based. Evaluative. Analytical. Imaginative. Responsive. There are highly credible organizations around this country that assist a system in its change process. A part of this assistance is the knowledge of how to leave the old behind—a process that will cause grief, despite the necessity for change and the time for change. Help is provided in assisting the new in emerging, and the organization in accepting this new container for its life. We must engage the best minds to walk with us in moving toward a system that is healthy and alive, attracting not only those who already call themselves Episcopalians, but those who will be newly compelled to become a part of this reformation. Stepping out in faith on an adventure has an energy that is contagious, that is compelling.

Be Willing to Adapt the Best Business Practices and Translate the Language to Meet the Needs of the System

Much time and effort goes into teaching leaders and congregations that the church is not in the hire-and-fire business, but deals in covenantal relationships; that we have bishops and mutual ministry reviews rather than supervisors. The downside of this careful language is that we have refuted the best practices of businesses for setting standards of behaviors. We need formal review mechanisms in place that document challenges and improvements. "We must be able to say, 'I'm not going to let you continue at this position, or move on,'" says a bishop. "We simply can't allow that kind of passing on of ineffective behaviors. No successful organization would do so. Why do we?"

The business of adapting best practices and translating the language to meet the needs of the church system will call for understanding, teaching, and practicing of covenantal relationships. These covenants include mechanisms for accountability, evaluation, and analysis in letters of agreement for parish clergy and in calls to serve on committees, commissions, and councils. "We have to stop saying that we cannot ask for accountability from people because they are volunteers," says one bishop. "Accountability is for everyone." St. Benedict's Rule of Life will remind us quickly that the matter of accountability has a long history in our own tradition, not just in the business world!

Put the Fear of People Leaving Behind

Clergy and laity alike identify fear as one of the major factors affecting the church today. The fears are far ranging, but one of the most consistent is the fear of losing members if expectations for healthy behaviors and accountability are too high. In pockets of the church, narrative data is beginning to show membership numbers growing when expectations for healthy behaviors are clear and high. The institution has yet to put its teeth into a church-wide expectation, for fear of losing people.

Says one bishop, "Fear seems to be out of proportion to reality. We talk about building capacity for healthy, effective leadership with high expectations for how we will live and work together. However, the reality is that if we lost half of our current membership out of unwillingness to become accountable for their own behaviors, over 40 percent of the U.S. population is not affiliated with a religious community. If we aren't interested in attracting some number of that unaffiliated segment of the population, we are in trouble." It's time to set aside the fear of losing people. A transition officer reports that phone calls from prospective clergy are increasingly asking if the diocese is a "safe place" to live and be in ministry. What is a "safe place"? Several individuals identify a safe place as "a place where people are expected to tell the truth, where people show respect for each other, and where there is high energy around doing God's work rather than doing each other in." It's a clear call for high expectations for accountability among clergy and laity, lest we eat each other alive.

Cultivate Buddies and Coaches Who Are Walking the Walk, Not Just Talking the Talk

At the beginning stage of choosing new behavioral options, it is important to locate a "buddy" or a coach with whom to reflect on the experience. Systemic change takes time—and a part of that time is spent developing a core group within the system on which to build strength. Buddies or coaches may be connected by computer, cell phone, Skype, or face-to-face visits. Both formal and informal networks already exist, and new ones form each time an individual makes the decision to take on the outrageous adventure. Beware, however, of those who have carefully cultivated the language without walking the walk. It is easy to confuse the two when one is looking for people to walk with. Says a bishop; "As I understand differentiated leadership, it means being clear and staying connected. Too often, the people I hear claiming that they are differentiated leaders may be clear, but they are not connected, or connected and without clarity."

Folks who share the common language of choosing healthy behavior for themselves, and *are being consistent about reflecting on it and modeling it in their given system,* need that network of voices to serve as mirrors for each other, building a community of support. If the language is common but the behaviors are not, look further. Those who are walking the walk will be working on their own self-awareness and looking for persons with whom they can process their own journey rather than the case studies of others.

In *A Failure of Nerve,* Rabbi Friedman looks at five leaders who were willing to "go first" to explore new ways and new worlds. He identified five aspects of their functioning which enabled them to lead an entire civilization into a new world, and which Friedman believes must be present in the leaders of any social system today to make a real difference.

1. A capacity to get outside the emotional climate of the day

2. A willingness to be exposed and vulnerable

3. Persistence in the face of resistance and downright rejection

4. Stamina in the face of sabotage along the way

5. Being "headstrong" and "ruthless"—at least in the eyes of others[29]

---

29. Friedman, *A Failure of Nerve,* 188–89.

Friedman stresses that what makes these attributes universal is that they are not related to personality, gender, or cultural factors, but are about the capacity to function well when the world about you is disoriented and stuck in a certain way of thinking.

The question "Could I be the one who is crazy?" continues to be important long after the first days of the adventure. Indeed, it is one of the marks of sanity that an individual can step back from their deepest beliefs and greatest passions to ask, *Is it possible that I am the one who is crazy?* No one is right 100 percent of the time. There is a fine line between self-confidence, knowledge, expertise, and a false sense of aggrandizement that borders on the pathological. The individual who is truly knowledgeable is also aware of the dangers of the presumption that they alone hold the truth. The ability to step back and ask the hard question—*Is it possible that I could be the one who is crazy?*—is a critical attribute of health.

Conversion and Reframing

Conversion of any sort may begin with a moment of absolute transfiguration, but conversion itself is an ongoing process. Those who have had the "ah-ha" often have a convert's fervor and are disappointed when they cannot change their local systems, much less the world, yesterday. Here is where self-awareness must be coupled with the other-awareness required for mature decision making based on emotional intelligence. An awareness of the others involved, where they are in the various stages of the system and its processes, what is important to them—and what they stand to lose with any change in the system—is key to constructive moving forward.

The conversion journey is also aided by taking time to help people reframe their experiences. Utilizing aspects of Appreciative Inquiry, reflect on times when individuals have been most effective, their church or group most engaged, their work apparently most effective.

Seek Different Perspectives and Ideas to Enrich and Enlarge the Journey

While the support of people who "speak our language" is important, we humans have a tendency to group ourselves with "likes"—people who think like we do, live like we do, etc. There is much we can miss if we don't deliberately seek out people who are different from us—people who can bring different ideas, a different background and training, or different questions to a group. As one bishop noted, after meeting with his most liberal congregation, he was feeling chewed up and spit out. He began to reflect on the last time he had felt that way. He realized that his previous experience had been with the most conservative congregation in the diocese. The ends of our philosophical and theological continuums, those who are at the edges, are least likely to have a mix of opinions and voices among them, and thus may miss not only new and critical information about the whole, but have no awareness that they are living in different paradigms from the people in the center. One end of the continuum joins itself with others who plant themselves firmly in an old paradigm and refuse to leave. The other has moved on to the new paradigm and see themselves as pioneers. The problem at either end of the continuum is lack of awareness that there are other ideas and experiences that need to be heard. Those who can adapt will go forward; those who can't will die along the way.

For one bishop, the image is of a fish tank on the beach, waiting for fish to jump into it. "There are only dead fish on a beach," he said. "Let the dead bury their dead. The live fish are in the water, and we have to go where the fish are. We will have to exercise muscles we've never exercised before, listen to ideas we've never wanted to hear, on our way to learning that the old way is not going to work anymore." He continued, "This is not a political statement, but a leadership statement. The Episcopal Church could learn from the experience of the Republicans in 2012. They missed it. They just plain missed where the culture was, and the reality that the old ways no longer work." In an entirely separate conversation, a lay leader noted that for him, the most stunning evidence of the church's need to hear voices other than "business as usual" were the televised images on election night: one, middle-aged and older, white, upper middle-class wearing dark suits; the other, exuberant young men and women of every color and creed, massed together in streets and parks across the country.

Amazingly, when we invite the different voices, and then listen carefully so we truly understand where and how we disagree, we will also discover glimmers of those areas where we actually do agree—and on that slim beginning, a relationship begins, and new possibilities appear. Linda, a vestry member, said with a little sigh, "Inviting different voices and allowing everyone not only a buy-in but a real role meant a hugely successful moment in ministry whose impact is still felt—and it didn't have any resemblance to the idea I originally brought to the table—it's much bigger!"

Pay Attention to the Grief That Is Omnipresent

In a society that does not do well with the losses associated with physical death, we do less well with the more daily, intangible griefs that are part of every human life—our own included.

One of the most important aspects of graduate training in counseling psychology was the work we were required to do on our own life's losses. Key to understanding loss in the lives of others while not being "hooked" by our own unexamined grief, this self-awareness and other-awareness is critical to all work of transformation. In the church, examples of dealing with such losses and their grief might include the parish where all trust in clergy has been lost after four successive rectors' marriages ended during their tenure, and a bishop who sold their property (for quite valid reasons) urged them to enter into a shared ministry experiment. Many in the congregation remained in such unrecognized and unhonored grief that the new rector could make no headway until the grief was addressed. In another diocese, a parish with an average Sunday attendance of 2,000 and some 200 different ministries could not agree upon a parish profile during their transition. A number of members did not believe the report was honest, as it reflected only the new vision and direction for the congregation, now in a new location, without reflecting the part of the story that included the grief over the loss of the old vision, direction, and building.

In both cases, when the grief was honored and attended to, and the people could recognize themselves as having a place in the story, they were able to move on together.

If we are going to work effectively, the awareness of grief over losses must be part of our lives. Perhaps the best model we have in modern times is the truth and reconciliation work sponsored by Bishop Tutu in post-apartheid South Africa. Most of us will never experience the grief and loss of that time and place. What was modeled for us in the truth and reconciliation process was the astonishing ability of people to hear the truth of other people's stories, and to accept and honor that truth without the need to defend or correct, *even when the truth differs from our own.* This model of hearing and respecting the hurts, disappointments, and grief of another in Holy Conversations is, indeed, holy work and hard. In many settings, after the stories are told and the grief named, the stories are laid on the altar and a liturgy of healing and reconciliation is celebrated.

In the last years of his life, the late John Schneider, author of the classic work on grief, *Finding My Way,*[30] was dedicated to helping people understand the difference between grief and depression. It was his concern that individuals be enabled to move through their grief in a natural, healthy way without being mistakenly medicated for depression. His research affirmed the significance of how individuals and groups address their grief over losses great and small, in daily life and in crisis situations.

---

30. John M. Schneider, *Finding My Way: From Trauma to Transformation: The Journey Through Loss and Grief* (Traverse City, MI: Seasons Press, 2012).

Human beings can deal with unbelievable losses *when they feel they have been heard and their loss has been honored*. When grief over loss is not heard or honored, humans tend to hang on with white knuckles, unable to let go. "But I *know* it was important! I *know* how sad I am to lose it!" an inner child wails. No matter how long ago, we continue to trip over these old, unacknowledged losses and griefs, bumps shoved under the carpet, often repeating the patterns that will lead to the same type of hurt, disappointment, and loss.

Another aspect of grief resolution is becoming an active participant in the decision regarding the change and loss: the purpose behind the change, and things chosen to be left behind. One bishop asks folks to join her in considering what is truly essential: the Gospel, the sacraments, the liturgy, the creed. "What are you willing to give up for the sake of the Gospel, to make disciples for Jesus Christ," she asks, explaining that we all have to give up personal preferences for the sake of the one not here, the people yet to come.

As bishops go about their dioceses, they see high anxiety; people know that the institution they love is struggling, and they are fearful of what they may lose. "I am equal part cheerleader for the good I see happening and pastoral hospice worker, listening, empathizing," says one. "I have to acknowledge that as we are trying to build capacity and try new things, there are people in our congregations who do not have the energy at this stage of their lives, for whatever reason, for these adaptive changes. And so we straddle two cultures—one birthing a new thing, and the other, a hospice ministry of some sort."

Recognizing and Honoring New Markers for Health

The church has historically utilized quantitative markers for measuring health and success in parish life. The numbers—people in the pews and dollars in the plate, ability to pay the diocesan assessment—have told the story. A bishop sat with his senior staff. At his request, the financial officer had prepared charts for each congregation, looking at the patterns of ten years indicated by graphs. The bishop handed pads of sticky notes to the staff members and asked that they study each individual chart, and then, on the sticky notes, write what they knew of the rest of the story. If there was a decline in numbers, what was the backstory?

As the exercise moved around the table, the staff members agreed that they were seeing different markers for health and success than those indicated by the graphs. They spoke of situations where the decline in both membership and giving looked negative *without awareness of the story,* but with an understanding that changes in the system and new expectations of healthy behavior had led to the departure of some individuals, the story became a more positive one. New patterns of behavior were clearly at work in these places. How it would affect attendance (as seekers recognized a safe place) and giving (as real stewardship replaced control and reactivity) would take longer to determine.

Certainly, there are operational costs in any organization, and mission and ministry require funding. Attending and giving *are* important. Yet as a church riding the waves of the cultural sea-change, we are unclear about what the evolving structure will be, church-wide, regionally, locally. We have no clue what role expensive edifices will play on a local level or what paid professional positions will exist. We are once again a pilgrim people, not yet arrived at a fixed point, but on a brave journey. And like all pilgrim people, we must identify new and different markers that confirm we are on a new path of promise—even if all of the landmarks are unfamiliar and uncomfortable. There are simply no roadmaps to the Promised Land.

Keeping "The Notebook" to Keep Sanity

A tattered spiral notebook reminds me regularly that when sanity is threatened by a system and I am in danger of believing I am the one who is crazy, I need a tangible way to reflect on what I am experiencing *in light of the foundational theories on which my personal belief and behavioral systems are built.*

During a particular institutional transition, it seemed evident that leaders had embarked on a course with predictable pitfalls, if not downright "disaster ahead" warning signs. There was growing anxiety in the system: any attempt to question the direction or make suggestions was met with great resistance from those in charge. Fear among staff members led to a widespread "no talk" norm. Perhaps, I thought, I *was* the one who was crazy?

In the spiral notebook, I made five side-by-side columns and began my strange "journal."

EVENT	WAY BEING HANDLED	PREDICTABLE RESULT	THEORETICAL CHOICE	RESULT
Staff taken to empty office of former boss to meet new boss	Lack of sensitivity	confusion, resistance, lack of cooperation	closure; grieve	cooperation; participation
"Silo-ing" of	Staff forbidden to talk to each other or anyone about process	no information available; distrust, tension heightened; acting out	Integrate and inform part of system; include	teamwork

The scribbles could not change the actions being taken; they could and did save my sanity! I was definitely *not* the one who was crazy! A little notebook and analysis based on proven theories helped me come to that conclusion. Sometimes it is consultation with a trusted confidante—preferably from outside the system who can look at the situation objectively—that helps one believe in their own sanity in the face of institutional craziness!

Holy Behaviors: Bullies Not Tolerated Here

Earlier, we defined bullying and other unhealthy behaviors. We've identified those behaviors clergy and lay leaders see repeated again and again throughout our systems, from one tenure to the next. Obviously, changing leaders does not make human beings behave differently. Only active awareness and intentionality can do that.

But as an institution, we *can* have an expectation that being part of the church means a new and different norm in behavior. I wonder what would happen if:

- we chose to let go of the fear that being honest about our darkside would make us unacceptable to God and to each other?

- we were honest about the dark side of our particular parish?

- every vestry, diocesan commission, and committee began every new year with a review of the "Episcopal playground," so we were clear we're all playing by the same rules?

- every "baby bishops" school included a session of interim ministry training and a session of transition ministry training?

- every Commission on Ministry and discernment committee were committed to finding the kind of leadership (lay and ordained) that can bring with them competencies for ministry in the reformation? This commitment would recognize that the call is also to be burned and crucified, to be creative and adaptable, to recognize the absolute absurdity and craziness of it all, and still to maintain a sense of humor and joy as they go about the work of the Kingdom.

- we were all aware that we are *all* in transition, all of the time . . . and took seriously the teachings of the interim ministry folks as important tools for life as well as for ministry?

- we stopped resisting being honest with ourselves and our congregations, and remembered that God knows us all "completely, absolutely, exquisitely, and perfectly," as one bishop said, recognizing that our lack of honesty is not fooling anyone? Perhaps this is the fundamental spiritual issue of being human.

• we share purpose and concepts, generation to generation, allowing each to own their version of truth, and speak it in their own vocabulary . . . letting go when it is time to pass the baton?

Remember the Essentials

A bishop states: The Gospel story never changes. It is always good news.

What is essential? The Gospel, the sacraments, the liturgy, the creed. Everything else is not.

What are we willing to give up for the sake of the Gospel?

What are we willing to give up to make disciples?

What of our personal agendas are we willing to give up for the sake of the ones not yet here?

REFLECTION: Revelation 21:1

Then I saw a new heaven and a new earth . . .

1. Scripture shows us that inspiration can drive change. How does the vision of a "new heaven and new earth" connect with the chapter I have just read?

2. SELF-AWARENESS: What moves me to be a part of bringing the "new heaven and new earth" to the institution of the Church? To my life? To my community?

3. OTHER-AWARENESS: What moves my community to be a part of bringing the "new heaven and new earth" to our part of God's Kingdom?

4. PRACTICE: What am I going to choose to practice to support my efforts and those of my community to do this work?

Be the Difference:
The Cost and the Promise

*"There is no **power** greater than a community discovering what it cares about."*

MARGARET WHEATLE

A number of years ago, I spent a week with clergy who were asked to consider the question of how visitors from another planet might identify Christians in our culture. How were they different from non-believers?

Since it is difficult to see ourselves as a stranger might, one of the experiential exercises sent teams from our workshop into different (non-Episcopal) churches in the community where we were meeting; we were asked to focus on the question outside our own familiar rituals. As I recall, several of the small groups, including my own, experienced some culture shock. Before we could begin to answer the larger question, however, we needed to consider what these strange-to-us folks appeared to care about and value.

It began benignly enough. Approaching the church, the crowded parking lot, with its mixture of rusting pick-ups and family cars, seemed to speak of a large and diverse community. Once inside, however, there was a decided shift. We felt more suspected than welcomed: Dressed down by our own standards (shirts and ties, no jackets or clerical collars for the men; flat shoes and casual dress for me, as the only woman in the group), we stood out among the extremely casual crowd. The men were offered the service bulletin and a welcome packet; I was not (as if I must be with one of the men and therefore could share the materials given to them). Members were asked to stand so that visitors could see them (leaving visitors to feel even more obvious). The sermon was on the "Rapture," and members were instructed to stop by the audio-visual booth before they left the service and pay $5 each to receive a tape of this instructional sermon to put with their most important papers at home. On this late October Sunday, men sat at tables beside the doors as we left, handing out packets of a political persuasion—why one candidate was preferable to the other to be president of the United States. Back at the retreat center, our report was unanimous: these folk valued control. They valued male and religious supremacy. We experienced the church and its people as dogmatic, judgmental, biased, unaccepting, suspicious, unfriendly.

There were already way too many places in the culture to experience these attitudes. We did not need to go to church to do so. It's an experience I have not forgotten, and one that makes me wonder:

I wonder what those outside our Episcopal culture see when they observe us?

For too long now, it seems to me, the answer to what we as Episcopalians care about has been characterized by a growing level of polarization and in-fighting that mirrors rather than leads the culture. We care, our behavior says, about being with people who look, sound, and act just like us—and when the differences become too great, we pick up our toys and go someplace else to create a more homogenous playground. We care about protecting life-long heterosexual marriage while politely turning our heads to extra-marital affairs and divorces. We say we care about the worth and dignity of every human being, but perhaps we care more about the beauty and dignity that enhance worship, as long as the candlesticks and chalice are properly placed. We care about our reputation as the church of the elite and important, and woe to the person who might publicly note that we are behind on our pledges.

A priest of the church, writing to me regarding this book, said, "In my experience, at the core of our issues is the need to define vocation. We are the last institution in the culture that is not defined in terms of purpose, priorities, partnerships, and accountabilities. At the heart of conflict, at the core of all the subjectivities that we are susceptible to, stands a lack of clear vision concerning our purpose, our calling. To frame a succinct and concrete purpose leads to identifying equally concrete priorities. We can't do everything. So what is it that God is calling us to do and what are we willing and able to do? What is our business? The answer, in so many words, is 'resurrection.' Now, how do we specifically and publicly express this?"

A bishop states, "I think it is a misunderstanding of the nature of Anglican theology that, instead of looking holistically and organically at our theology and our work in human growth and behaviors, we have made an artificial line of demarcation that says this is theology on the one hand and this is touchy-feely stuff on the other. We're not willing to see it all as a whole. Study shows us that there is direct line from Augustine, the father of introspection, who taught us how to look into our own souls, and Benedict, who taught us how to relate in community, to Anglicanism. We ought to be gushing over the opportunity to do this kind of work, not sealed off from theology and mission."

Another bishop says: "There will be a cost to making this kind of change. It is the cost of life as we know it. Even for those who know the change has to come, and are willing for it to come, it will cost something. I don't even know yet what that cost will be to me personally. But I know it will be some point of privilege that is working for me—and I will have to give it up if we are to survive."

Others remind us that infrastructure and finances will struggle mightily in the transition to whatever is to come. How ministry and mission are financed and kept alive are real questions that need real answers as our structures evolve.

A young lay leader reflects thoughtfully that it's all about evangelism. To him, the cost of not changing is both huge and unthinkable. Yet he is aware that there are those restraining forces that will fight to maintain the status quo. "It's hard to be excited about bringing friends into a place where people are fighting about things like styles of worship or music, or something else that really isn't that important in the great scheme of things. So it scares me to think that we'd be content to just rock along in this same old dysfunctional way until we disappear. To me, there is no cost too great for changing the way we deal with each other. The promise is that we get to realize God's gospel imperatives to deal with issues head on, confront them, and more importantly, get on with the work of the Gospel—which is why I go to church in the first place!"

Add the bishops, "The promise is an entirely new way to serve God's mission in this time in a substantially healthier way and that's worth about everything. This is a chance to do something really exciting—for Christ's sake."

It's an important promise.

Outside our church doors, there was nothing even remotely civil about the most recent political campaigns. Plural. From local runs for mayor or county official to the nation's highest office, name calling, truth stretching, denigrating the "other" and what they aren't rather than establishing what one *is* . . . the ugliness flowed across the nation via TV screens, social media, and newspapers; a stream of toxic negativity that pushed polarization to unprecedented heights. We've also heard dark stories of athletic abuse finally called by its proper name—child sexual abuse—and the pretense of being individuals above suspicion that allowed that abuse. As athletic temples cleanse their rolls of those who don't win enough, rabid fans scream, "I don't care what else he's done, so long as he wins!" The fan in the stands with the loudest voice just might be bringing the same "win at all costs" attitude to the vestry table.

Far from being counter-cultural and behaving in ways that are congruent with the life and teaching of Jesus Christ, we have brought the hostile, the polarizing, the toxic with us into our naves and parish halls. There are those who cry loudly about the effect the culture has on the church. This is not about modern culture seeping into naves and parish halls, puffs of smoke under doorways and through vents and windows like poison gas, but about unholy behaviors marching with us right into our pews, becoming acceptable parts of the very fabric of our lives.

"We've gone beyond corporate-think and corporate-speak and into 'Survivor' mentality," a man said. "Who are we going to vote off of the island?"

American Public Media's Krista Tippett offered a series on the most polarizing issues in our country on her syndicated program, "On Being." Former arch-enemies Jonathan Rauch and David Blankenhorn battled mightily, and publicly, over protection of heterosexual marriage and advocacy of gay marriage before becoming friends and collaborators. Listening to them, these words jumped out at me: "We are at the lowest level of public conversation ever in our county . . . it is bad for our country; it is bad for our souls." Echoes of Rabbi Friedman's "the greatest threat is not external, but internal."

Rauch and Blankenhorn's dialogue was one of those sit-in-my-car-because-I-don't-dare-miss-a-word times. I wanted everyone in the world to join me in hearing how these two went from enmity to friendship, moving beyond their strong differences and experiences to agreeing that their country was more important to them than being "right." "There's nothing soft and squishy about that," said one. "There's something higher than being right."

Scribbling furiously on the back of an envelope, I wrote down:

Model on a small scale wherever you can that there is a different way of talking to each other.

Be rigorous.

Be powerful.

Be funny.

But don't be mean.

And remember three behaviors:

Be curious.

Be polite.

And admit that there may be something you may not know until you put yourself in the other's shoes.

Working as a consultant with two long-conflicted colleagues in a non-church system, I introduced the behavior/impact exercise. The war between the two had been waging far too long to the detriment of their department, and all previous attempts to mediate had failed. The glimmer of hope had begun when, after naming the times they had observed dysfunctional behaviors in the system, they had named and owned times they had been sucked into such behaviors themselves, making a list of the impact on their colleagues and clients. Silence had filled the conference room for a number of minutes. Finally, one of the pair spoke. "You are basically asking me to change how I am in the world," he said. "My attitude, as well as my behavior. That's really hard."

He was right. It *is* hard. We want it to be easy, but it is not. The acceptance of that reality—that being the difference, making the change is hard, hard work—is a moment when a truth is named and taken inside the heart, mind, and spirit in a way that changes everything.

The "ah-ha" moment that recognizes the difficulty of the task precedes the determination to *be* the change you want to see in the world. In her book *Turning to One Another: Simple Conversations to Restore Hope to the Future*, Margaret Wheatley shares a story from the Aztec people of Mexico:

> It is said by our grandparents that a long time ago there was a great fire in the forests that covered our Earth. People and animals started to run, trying to escape from the fire. Our brother owl, Tecoloti, was running away also when he noticed a small bird hurrying back and forth between the nearest river and the fire. He headed toward this small bird.
>
> He noticed that it was our brother the Quetzal bird, running to the river, picking up small drops of water in his beak, then returning to the fire to throw that tiny bit of water on the flame. Owl approached Quetzal bird and yelled at him: "What are you doing brother? Are you stupid? You are not going to achieve anything by doing this. What are you trying to do? You must run for your life!"
>
> Quetzal bird stopped for a moment and looked at owl, and then answered: "I am doing the best I can with what I have."
>
> It is remembered by our Grandparents that a long time ago the forests that covered our Earth were saved from a great fire by a small Quetzal bird, an owl, and many other animals and people who got together and put out the flame.[31]

It happened on the road to Emmaus. It is the grace of transfiguration. In this post-Christian time in our church, it continues to happen.

A few weeks ago, a priest, part of a diocesan leadership team, was in a small rural parish. It was the second week of a three-week series, and the

---

31. Wheatley, *Turning to One Another*, 158.

152   Becoming the Transformative Church

>> >>

"Holy Conversations" had moved from stories of times they had been most engaged in their parishes to times they had been hurt and disappointed. For many years, this small group of faithful people had lived in the fear that someday, for some reason, their church might simply disappear and with it, the opportunity for an alternative to the fundamentalism in their area. At times, the tension brought anxieties which threatened to destroy them from within. In these brave and honest conversations, they were naming the behaviors that had held them hostage, determining to take specific steps to not just survive, but do mission and ministry in their community. Above all, they were determined not to allow the return of the destructive behaviors that were the true threat to their survival.

"As I listened," the priest said, "I was overwhelmed with emotion at their faithfulness, and at the importance of what they, and we, are doing. I am aware that these things require time, as well as psychological, spiritual, and emotional energy, and that sometimes it's just easier to follow some program from somewhere than it is to build healthy relationships. We have lots of metrics for measuring efficiency and what we call effectiveness. We don't have metrics for faithfulness and wholeness. And I was so thankful that I am a part of something where we're not taking the easy route—for this work deserves all of the support that we can give it."

The good news is that all of us have the opportunity to be the Quetzal bird, or one who joins the Quetzal's brigade. The additional news is that we must continue hurrying back and forth with the water, for the fire is large and spreading rapidly. We will grow weary and want to quit. Putting out the fires of damaging behaviors requires endless repetitions, time, and psychological, emotional, and spiritual energy.

Shinichi Suzuki, the Japanese violin pedagogue, tells his students that in order to incorporate a change in their playing, the new way must be repeated at least one hundred times in succession. If the old way intervenes, the count begins again.

Repetition, repetition, repetition.

Change *is* hard. But the cost of not changing is unthinkable. And the gift you pass on to your part of the world could be good patterns of functional behaviors, congruent with the life and teachings of Jesus; patterns that free us to respond fully to our charge to bring the Kingdom of God to earth here and now.

Pockets of this Kingdom work exist today: local efforts spotted across the face of the Church. History reminds us that when local efforts become connected, amazing things can happen. As long as those efforts exist in isolation, nothing will change. But the connection of local simultaneous actions can result in something much more powerful than the sum of their parts. As the transformation comes, we must hold it high and sing its song, so that others will see and know that it is real and here to stay.

We are presently in a between-time—on a bridge between where we have been and where we must go. The way ahead is not clear, which makes it difficult to step out in faith. Like Abraham and Sarah, if we choose to answer the call that means new life, we will leave much behind. One of the things that we will leave behind is the need to know now. And with us, we will take the awareness that we are embracing a new and foundational call that must continue with us, beyond our time, perhaps forever. It is hard to imagine a time when living and working together would not be a priority!

True leadership is generative. It provides replicable models, not rigid prescriptions to be mimicked without thought or integration. This kind of life-giving leadership, at all levels of our life together, is within our grasp, as we choose to walk into the light of God's new heaven and earth.

The poet David Whyte, writing in the Afterword of the book *Leading from Within: Poetry that Sustains the Courage to Lead,* references those who are "students of leadership."

> Students of leadership, are, I believe, of all ages, all descriptions of humanity. I hope to always be one. I invite you to be one, too—enabling the change you want to see in the world. Some of you will speak with words that the leaders of today do not know, for they do not yet exist. You will create ways we cannot imagine for situations unknown to those of us alive today. If the church and the world are to survive, the concept you will make your own is this one thing: we must find a way to live and work together.[32]

We began this journey with a leadership story from a new generation of leaders, represented in this book by then fifteen-year-old Virginia.

When Virginia was about ten years old, we were driving through the rolling lands of Kentucky, having one of those in-the-car conversations, when she told me that she wanted to create a "School for Listening." It was all perfectly clear in her head. People would be gathered together in groups and learn how to listen to each other, whether or not they were of the same opinion. "Think of the things we might learn from each other," she said, wide-eyed. "Think of how good it would be!" Her hope filled my heart and soul—joining my hope with hers that it could be so; praying that her hope would not be destroyed.

Another long-ago Virginia wrote a child's letter to the editor of the newspaper, asking if, indeed, Santa Claus really existed. A sensitive editor's insightful response about faith and hope continues to touch people each year,

---

32. David Whyte, in "Afterword," *Leading from Within,* 239.

even in these cynical times. I believe it says something about a need that we know that we all have, that the "Dear Virginia" letter about belief is a classic of every Christmas season.

To the Virginias of the twenty-first century and beyond, we say, "Yes, Virginia—there is hope, for a church and a world in which we listen to each other, work and serve together. We want to pass it on to you in better shape than we found it, and trust that you will do the same for the generations that follow you."

REFLECTION: Matthew 28:19-20; Acts 2:42-43

Go therefore, and make disciples . . . teaching them to observe all things that I have commanded you . . . They devoted themselves to the apostles' teaching and to fellowship in the breaking of bread and in prayers; and everyone was filled with awe at the many wonders and signs . . .

1. Scripture reminds me that I am part of God's continuing development of His church, which has been moving forward since the time of the apostles. How do these two readings connect with this chapter and its emphasis on being the change I want to see in the church and the world?

2. SELF-AWARENESS: What is God calling me to specifically? What is important to me beyond my own comfort in my church? Who are the "Virginias" who call me beyond my own needs?

3. OTHER-AWARENESS: What is God calling my community to? What is important to my community beyond its doors? Who are our "Virginias" and what do we want for them?

4. PRACTICE: What next step am I going to take? When will I take it? How will I take it? What support do I need? To whom will I be accountable and from whom will I get feedback?

Glossary

Vocabulary can be particular to a system, or may have differing meanings in different systems. This glossary is intended to familiarize the reader with particular terminology from leadership theories, the Episcopal Church system, and transition work. While examples used throughout this book are particular to the system known as the Episcopal Church, leadership and transitions are areas that cut across religious, academic, athletic, corporate, and family systems. The definitions offered here explain how the words are utilized in this particular book.

Accountable Acknowledge and assume responsibility for actions.

Adjudicatory The defined legal territory unit and administration of an organization. In the Episcopal Church, the diocese is the adjudicatory unit.

Anxiety Feeling of concern and unease, which can range from low-key chronic to dreaded feeling about something that appears frightening and can become more acute.

Bishop The Episcopal Church takes its name from the Greek term "Episcope" meaning "bishop." The bishop is the chief pastor of the diocese.

Boundaries The intangible line or "fence" that mentally, emotionally, physically, and spiritually separates one person from another.

Bowen Theory A theory of human behavior that views the family as the basic emotional unit and uses systems thinking to describe the complex interactions in the unit.

Bullying The use of force or coercion to abuse or intimidate; can be emotional, verbal, or physical.

Call A spiritually based indication that a community and an individual have mutually discerned that they are to serve together.

Canon to the Ordinary An officer of the diocese who serves as the assistant to the bishop.

Commission on ministry The appointed diocesan body that meet with candidates for holy orders to assist in discerning their call and next steps.

Competency The estate of being well qualified intellectually, emotionally, physically, and in the Church, also spiritually.

Conflict A clash or disagreement between opposing groups or individuals.

Consultant An individual trained to guide a particular process or action (may include in this system: design consultant, transition consultant, other consulting areas). The general term of "consultant" covers a broad spectrum of expertise and practice; where named in this book under "Best Practices" or "Counteract," or in narrative accounts of positive experiences, it denotes individuals who have been trained in the areas listed under "fundamentals."

Conversion The awakening of knowledge or understanding within a human who had no previous belief or concern in religious or spiritual matters, or a reawakening to new moral and spiritual realities that precede a transformation of lifestyles and patterns over time *as opposed to* one-time wholesale adoption of a set of beliefs.

Covenantal A binding agreement or promise entered into with understanding that it is philosophically based on the scriptural model of God's promise to the human race.

Cut-off Completely ending a relationship, without hopes of reconciliation.

Deacon A person who is ordained to servant ministry.

Diocesan council The elected diocesan body that, with the bishop, conducts the business of the diocese between annual conventions.

Dioceses The Episcopal Church is divided into geographic regions known as dioceses, each served by a diocesan bishop.

Discerning a call An ordained person follows a reflective process to discover whether or not they believe they are called to a particular position. A congregation, through their search/nominating committee and vestry, discern among candidates who they will call to be the spiritual leader of their parish.

Discernment An organized way of bringing thoughts and feelings to bear on a particular decision.

Discernment for ordained ministry Following a stated process to see if the religious community as well as the individual agree that they have a vocation to ordained ministry.

Dislocation The emotional state of having been separated from something familiar.

Distancing Moving away from, withdrawing without leaving completely.

Emotional intelligence The ability to identify, assess, and control the emotions of oneself, and to utilize this ability to work more effectively with others, and with groups.

Experiential learning The process of making meaning from direct experience; having an experience, whether staged or real, and reflecting on it in an organized manner to extrapolate meaning.

Feedback Information that is sought from or offered by one individual (1) to another (2) about how that individual's (2) words or behaviors affected them (1); feedback offers the opportunity for repeating or changing words and behaviors in the future based on whether or not the impact reported was positive or negative.

Formation The act of shaping, developing a person in the spiritual life.

Foundational The basis on which something is built, stands, is grounded. The fundamental assumptions from which something develops.

Generativity The impulse within a system to create, produce, or generate new content to pass on to a new time. In Erik Erikson's Stages of Psychological Development, generativity in the psychological sense is the concern for establishing and guiding the next generation and is said to stem from a sense of optimism about humanity.

Group processes; group development Predictable stages that a group will move through during its lifetime.

Human relations training Originally a form of group psychotherapy that sought to improve work performance, employee satisfaction, and productivity through better interpersonal relationships, moved out of the workplace, promoting the awareness of self and others as a way of improving relationships in society at large.

"I" messages Using the first person when speaking—"I think," "I want," "I feel," etc.

Impact A measure of the tangible and intangible effects or consequences of one's actions or influence on another.

Intent A person's *intent:* what they meant to do or say; may or may not be accompanied by forethought or planning; often declared after the fact.

Intentionality; intention Determining to do a specific thing; thoughtfully planning a particular course of action.

Laboratory learning Laboratory learning believes that knowledge must be discovered by the learner if it is to mean anything to him or her, or make a difference in his or her behavior. In laboratory learning, the teacher's or leader's job is to set up conditions where the learner can experiment, try things out, see what works, and generalize for him or herself. The test of learning is not responses on a classroom test, but whether or not the learning makes a difference in the learner's life.

Laity In a religious organization, the laity consists of all members who are not a part of the clergy.

158   **Becoming the Transformative Church**

>> >>

Leadership development As used here, an intentional approach to providing curriculum opportunities that build competencies in leadership skills. Not to be confused with irregular and random offerings, which may or may not build capacity.

Ministry A person or entity through which service or office is accomplished.

Ministry of the baptized All persons who have been baptized are considered ministers of the Church, called by God to serve others.

Mission Base of ministry practice; sometimes defined or spelled out in a mission statement.

Model A physical representation of a behavior; a moral example to others.

Mutual discernment A parish and a candidate discern simultaneously regarding a potential relationship.

Naming Calling a specific act, person, or event what it is.

Non-stipendiary Receives no pay for services rendered.

Norms Behaviors and practices commonly accepted as "normal" for an entity or system.

Openness A philosophical and psychological position that is accessible, not concealing, willing to consider or deal with something.

Options for discernment Dioceses generally offer several different options or choices for the way in which the call of a clergy person can take place.

Over-functioning Routinely take on more than one person can handle; may act like a martyr; more talking than listening; generally does not delegate; does for others what they could do for themselves.

Owning Admit or acknowledge that something is the case.

Patterns A repeated theme; recurring events.

Personalness Revealing intimate information in an effort to be close to someone.

Polity The form of government of a religious institution.

Priest An ordained minister.

Priest-in-charge Title given to a priest who is appointed to serve in a particular jurisdiction for a set time.

Process (n.) A method or way of doing a particular thing; (v.) to reflect on and analyze.

Program life Churches have various program offerings on the local level which are often called the "program life."

Provisional try An expected normal practice of the opportunity to try new things, whether or not they are "successful" or become incorporated.

Purpose The object toward which one strives or for which something exists.

Reactive Ready or rapid response to a stimulus, generally without prior thought or analysis.

Rector The priest who has been called to serve a congregation as its chief pastor.

Rector-in-the-interim A priest who serves a congregation in the transition or interim period between rectors. There are interims who have designated training and those who do not.

Red flag check The call made by one transition officer to another during a search/nomination check to determine if there are any serious impediments in a candidate's life. This is a confidential call between colleagues, who are pledged to honesty regarding a candidate.

Reformation The act of reforming or the state of being reformed; widely believed religion currently in state of reformation; historical reference to Protestant reformation within sixteenth-century Western Christianity initiated by Martin Luther, John Calvin, and other early Protestants.

Reframing A general method of looking at an issue or event from a different perspective to allow other possible interpretations of its meaning.

Resistance The act or power of opposing or withstanding something or someone.

Responsive Answering or responding to words or actions promptly, thoughtfully, and appropriately.

Sabotage A conscious, planned, passive-aggressive, or unconscious effort to stop a particular plan or action.

Search committee A group of church members appointed by the vestry of a congregation to serve as the representatives of the congregation who will conduct the search for a new rector.

Self-awareness The ability to look at one's own thoughts, feelings, and actions with a kind of objectivity, for the purpose of understanding how one's behavior impacts other people.

Self-differentiation A term coined by Family Systems pioneer Murray Bowen to define the process of becoming an adult who is clearly separate from others yet capable of being together with them. The opposite of differentiated is to be *fused,* placing responsibility on others or on situations or predicaments for the way in which our lives develop.

Self-reflection The capacity of humans to exercise introspection and the willingness to learn more about themselves.

Senior warden Member of the vestry appointed or elected to be the leader together with the rector.

Siloing The separating of individuals or entities from each other, so that each stands alone, without interface or interaction with the others in the system.

Standing committee The elected body of clergy and lay people second in ecclesiastical authority to the bishop.

System The combination of interrelated and independent parts forming a unitary whole which continually influence each other directly or indirectly.

Systemic Something that is spread throughout the system, affecting all its parts.

Theory; theoretical A contemplative and rational type of abstract of how something works; "theoretical" may be used to describe ideas and empirical phenomena not easily measurable.

Training The practice of building capacities in interpersonal and group skills through laboratory learning modules.

Transformation The state of being transformed.

Transformative A marked changed, usually for the better.

Transition A time between; a bridge time between what has been and what will be next.

Transition officer The person in each diocese who guides the transition or deployment process for congregations and clergy.

Transparency A metaphor implying visibility and openness regarding behaviors; performing in such a way that it is easy for others to determine what is right or wrong; access to information held by points of authority.

Triangulation When one person will not communicate directly with another, but will bring a third party into the communication loop, creating a triangle.

Tutu Archbishop Desmond Tutu, primate of South Africa during Apartheid, who moved the South Africans through the process of Truth and Reconciliation.

Typology Jungian-based concept of inborn preferences in personality regarding how energy is obtained by the individual; how they give and receive information; make decisions and orient themselves. Most frequently experienced through the Myers-Briggs Personality Inventory.

Under-functioning Little or no initiative or follow through; often gets others to do things for them; frequent emotional or physical illness.

Vestry The elected body of a congregation who are the legal governing and decision-making body of a parish church.

Via media The middle course or way between two extremes; a description claimed by Anglicanism and the Episcopal Church.

APPENDIX A
The EIAG

The EIAG (Experience/Identify/Analyze/Generalize) is a procedure that can be used to process a situation of conflict. There are two necessary ingredients to using the EIAG: (a) that all participating experienced the event, and (b) that there is agreement among those who had the experience to participate in this reflective process.

E - Experience

All that is happening in a group at an identified time

I - Identify

- A specific behavior that all can recall
- An incident that influenced/impacted the group
- One that the initiator (X) has given permission to explore

A - Analyze

Invite each observer to respond (anyone can pass); analyzing the effect of X's behavior—affective/cognitive/behavioral)

Internal reaction at the moment of the incident:

"When X . . . I felt _____."

"When X . . . I thought _____."

"When X . . . I observed _____." (your internal vision)

External behavior at the moment of the incident:

"When X . . . I did/said _____."

Assumptions/projections:

"When X . . . happened, I assumed, projected _____
(which may have caused you to react the way you did).

Process opinions:

(Ask X . . .) "What was your intention?"

G – Generalize:

Transfer to other situations:

(Ask X . . .) "Based on your intention and the group's responses, what have you learned?

(Ask others . . .) "What have you learned?"

(Suggested format for stating generalizations:)

Infer: "I have learned _____ about myself."

Reinforce: "Behavior I affirm and will try again
_____."

"A new behavior I might try is _____."

Apply: "Another situation in which I might apply this learning is
_____."

APPENDIX B
Integrating the Interim and Nominating Processes: The Diocese of Lexington

The following recommendations were made by the Advanced Leadership/ Design Team in a workshop session as ways to integrate the work of interim rectors with the nominating process, enhancing and extending the educational aspects of both.

These recommendations are listed under topics of the goals for each step, in the form of a timeline.

GOAL:	TIME IN PROCESS:
Preparation for transition	Vacancy-to-be announced

BISHOP AND TRANSITION OFFICER MEET WITH VESTRY

TRANSITION OFFICER ASSISTS IN SECURING INTERIM

TRANSITION OFFICER PREPARES VESTRY FOR DUTIES OF VESTRY/INTERIM/NOMINATING COMMITTEE

Interim in Place	

INTERIM and TRANSITION OFFICER meet for planning and understanding of what each brings to the process; TRANSITION OFFICER clarifies Diocesan Process; INTERIM IN EARLY STAGES OF LOOKING AT PARISH ORGANZATION AND ISSUES, AND BEGINNING WORK ON DEVELOPMENTAL TASKS.

Preparation for Nominating Process	Interim settled and ready

INTERIM will introduce timeline (version that identifies when person came to parish and what was going on in their lives and world when they came—NOT the more analytical version). This should help the interim become better acquainted with the parish and give background info to the communicants which will be helpful in Holy Conversations.

INTERIM AND SENIOR WARDEN will meet with BISHOP to determine readiness for NOMINATING COMMITTEE to be formed.

INTERIM WILL include in his/her TEACHING AND PREACHING topics such as change and importance of healing ministry; building on the past but looking into the future; shifts in power and leadership.

TRANSITION OFFICER meets with VESTRY TO TRAIN FOR appointment of Nominating Committee.

TRANSITION OFFICER TRAINS NOMINATING COMMITTEE and assists in preparations for Holy Conversations.

TRANSITION OFFICER AND LEADERSHIP TEAM LEAD HOLY CONVERSATION #1

NOMINATING COMMITTEE hangs newsprint and is available on Sundays after services to help those who did not attend Holy Conversations to add their stickers to the newsprint.

INTERIM includes preparation for concepts of reconciliation and healing in their teaching and preaching in preparation for Holy Conversation #2; please take every opportunity to explain how crucial it is not to continue to sweep things under the rug, that it is normal for people to look at the immediate past, but the collective past ghosts is what we are after—that sadness and loss unnamed and unprocessed turns into bitterness and contaminates the next tenure, etc.

TRANSITION OFFICER AND LEADERSHIP TEAM LEAD HOLY CONVERSATION #2 on Telling the Story of Hurts, Angers, Disappointments, and Ghosts; **Bishop** serves as celebrant for the Service of Healing and Reconciliation and usually preaches; he/she *may* request that the *INTERIM* give the homily.

Interim is prepared for pastoral follow-up; Nominating Committee follow-up with newsprint as in last week.

INTERIM includes focus on response to change as an important preliminary to wishes, hopes, and dreams for the future.

TRANSITION OFFICER AND LEADERSHIP TEAM LEAD SESSION #3 on Wishes, Hopes, and Dreams, which includes a section on change.

NOMINATING COMMITTEE AGAIN MANAGES NEWSPRINT.

Interim includes focus on diversity in spirituality and worship preferences as part of the healthy whole in preparation for and follow-up to Session #4.

EACH PARISH WILL HAVE A SPECIFIC TEAM ASSIGNED TO IT
FOR HOLY CONVERSATIONS. THERE WILL BE A SPECIAL SHEET
OF RATIONALE PREPARED TO GO WITH THE TIMELINE/TASK
ASSIGNMENTS.

Whenever it is possible, we would like the team and the Nominating
Committee and Vestry to meet together before the conversations begin
in order to stress the importance of set-up and process going according
to protocol. Every step of the Holy Conversation process is carefully timed
and planned to allow a parish to have an efficient and effective meeting.
The Interim Rectors can be of great assistance in helping their leadership
understand that following the protocol is essential to this success, and that
no matter how many times all of us give instructions, there will still be
some confusion and lack of understanding—so all of us working together
can make a huge difference!

APPENDIX C

The Nominating Process
in the Diocese of Lexington

Step by step through the process followed by each parish in transition

Check the bullets . . .

- Bishop notified of impending vacancy; meets with wardens and transition officer   ____

- Bishop and Transition Officer meet with vestry   ____

- Priest leaves   ____

- Transition Officer vets Interims; when approved by Bishop, gives to Vestry; Interim selected   ____

- Consultant meets with Vestry   ____

- Vestry receives applications for Nominating Committee   ____

- Nominating Committee formed/trained/commissioned *CONSULTANT PRESENT   ____

- Nominating process begins   ____

- Self-Study Holy Conversations *CONSULTANT-LED   ____

- Analyze Data *CONSULTANT-LED   ____

- Set parish goals/approve by Vestry   ____

- SEND TO CONSULTANT FOR APPROVAL BY BISHOP   ____

- Develop profile/approve by Vestry   ____

- SEND TO CONSULTANT FOR APPROVAL BY BISHOP   ____

- Receive Position Open Form from CONSULTANT and return to CONSULTANT   ____

- CONSULTANT declares position open with Office of Transitional Ministry at the Church Center   ____

- Prepare nomination form as shown in manual for use by parish
  (all names go to Bishop through Consultant/Transition Officer) ___
- Bishop vets all names of applicants, nominees, and computer matches
  for known problems ___
- CONSULTANT delivers names of potential clergy to Nominating Committee ___
- CONSULTANT trains Nominating Committee for final process ___
- Vetting begins ___
- Written questions, SKYPE interviews ___
- Reference checks; Committee, Transition Officer, Bishop ___
- Visits (with NC and Bishop); work with CONSULTANT and BISHOP'S SECRETARY ___
- Committee recommends to Vestry (CONSULTANT FACILITATES MEETING) ___
- Vestry reflects on recommendation and elects new rector
  (CONSULTANT MAY BE PRESENT AS NEEDED) ___
- Notify Bishop ___
- Issue Call ___
- Negotiate Letter of Agreement ___
- Announce to parish ___
- Celebrate and close Interim period ___
- Celebration of New Ministry ___
- Process complete—Praise the Lord! ___

Letter from Consultant

Dear (name of parish),

It is my privilege to serve as the guide in the Nominating Process for your new rector.

My job is three-fold:

1. To guide you through a complex process that most parishes experience perhaps once a decade, and we at the Diocese experience several times a year. We have all of the latest information from the Episcopal Church Center in New York, and updates to guidelines, and will be able to help you move efficiently and effectively through the different stages. There is no question that is too large or too small for you to bring it to our attention!

2. To input the official information from your self-study into the positions open forms at the Church Center and be the contact for all who wish to have further information about your parish.

3. To provide the names as vetted by the Bishop for your consideration, and to be the bridge between the Bishop's office and the Nominating Committee.

I look forward to being a part of your community as we move forward on this exciting adventure of discernment.

Faithfully,
Kay Collier McLaughlin, PhD
Deputy for Leadership Development
Diocesan Consultant
The Diocese of Lexington
859-252-6527

Suggested Box for Web Pages
for Interested Candidates

IF YOU ARE INTERESTED IN DISCERNING A CALL TO SERVE AS RECTOR OF _____.

If you are visiting our web site, and feel that you might possibly be one in discernment of a call to our parish, we hope that you will begin to know us through these pages. The faces of our people, our worship, our ministries, and the place we gather are all depicted here to give you some idea of who we are. Please know that as you are praying for your own process of discernment, we also are praying for all those whom God may be calling to enter our process, as well as for our parish. May all of our journeys be rich in growth, and in possibility.

APPENDIX C1

Sample Nomination Form for Nominating Committee Membership

Applicant Name_____

Address_____ e-mail_____

Preferred Telephone Contact _____

As an applicant for membership on the Nominating Committee, I understand that this committee would involve a big responsibility and major time commitment. I understand that this responsibility must take priority over virtually every other kind of meeting until the task is completed. Meetings will be at least weekly, and are mandatory. The only exceptions will be illness or family emergency. I am prepared to see this through, and am available for the Nominating Committee Formation Retreat on _____ from 10–2 at Mission House.

I am also available for the Holy Conversations on the following dates:

Session #1 _____ Session #2 _____ Session #3 _____ Session #4 _____

I understand that the vestry is seeking the most complete representation possible of our congregation, and to achieve this balance, will be considering areas of parish life represented by each nominee, as well as skills which each bring to the committee.

I believe that this nominee represents the following demographic groups in our parish:

Young adult/young family ___   A representative of the Outreach ministry ___

Mid-life ___   A representative of youth ministry ___

Older adults ___   Balance gender, ethnic, etc. ___

Single adult ___   A representative of 8 a.m. service ___

A member for 3–5 years ___   A representative of 9:30 a.m. service ___

A member for 10–15 years ___   A representative of 11 a.m. service ___

A member for 20 plus years ___   A representative of music ministry ___

A member for 30 plus years ___   A representative of education min ___

Social/economic spread ___

Other _____

*I believe this individual brings special qualities and skills to the work
of the committee in the following areas:*

Personal spirituality foundational to discernment process __

Knowledge of Episcopal Church and polity __

Is known as a bridge builder, not in any "camp" __

Collaborative and cooperative __

Works well with others __

Understands and respects the role of the Bishop and Diocese __

Listens well to others __

Experience in interviewing __

Respectful of differing viewpoints __

Positive, hopeful attitude __

Not on any former Nominating Committee __

Not overtly "pro" or "con" immediate past rector or other previous rectors __

Not overtly "pro" or "con" Bishop and Diocese __

Can represent several constituencies, recognizing importance of ones he/she does
not represent __

Has a good overall perspective on the parish __

Not known as "anti" any particular groups of laity or clergy within or without the
congregation __

Open minded to consider all qualified candidates __

Willing to make this committee a priority for the time required, including weekly
meetings __

Knowledge of larger church __

Attention to detail __

Respectful of process __

Ability and willing to travel __

Ability to work for consensus __

Legal expertise __

Financial expertise __

Ability to maintain confidentiality __

Ability to avoid triangulation and rumor__

Personal emotional intelligence leading to understanding of emotional Intelligence and
healthy human interaction on the part of others __

OTHER:

I am aware that the final responsibility for selection of a balanced commit-tee lies with the vestry, and that the names of committee members will be announced on the web site and in the newsletter as soon as the selection process is completed.

Signed: _____

Date: _____

Please place this completed form in the envelope provided. It may be placed in the offering plate or mailed to the Church Office no later than _____.

APPENDIX C2

Choosing a Convener for the Nominating/Discernment Committee

The Convener of the Committee is chosen by the Nominating Committee at the conclusion of the Formation Retreat.

Criteria for Convenor of Nominating Discernment Committee:

1. A person of deep personal faith and prayer

2. A team builder—A "Bridge Person"—who is known to build bridges between all people, rather than a "troll" person who guards the bridge from being crossed

3. A well-organized person who understands and uses group process effectively

4. A person who is able to delegate, and is not a control freak

5. A person who is able to put the needs of the Church before personal "want," and does not bring personal bias, unfinished business with past rectors or vestries in this or other parishes (positive or negative) or personal/political agendas into the work of discernment and nomination

6. A person who is able to use e-mail

7. A person who listens carefully and hears at least equally to the amount they talk

8. A person who understands the roles and value of the Consultant and the Interim, and is positive about working with both

9. A person who understands Episcopal polity and process—i.e., the role of the Bishop, Deployment Officer, and Diocese in an Episcopal process; and the process itself as explicated for the option chosen for discernment and nomination—and will work to keep channels of communication open and process followed

10. The Chair should be someone who will not attempt to dominate the Committee, but will trust that the Holy Spirit will work through the Committee and the Process.

APPENDIX D

Diocese of Lexington: Office of Transition Ministries: Preparations for Vestry Training for Nominating Process

- Senior Warden and/or Interim set a date with the Transition Officer for a 2-hour session with the full vestry, which may be done in conjunction with a regular vestry meeting (i.e., brief break after business session for light supper; reconvene for 2-hour training) or at a separate meeting.

- At this meeting, the vestry will go through exercises regarding the demographic break-outs of their parish; explore the differences between political or personal constituencies and demographic balance; and look at qualifications for membership, how to keep both transparency and confidentiality, which are important to the level of trust and anxiety in the parish, as well as the pros and cons of vestry selected/committee elected chair and considerations for that position.

- The vestry will also consider at this time the mandate they will give to the nominating committee, and their own buy-in to the process of nomination.

By the very nature of the work, each parish Nominating Committee is composed of busy people with demanding lives—the kind of people who bring excellent skills and resources to the work. One cannot convene a balanced committee of people who are all retired, all don't vacation in warm climates for a month in the winter, all of whom, etc., etc. WHATEVER THEIR LIFE CIRCUMSTANCES, the individuals asked to be a part of this committee must understand that this is NOT AN HONOR; IT IS WORK—work which must, for the time of the process, take priority over many other commitments.

Obviously, you are not going to ask them to miss family weddings or vacations or important work commitments. But should they be members of a group of any sort which meets every week and it conflicts with the time the majority of the Nominating Committee agrees to meet, can they take a sabbatical from the previous commitment for this pressing task? How is the vestry going to present the seriousness of this work to those asked to be on the Committee?

- The vestry will also be aware that a FORMATION RETREAT must be scheduled with 100 percent attendance of the Nominating Committee present at least 4–6 weeks prior to the first Holy Conversation. Normally, the dates for the Holy Conversations are scheduled by the Nominating Committee at their retreat, and around the need for the Bishop to be present for the Liturgy of Healing and Reconciliation at the 2nd session. (This date can be worked out with the Transition Officer/Consultant at the Bishop's Office.) In those instances when the dates for the Holy Conversations need to be set prior to the formation of the Nominating Committee, it is an excellent opportunity for the vestry to use this opportunity to demonstrate their buy-in to the Nominating Process, and to work with the Interim and the Transition Officer/Consultant on the dates for the Holy Conversations.

- The Holy Conversations are led by members of the Diocesan Leadership Team—a select, unpaid volunteer group of trained men and women from across the Diocese who offer as part of their personal ministry their time and talents to serve as presenter/facilitators for parishes in the Diocesan family who are going through transition or other congregational situation which benefits from a design/implementation by this group. Since the Holy Conversations are held in the evenings, team members often drive several hours at the end of a work day to share in the self-study sessions. While the Nominating Committee will work more explicitly with the Leadership Team and set-up, we ask the vestry to consider that they will be welcoming from 3–12 sisters and brothers into their congregational lives, and ask that these leaders be offered every hospitality—something we know we can always count on from our parishes.

The FORMATION RETREAT is a full-day meeting, generally scheduled on a Saturday from 9–3 at Mission House. The general practice is for the Transition Officer/Consultant to offer several dates to the parish, to be specified at the time individuals are asked to be on the committee. If the groundwork for commitment has been laid by the vestry when individuals are asked to serve on the committee, there is generally no difficulty setting the date—even with very busy people. (We have not yet worked with a parish or committee who are not VERY BUSY. There is a sense of self-importance and entitlement that go with being "too busy" to compromise over dates that must be watched out for!) When the setting of the initial dates for vestry training and formation retreat go well, it is a strong indicator of the commitment of the parish to do this work in a spiritually grounded, deeply committed way. Experience shows that what follows is an excellent process in which large numbers of the members of the parish follow the example of the vestry and nominating committee in attending Holy Conversations for self-study, and prayerfully supporting the ongoing work.

The reverse can also be true. When there is difficulty around setting dates with the vestry and nominating committee, the experience is of less modeling for the parish, less engagement by the parish, and many delays in the process.

These early stages are crucial—and we thank you for your hard work and dedication to get the Nominating Process at your parish off to the best possible start!

APPENDIX D1

TO: Members of the Nominating Committee
           Members of the Vestry

FROM: Kay Collier McLaughlin, PhD; Deputy for Leadership Development
           Office of Transition Ministries; the Diocese of Lexington

Friends —

How exciting it is to arrive at this point of discernment. Anticipation
is high as the Nominating Committee hosts the final candidates and we
await their recommendations for the Vestry to consider as they issue the
call for the position of Rector—and along with anticipation comes anxiety! I want to clarify a few things before us so we all are able to continue
to move through these final stages according to the diocesan process.
I have to tell you all that this Nominating Committee has been a poster
child for how to follow process—with the results soon to be before you.
A member of another nominating committee has kept track of the hours
spent PER CANDIDATE, and tells us that approximately 350 hours have
been devoted to the study and interviewing of each candidate by the time
they arrive for their local visits! Congratulations to the Vestry for their
selection of this outstanding group—and to the committee for their hard,
hard work. As we move into this final phase of the process, let us all
remember that the Nominating Committee is an entity OF the Vestry,
created BY the Vestry, with representatives FROM the Vestry, and has
been in regular contact WITH the vestry. The Bishop and I want to commend you for the wonderful way in which you have honored each others'
tasks in the interim. That respect for each other will be highly important
as we move forward.

You all selected Option B as the guideline for the committee's work. Under
Option B, we are now at the stage in the process for the Vestry to meet
with the Nominating Committee in two ways: First, and upcoming, to
join the nominating committee and candidates at a SOCIAL OCCASION,
where as the Nominating Committee completes this next-to-final step of
their process, the Vestry has the opportunity for face-to-face SOCIAL EN-
GAGEMENT with the candidates; and second, to receive the recommendations and rationale from the Nominating Committee who will then turn
their data over to the Vestry so that the Vestry can do their work prior to
issuing the call.

The old standard (national) process recommended visits to the candidates
in their locales, with follow-up visits to our diocese. Option B, as exercised

in both this and other dioceses, respects both the economic times and how technologies such as SKYPE can assist us in getting acquainted without quite so much expensive travel.

It is really important that we maintain clear boundaries between the work of the Nominating Committee and the work of the Vestry throughout the candidate visits and the remainder of the process. Every guideline that is given for the nominating process states that the candidates must NOT be put in double jeopardy—i.e., made to feel that the Vestry does not trust the work of the Nominating Committee and is endeavoring to re-do or duplicate their work. This sends wrong messages to the candidates and can possibly jeopardize a call itself! None of us want that to happen.

As we head into the candidate visits this month, and then our joint meeting of the Vestry and Nominating Committee which I will facilitate, hopefully this will help those who are new to the Vestry this year and thus new to this nominating process, the Vestry as a whole, and the Nominating Committee be on the same page:

- The nominating process in which we are engaged is based in three important concepts: THOROUGH SELF-STUDY, COMPETENCY, and DISCERNMENT. From data generated through the interactive self-study emerged the GOALS AND CHALLENGES which you as a Vestry approved, and which the Bishop approved. Holding these goals and challenges before them, the Nominating Committee was trained in the reading of OTM profiles of candidates in order to find the COMPETENCIES and SKILLS that support the GOALS and CHALLENGES. With this information before them, they engaged in a process of discernment in which they opened themselves to be led by the Holy Spirit in prayerful consideration of which of these well-qualified individuals might be the best "fit" for Calvary Church at this time.

- ENJOY meeting these finalists at the planned social occasion, which is HOSTED BY THE NOMINATING COMMITTEE AND IS THE RESPONSIBILITY OF THE NOMINATING COMMITTEE. You are there as their guests to meet the candidates in a STRICTLY SOCIAL MANNER. No member of the Vestry should ask any "business" questions at this time. The ball has not yet moved to your court! There is much to be learned through social engagement and observation, which is what this event will be about. YOUR TURN COMES LATER!

- The Nominating Committee will have their final discernment meeting and set a date for a joint meeting of the Vestry and Nominating Committee, with the Transition Officer/Consultant serving as facilitator.

- The Nominating Committee will bring with them to the meeting large newsprint statements of the goals and challenges to post as the foundation for all discussions. The Vestry is asked to continue to keep these materials before them as they move forward in discernment.

- Vestry members: remember you are under strictest confidentiality regarding any information that is shared with you from this point on, and you must sign the same confidentiality statement that members of the Nominating Committee signed (to be provided by Conveners). Confidentiality means that no spouses, partners, or family members are to be privy to information until after the call is finalized.

- You will be provided the written questions and answers from each of the two/three finalists, as well as the means to view their sermons. You will also be provided with a summary of the telephone questions and answers to review.

- You will have an opportunity at the joint meeting to question the Nominating Committee in areas in which you individually need further clarification.

- When all of the above data has been carefully studied and digested by members of the Vestry, they are asked to determine what further information they need, and how they would obtain it (SKYPE interviews, personal visits, etc.).

- As the Nominating Committee continues to hold the Vestry in prayer, the Vestry is asked to move into prayerful discernment, in the context of the Holy Eucharist, aware that this is a sacred process that involves all parties listening for God's voice.

- The Vestry is also asked to be aware that this is a process of MUTUAL DISCERNMENT, which includes discernment BY EACH CANDIDATE as to whether God is calling them to Calvary Church. It is also important to remember that THERE IS MORE THAN ONE RIGHT ANSWER! It is also important to be aware that the candidates are likely also engaged in other nominating processes. While it is important that the Vestry not feel rushed to conclusion, it is equally important that they continue the gracious consideration that has been shown all candidates by the Nominating Committee by keeping them apprised of possible timeframes, and by respectful contact of those not finally called as Rector. Once the Vestry has a firm commitment from the rector-elect, it is appropriate to contact the other candidates directly, before word reaches them from other sources. Past experience and history reveal to us that some of our parishes, "most dearly beloved rectors" were second, third, or fourth choices!

- When a decision has been reached, the Senior Warden will contact the Bishop with the name of the person to be called as Rector of Calvary Church. AFTER THE BISHOP HAS GIVEN PERMISSION, the Senior Warden calls the individual and issues the call. The Senior Warden also informs the Chair of the Nominating Committee of the decision. All parties remain under confidentiality. It is possible for these calls to be made from the meeting itself; it is also possible for connecting with the necessary parties to take a matter of hours or even a day or two.

- When the Vestry, the rector-elect, and the Bishop have signed the Letter of Call (see Transition Officer or Canon to the Ordinary for template), and the rector-elect notifies the Senior Warden that they have announced their departure to their present parish, the announcement may be made to the congregation.

I look forward to being with you in these final exciting stages of the process. It has been, and continues to be, a privilege to walk this path with you.

Faithfully,
Kay

›› ››

APPENDIX D2

The Presentation Packet for Nominating Committee Presentation of Candidates to the Vestry

The following materials should be assembled in this order for each candidate that is to be presented to the vestry by the nominating committee:

- A sheet with the goals and challenges as established in the Holy Conversations and approved by the vestry and Bishop

- A 1- to 2-page summary showing how the COMPETENCIES, SKILLS, and EXPERIENCES of the candidate will support the goals and challenges; and summation of how interviews and sermons have brought the DISCERNMENT of the committee to recommend this individual as the first, second, or third possibility to serve as rector

- Document of size of parish and leadership characteristics from nominating committee materials

- The cover letter, résumé, and OTM materials as received from the Bishop

- Answers to the written questions asked by the Bishop

- Answers to the written questions asked by the committee

- A summation or transcript of SKYPE interviews

- A copy of or link to recorded sermons

- A summation or transcript of on-site interviews

- Any other supporting documentation

Materials for each candidate should be clipped together, and all materials placed in a presentation envelope or folder for each member of the vestry and each member of the nominating committee.

The Joint Meeting of the Nominating Committee and Vestry for the Purpose of Receiving Recommendations of Names

The convener of the nominating committee confers with the consultant for possible dates they are available, and then works with the senior warden of the vestry and rector-in-the-interim to set the date for the joint meeting.

- The consultant sends a joint letter to both groups regarding the purpose for the joint meeting and expectations of that meeting.

- The consultant, convener, and rector-in-the interim confer on logistics and agenda.

- The consultant serves as facilitator for the meeting, freeing all members of the nominating committee and vestry to be full participants in the process.

- The consultant calls on the rector-in-the-interim to open the meeting with prayer.

- The consultant then briefly summarizes the process that has brought the two groups to this meeting.

- The consultant asks the convener and co-convener to verbally present the names and rationale for their recommended candidates, one at a time. Following each presentation, other members of the nominating committee are asked to add anything additional about a specific candidate. When all have been heard, the consultant asks the vestry for further questions regarding this particular candidate.

- When all candidates have been presented in this manner, the consultant asks if there are further questions from anyone on the vestry.

- The consultant asks the conveners to hand the materials to all present. The group is given 10 minutes to sift through the materials and see if they have further questions at this point.

- The consultant then addresses "next steps" to be taken by the vestry, options available to them, and asks that they remember that final discernment is to take place in the context of the Holy Eucharist. The consultant also reminds the vestry of the sequence of phone calls to the Bishop PRIOR to the call to the newly elected rector-to-be, and the contingency that there must be agreement between the rector-to-be and the senior warden on the date for announcing the name of the new rector, and the conditions of the Letter of Call.

APPENDIX E
Reflective Process
and Patterns

It has often been said that "experience is the best teacher." However, experience can only teach us if we *examine* the experience in an orderly manner, and *reflect or consider* what it meant and *what it tells us* about our story, in combination with other experiences. In other words, is it an isolated experience, or is it part of a pattern of experiences in the life story of this place?

To reflect is to pull back the curtain on an experience, and view it much as one might view a stage production. What happened? What did the characters in this event do? Say? What did they think? Feel? What might be generalized about it? How can we learn from it?

To reflect is to ponder seriously, to shed light on an event in order to learn from it.

We will be using reflective process to consider the story of our parish, beginning today at this Formation Retreat, and continuing through the Holy Conversation data-gathering process and data analysis.

Our first reflection will be on the previous rectors. We're going to list them, and list what we know of their strengths and their weaknesses:

NAME	STRENGTH	WEAKNESS
Rector (Name)	Strong preacher	Didn't do hospital
	Gifted teacher	Vain
	Good administrator	Didn't socialize
	Good with money	
Rector (Name)	Pastoral	Read sermons
	Good at crisis, illness	Didn't like teaching
	Loved in community	Poor administrator
	Wonderful prayer groups	Drank a lot

NAME	STRENGTH	WEAKNESS
Rector (Name)	Good at Capital Campaign	Not in office enough
	Great community leader	Not visit
	Strong preacher	Drank a bit too much
	High energy, gregarious	Cliques
Rector (Name)	Very warm and loving	Spouse drank too much
	Very spiritual	Not good preacher

From the sample above, you can begin to detect patterns.

"Ghosties and Ghoulies and Long-Legged Beasties, and Things that go 'BUMP!' in the night. . . ."

This line from an old prayer does a lot to inform us about "family secrets"—those things we sweep under the rug and never talk about—and which are guaranteed to trip up a new rector—as they go "BUMP!" in the life of the parish. We need to be able to name those family secrets and get them out on the table—or we are destined to repeat the patterns of dysfunction again and again.

Let's remember we are in a confidential setting, and you are free to either share or ask questions about the family secrets.

›› ››

APPENDIX F

Description of
Holy Conversations

"Holy Conversations" is the name given to the self-study process in the Diocese of Lexington. Holy Conversations are based on several modalities:

- Appreciative Inquiry
- Three-phase Leadership Training
- Concepts of grief, loss, and recovery
- The work of reconciliation of Desmond Tutu

Holy Conversations are led by a team of trained presenters and facilitators from the Diocesan Leadership Team.

When the Bishop, the Interim, and Senior Warden have agreed that it is time for the self-study to begin, the Interim and or Nominating Chair will work with the Transition Officer/Diocesan Consultant to set the dates for the conversations, and to understand the responsibilities of the parish in advertising and managing the conversations.

Format: The conversations take place in the largest gathering space outside of the sanctuary. There is a need for a podium and mic for the presenter, and seating at tables (preferably round tables, but a circle of chairs will accommodate if those are not available) with eight chairs per table, and a flip chart stand and flip chart for each table. Holy Conversations may include a three session format or a four session format. The average length of the gatherings for sessions #1, #3, and #4 is two hours. Session #2 includes a worship service, so we ask participants to include that in their plans.

Summary of Conversations:

Holy Conversation #1: "The Things I Value . . ."

Using the concept of Appreciative Inquiry, the presenter introduces the idea of being people of The Story. The table groups then move into answering questions regarding the experiences that have been most important to them in their parish, and including contributions they have made to the parish. In the report-back period, each table group listens to the individual stories and decides what QUALITIES are represented in the story. The table leader records the qualities on the flip chart, and then reports the qualities that are valued by their table group back to the full gathering.

Holy Conversation #2: "When I Have Been Hurt, Disappointed, or Angry . . ."

With a safe structure established for telling stories, Session #2 is introduced by concepts of loss and grief, and the need for getting the ghosts out from under the carpet so that the next rector is not tripped up by them. The same format is followed at the tables, with participants being given one sheet regarding hurts, disappointments, etc., which they use as in the previous week. Stories are shared at tables, with the facilitator capturing *qualities of the event which hurt or disappointed* on newsprint. In this session, it is particularly important for facilitators to use their training and skills to be sure that each story is heard respectfully, without contradiction or defense, so that participants experience being heard and honored in difficult conversation. Facilitators report out to the full group. Following this exercise, the group moves to the sanctuary for the Liturgy of Healing and Reconciliation. The individual papers and newsprint are placed on the altar at the offertory.

Holy Conversation #3: "When my safe place changes: looking across the bridge to God's future for . . ."

This session deals with how participants have experienced change in the past, particularly in their parish, before turning to visioning for the future and having an opportunity to express wishes, hopes, and dreams, and things they specifically and individually are willing to do to make those hopes and dreams come true. (Session #3 and #4 *can be* integrated to create one session rather than two. This format makes for a very tightly managed evening, but it is possible to do! When the **Three Session Format** is used, the "change" session takes the form of the presenter asking the group what feelings they have when they hear that change is coming. Facilitators capture the words at their table on newsprint and report them out at the beinning of their final report to the group. This shortened form of the change exercise should take a maximum of five minutes.

Holy Conversation #4: "The way I connect with God; the way others connect with God": foundations of our wishes, hopes and dreams.

Utilizing the concepts of Urban T. Homes' spiritual quadrants, the participants self-assign to corners of the room where team members introduce in "dramatic definition" the Head Spirituality, Heart Spirituality, Mystic Spirituality, and Kingdom Spirituality—to the question: Which is the place that you are most comfortable or feel most connected to God? They are then asked to move to a second or auxiliary corner, and last of all, to the place they feel least comfortable. Following the exercise, there are table discussions, and then a closing teaching regarding the strengths and excesses of each and how, together, they form the whole of God's people. Following this interactive exercise, the participants are then asked to fill out a sheet with their wishes, hopes, and dreams for their congregation (or diocese), and indicate beside each *what they are personally willing to do to make that particular wish, hope or dream a reality.* The format of previous evenings is followed in sharing at table and in the full group.

The evening concludes with a short narrative from the presenter on how God is constantly making all things new—particularly reminding people that they have heard *qualities* they appreciate and want to take forward, as well as *qualities* that have been hurtful or disappointing, and they would like to leave behind. Just as there was a time when some of the specific things they valued were unknown to them, so in God's future for us, there are things beyond our imagination, which will also become valued. The evening ends with the group holding hands and saying the Lord's Prayer.

APPENDIX G

Preparations for
Holy Conversations

PLEASE be aware that each step of this process has been carefully thought out, tested, and WORKS! If you have any questions about this process, timeline, checklist, or rationale which follows for each aspect, PLEASE CHECK WITH YOUR CONSULTANT BEFORE CONSIDERING ANY CHANGE. Remember—"if it ain't broke, don't fix it!" This detailed process was created to assure that the self-study, data analysis, and creation of the brochure and living portfolio are as successful and expedient as possible. THERE ARE NO EXCEPTIONS! Trust it! We use this successfully many times a year, while an individual parish may go through the process every 5–10 or 15 years. THANK YOU FOR YOUR COOPERATION!

*Where there is a nominating committee in place, the nominating committee is the responsible group. Where the vestry is functioning as the nominating committee or decision-making body for other transition questions, the vestry is the responsible group for all preparations. When the **process known as** Holy Conversations is used for other purposes in the parish, either the vestry or a special committee should work with the Deputy for Leadership Development. IT IS HELPFUL TO HAVE AN OVERALL CHAIRPERSON OR POINT PERSON TO ASSURE THAT THIS EVENT RUNS SMOOTHLY AND EVERY DETAIL IS ATTENDED TO. Preparations are an exercise in event planning and management!*

Timeframe: Experience has shown that the most effective timing for Holy Conversations is on three–four consecutive weeknights, from either 6–8 p.m., 6:30–8:30, or 7–9. The basic format calls for presentations on the theme, followed by table discussions and report outs. Session #2 includes a liturgy of Healing and Reconciliation as an integral part of the evening, and will take an additional 30 minutes.

The Holy Conversations are facilitated by members of the Diocesan Leadership team—trained volunteers who come from across the Diocese to assist parishes in the Diocesan family. Each team will have a team leader and a facilitator for each table.

Invitation and Recruitment–Vestry/Nominating Committee

TASK:	COMPLETED:
• One month before: announcement in newsletter	_____
• Mail or e-mail individual invitations to EVERY household	_____
• Two weeks before: call every household for reservation	_____
• One week before: call anyone who has not made a reservation	_____
• Based on reservations, assign people to the number of tables required for reservations (no family or interest groups at same table)	_____
• Make master list of groups for facilitator and registration table	_____
• Make nametags with table number on nametag	_____
• Make corresponding numbered sign for each table	_____

EQUIPMENT AND SETUP–Vestry/Nominating Committee and sub-committee

• Secure the use of sturdy flipchart stands (may need to borrow from school, university, or another church) or purchase charts, which sit on each table.	_____
• Stands should be set up at least $1/2$ hour before start time.	_____
• Podium for facilitator if available (set up $1/2$ hour before start).	_____
• Round tables should be set up, ready to go (pencils on each table, etc.).	_____
• If round tables are not available, set chairs of 6–8 in circles with a card table in the middle.	_____
• PR system for presenters* extremely important regardless of the size of the parish or room–hearing what is said by all is critical to the process.	_____
• REGISTRATION TABLE should be set up with alphabetized nametags, extra nametags for walk-ins, and at least two nominating committee or vestry members to be sure family members, etc. are assigned to different tables as walk-ins arrive, one to point them to tables, etc.	_____

FOOD PREPARATION AND SERVING–Sub-committee

Generally the Holy Conversations take place around a light supper or refreshments. In order to free the nominating committee or vestry for their other responsibilities, it is helpful to have a sub-committee working with the nominating committee or vestry that is responsible for food and setup to assure that it happens quickly and can be managed *while the conversations are taking place. The following has proven to work and is very simple:*

- A platter of sandwiches, chips and cookies, plus drinks are available in the team prep room 45 minutes prior to the start time for the leadership team. _____

- A platter of sandwiches, chips, and cookies, and paper plates and napkins are placed in the center of each table just before the time for the Holy Conversations to begin. Pitchers of water, tea, lemonade, and paper cups should also be on the tables. _____

- Sub-committee quietly collects trash between nominating committee exercises. _____

Analysis of Data from Holy Conversations—Nominating Committee/Vestry

- After each Holy Conversation, the Senior Warden or Nominating Chair collects newsprint and individual forms from table leaders (* for the service of reconciliation and healing following Session #2, the newsprint and individual forms will be presented at the altar during the offertory). _____

- The nominating committee or vestry will meet with the consultant to be briefed on analysis of data and goal formulation. _____

- Depending upon Option, the data will either be:

  —Presented to the Bishop/Transition Officer in form of report (Options C, N, SCMC) _____

  —Utilized to draft brochure for Living Portfolio (A and B) _____

Moving from Data Analysis to Living Portfolio/Brochure—Nominating Committee/Diocesan Designer

- Look at models of Living Portfolios and brochures in relation to CDO requirements. _____

- Establish goals. _____

- Define challenges. _____

- Write parish description. _____

- Collect parish photos. _____

- Contact the Diocesan designer to arrange for meeting. _____

- Goals to be approved by vestry and Bishop _____

- Brochure design to be approved by vestry and Bishop _____

- Printing estimates _____

Rationale

Holy Conversation schedules are very full. The goal is to maximize information while promoting fellowship and keeping to a timely program that respects the needs of the participants. Every step under "Preparations for Holy Conversations" has been designed and tested for efficiency and effectiveness. Please read the following carefully so that you understand the reason for each step, and will not think that any step can be short-cut! Trust this process—it WORKS!

Invitation, Recruitment, Nametags, and Table Groups

The *mailed, distinctive invitation* makes a statement about the importance of these conversations, which is underscored by e-mails blasts, follow-up calls, and announcements in both newsletters and at services.

REGARDLESS OF THE SIZE OF THE PARISH, reservations are necessary for *each session,* in order to create *nametags* and *table assignments.*

It is easy to think that everyone in a parish knows each other, and therefore, nametags are not necessary, especially in smaller parishes. It is always amazing to discover that there really ARE people who do not know everyone's name, or may not know each other if they attend different services. There may be people who are new to a parish. In addition, the *facilitators* need to know names to go with the faces at their tables!

The nametags should be available at the door. Generally, they are created on the computer each week from the reservations for that week. They may also be hand-printed, in LARGE, BLOCK LETTERS made with a BLACK SHARPIE. (Black is important as it is easiest to read.)

As each person picks up their nametag, a member of the nominating committee should be there to escort them to their assigned tables.

Reservations and Table Assignments:

For the self-study Holy Conversations, every participant should be assigned to a table group that allows them the greatest freedom to tell their own story, and express their own hopes and dreams without feeling pressure to conform to any other individual's or group's needs. Therefore, reservations and follow-up are necessary to maintain the balance and distribution of the tables from week to week.

Family members should be seated at different tables, as should members of special interest groups. Vestry members and nominating committee members should be distributed among the tables. Depending on the number of tables and size of the congregation, it is preferable to have (in parishes where 7 or 8 tables are sufficient) a nominating committee member and a vestry member at each table, or (in parishes where 15–20 tables are required) either a nominating committee member or a vestry member at each table.

The nominating committee should provide a sign-up sheet each week for subsequent weeks. These sheets can be placed on each table, with a nominating committee or vestry person at the table responsible for seeing that participants at their table confirm their reservations in this manner.

Nominating committee members are encouraged to get a definitive response—emphasizing to congregants that a "maybe" does not assist the process—that, whenever possible, a definite reservation is preferred!

Equipment and Setup

Flipcharts and stands may be of the following variety:

- Sturdy flipchart stands (most parishes own at least one or two, which may be supplemented by borrowing from other churches, a school system, or a business)
- Flipcharts (pads of newsprint which may be purchased from OFFICE DEPOT or other office supply)
- Table-top newsprint easels

There must be *one flipchart and stand for each table, and one at the front of the room near the podium.* The newsprint is an important component of continuing the conversations between sessions, as it will be posted in the parish house, with nominating committee members encouraging those who were not able to attend the Holy Conversations to study the newsprint and add their opinions through the use of adhesive colored dots. The newsprint is then utilized for data analysis.

Setup MUST be completed each week at least 30 minutes BEFORE the established time for the program to begin. (See introduction on goals and tight schedule!) The Leadership Team arrives 30 minutes prior to the meetings and needs to assess the area they will be using, as well as hold their team meeting.

IF AT ALL POSSIBLE, there should be a PA system, with the mic at the podium. When several tables of individuals are in a room, the mic is a great assistance in keeping the interest level and being sure everyone can hear everything. It is well worth the time and effort to rent or borrow, if the church does not own one!

In large parish halls (this would be the 10–20 table meetings), it is most helpful to have two standing mics out among the tables for reports from table leaders, in addition to the mic at the podium.

Room Setup:

- WHEN THE PARISH HALL IS EQUIPPED WITH ROUND TABLES: Each table should be marked with a "tent" sign with its table number (which corresponds to the numbers for table assignments for participants) and have 8–9 chairs around it.

- IF THE PARISH HALL IS EQUIPPED WITH RECTANGULAR TABLES: *FOLD THE TABLES AND PUT THEM AWAY. Arrange the chairs in circles of 8–9, with a small table of some sort in the middle of the circle for coffee cups, etc. The Leadership Team will provide clipboards or writing boards for people to use. Rectangular tables are an absolute no-no because it is impossible to see and hear each other adequately.*

There should be a flipchart stand at each table.

Food Preparation and Serving

Food is always a wonderful, welcoming way to start an evening! The trick here is to provide hospitality and comfort while maintaining the tight schedule—quite a challenge! Whatever food is provided must be planned with these goals in mind. Therefore, the preference is to have plates of sandwiches or cookies in the center of each table, with self-serve drinks to be picked up by individuals on the way to the tables.

Please be mindful that your Leadership Team members come at their own expense and on their own time from across the Diocese, generally coming directly from work and without time for dinner. Your hospitality to the team is greatly appreciated! Please be sure they have something to drink and whatever refreshments are available.

Analysis of Data from Holy Conversations

The collection of newsprint and individual paperwork can appear to be an overwhelming amount of disorganized information! As soon as possible after the final Holy Conversation, the nominating committee and the consultant meet to begin the process of data analysis—an interactive process that allows the committee to discern how their *experience* of Holy Conversations and the data on the newsprint come together to formulate the goals for the parish. It is important to remember here that the *goals are parish goals—not a list of wants and don't wants in a rector.* Once the goals have been formulated and approved, they will be supported by a list of *ministry skills* taken from the MINISTRY SKILLS MANUAL which BEGIN to define qualities, attributes, and skills needed in a rector.

Moving from Data Analysis to Living Portfolio/Brochure

Part of the research done by the National Transition Office involved meeting with clergy focus groups to discover what was working and what was not working in transition/search processes. One of the biggest "not workings" revealed by this study involved the former profile brochures—printed materials ABOUT a parish. The clergy referred to them as "Chamber of Commerce puff pieces" that bore little relation to the actual experience of the parish. SHOW US WHAT YOU DO; don't tell us about what you do . . . the clergy said.

THE LIVING PORTFOLIO and a template for a brochure are a DIOCESAN DESIGN paid for by the Diocese of Lexington and executed by a professional graphic designer in conjunction with the Transition Office to:

- Insure that all of the ingredients required by the Transition office in NYC and the Diocese are included and match the position open profile.

- Save the parishes money with a design that can be personalized for each.

- Save the parishes time by ensuring that all is at the "go" stage when it reaches the Bishop for approval.

- Offer a baseline for printing (the parish is also free to get other estimates).

The designer also assists the nominating committee in selecting a design for the cover of the portfolio or folder, and executing that cover.

In this manner, it is possible only to print the number of portfolios needed (approximately 30) rather than paying for several hundred booklets, the majority of which collect dust in a basement.

APPENDIX H
Training Notes
Overview of Holy Conversations

Necessary Ingredients for Conducting Holy Conversations Self-Study

- Senior Trainer/Presenter (often Transition Officer or other Leadership Development Resource*) *If the latter, it is crucial that the senior trainer as well as all consultants have internalized knowledge of systems theory, as well as church systems, polity, and practice)*
- Table Facilitators (trained by senior trainer)
- Integration with Trained Interims in Parishes
- Integration with Consultant
- Support of Bishop for above

What Training Is Necessary to Begin this Process?

- The senior trainer needs a strong background and training in

  Group Dynamics

  Systems Theory

  Emotional Intelligence

  Appreciative Inquiry

  Bereavement Theory

  Typology

  RESOURCES: Center for Emotional Intelligence and Human Relations (Roy Oswald)—Offers foundational training in Human Interaction and Group Development in five-day modules planned for clergy and church professionals in both scheduling and cost. Also offers a three-day overview training for Bishop/adjudicatory heads to provide the theoretical and experiential base for necessary support from the top.

- Table facilitators must attend a day-and-a-half basic training. It is helpful to begin with facilitators/leaders who have previously been trained by such entities as EfM Mentor Training, DOCC, or three-phase leadership training through (now defunct) systems such as MATC, etc. or CDI. The Diocese of Lexington Leadership Development Curriculum is available to train leaders.

The training is *experiential,* giving participants an opportunity to EXPERIENCE working in small groups and then REFLECT ON THE EXPERIENCE with theoretical constructs taught to support the EXPERIENCE. The GOAL is to provide the leaders with skills that enable them to think on their feet and to have resources that are integrated into their thinking and behavior, allowing a natural response to any situation that might arise, rather than a PRESCRIPTIVE approach, which leaves a leader without resources if individuals deviate from the script (which they always do).

RESOURCES: The EQ-HR units are outstanding training for any interested person. The most expedient way to begin training a team, however, is to get commitment from a core group of 15–25 leaders and have invited trainers come to do the initial training. (Investment of $2,000-$3,000).

- OF BISHOPS, INTERIMS, and SEARCH/NOMINATING CONSULTANTS: This work is most effective when there is:

1. Buy-in of the process (Bishop and LL developing together for their particular diocese) which undergirds

2. Mandate that TRAINED INTERIMS and TRAINED SEARCH/NOMINATING CONSULTANTS will work together with the transition officer for an integrated approach to transition, particularized when necessary to meet the special needs of a given parish.

3. Regular meetings of interims, transition officer, and Bishop

4. Careful blending of the work of interims and consultants to both hold the necessary boundaries that separate the developmental tasks of the interim period for which the interim is responsible and the tasks of the nominating process for which the consultant is responsible, with regular communication that allows an organic approach to issues and patterns that may emerge in the work of the nominating committee and process (responsibility of consultant) AND be reflective of systemic issues that need attention (interim).

The Back Story of Leadership Development/Transition Ministries in the Diocese of Lexington:

It has been said that luck is when crisis meets preparation and opportunity. Add the elements of timing and demands of economic downturn—and the vision of Stacy Sauls.

After a year in which the Bishop and Canon to the Ordinary had spent more time than either had available hoping to iron out the difficulties in a conflicted parish, Bishop Sauls called on a member of his staff who, while serving as communications officer, had for many years worked as a consultant in church systems. Would it be possible to design a series of congregational meetings to assist in resolving this situation?

The draft design was called "Holy Conversations" and would offer three consecutive meetings over a three-week period in which the congregation would look at:

- The history of their congregation (timeline) and tell stories of times they had been most excited and energized in order to determine what they truly value (Appreciative Inquiry)

- Hurts and disappointments they have experienced over the years (Bereavement Theory; Tutu's Truth and Reconciliation Theories), culminating in a Liturgy of Healing and Reconciliation

- What happens when a safe place changes (Transition and Change Theory) and how it is the bridge to wishes, hopes, and dreams for the future, and personal commitment to make those dreams come true

Critical to the design were :

- Trained, objective facilitators from outside the parish who would, by their presence, be the non-anxious presence to keep the work on task in a safe environment and represent by their presence the support of the Diocesan family for each parish: they were named "The Diocesan Leadership Team"

- Forming groups where families, interest groups, and various constituencies were separated for purposes of freedom of expression

- Nametags and reservations to emphasize special nature of the work, and be sure that people truly knew each other

The design was later utilized with a congregation facing their first nominating process.

While this work was going forward to deal with unique situations, several parishes in the diocese were experiencing a different kind of crisis—but one too familiar across the church. Three parishes, which ranged from large and successful to average in size and attendance and holding their own if not setting the world on fire, entered transition periods served by "interims"— i.e., retired clergy—and began their nominating processes. Less than three years later, when all three "new" rectors had come and gone, with emotionally, spiritually, and financially damaging dissolutions of pastoral relationships, reflection on the experiences revealed:

- The so-called interims were more involved in the nominating process than was appropriate, and not attentive to work within the system on real issues of transition; often pushed the Nominating Committee to "hurry."

- The Nominating Committees were resistant to the guidance of the Deployment Officer.

- The self-studies (surveys) were inadequate, and revealed little of the real story and needs of the congregations.

How could the work that had begun in response to special situations in congregations inform and assist in a "normal" aspect of diocesan life– transitions?

When economics called for creative reorganization of staff to meet both budget and demands of the community life, one of several new con-figurations of positions would be known as "Deputy for Leadership Development"—a position that would encompass Transition Ministries and provide a means of designing and training for emerging needs in the Diocese as they were identified.

An intensive revamping of the interim requirements and the transition/nominating process was approved by the Bishop, who was clear in his expectations that all parishes would follow this process and would work under the guidance of the diocesan consultant rather than having an op-tion of whether or not to have a process consultant and hiring indepen-dent consultants.

What makes it work?

Information and training

Building of trust

The following bulleted steps from the announcement that a vacancy will be happening to the call of a new rector are fleshed out in the manual for nominating process. The bullets themselves reveal the process of building trust and relationship, and providing constant information and training:

- Parish informs Bishop of impending vacancy.

- Senior warden meets with Bishop and transition officer (TO).

- TO begins search for TRAINED INTERIMS—provides three names to the Bishop for approval and then to parish.

- TO meets with vestry to explain Diocesan Process.

- TO works with parish on placement of interim.

- Interim meets with TO, Bishop, and other interims on monthly basis.

- Interim, warden, and Bishop meet to determine when Nominating Process ready to begin (interim demonstrates how developmental tasks of interim period have been accomplished or where they remain).

- TO trains vestry on how to develop a balanced nominating committee.

- Nominating committee is appointed: must be available for pre-set date of Formation Retreat and Holy Conversations.

- TO leads day-long FORMATION RETREAT for nominating committee.

- Holy Conversations take place under direction of Leadership Team.

- TO meets with committee to train in data analysis and goal setting.

- TO on all e-mail and communications of committee to review in draft form the brochure and materials.

- POSITION OPEN.

- Process continues.

200   **Becoming the Transformative Church**

›› ››

APPENDIX I

The Office of Transition Ministries the Diocese of Lexington

Dear Friends,

Perhaps you are feeling a little bit like an anxious host or hostess, about to welcome what you hope will be a large crowd to a party in your home. Or maybe like an expectant parent, checking off the stages in the long months before an actual birth. There is truth in both metaphors—and I am going to ask you as Vestry and Nominating Committee to take a few minutes and think about what the impending event(s) is about for YOU.

We are now approaching the all-important data-gathering process—the time when we will begin to hear the stories of the people, from which the goals and challenges of your congregation will be revealed. It is a time when you have the opportunity to lay down your leadership role for a few hours on four different evenings, and allow yourself to simply be a member of your parish, with your own stories, wishes, hopes, and dreams.

For those of you in the inner circle of leadership, this can be as much of a challenge as it is an opportunity. You are accustomed to leading the conversation, and having major input in the decisions; to knowing something of what led to different decisions, and to loyally supporting and defending the decisions made and actions taken.

The Holy Conversations are a time for a different kind of leadership—one which is able to allow the *other* circles of your parish to feel equal in voice, experience, and opinion to those in the inner circle of elected leadership. You can do this best by being at your table as simply one communicant of your congregation—with no greater or lesser stories to share than anyone else at the table.

You do not have to worry about guiding the conversation, as the facilitator at your table will provide that leadership. You can set the tone for participation by willingly sharing your own stories, and by listening with great respect to every story that is told.

Often, those in the inner circles of leadership have inadvertently challenged someone else's truth, by their own word or actions, as they attempted to carry out the mission and ministry decisions of a particular tenure. So even if the stories are about a time when you were not in an elected leadership capacity, you may represent another "inner circle." The best posture for leadership is to be fully present, listen respectfully, and if asked for opinions or rationale on ancient or recent history, support the facilitator by saying something like, "Let's stay with the process, ok?"

Please remember, that with each circle of congregational participation outside the inner circle of leadership, there may be less actual detailed knowledge, but no less passion for the work of the church. There will also be circles of worshippers who appear to be more on the fringes, appearing most frequently for worship, and seemingly less involved in the operation of the parish—and perhaps unfamiliar with most of the stories. It takes ALL of these circles of men, women, and children to make up a congregation. While there may be movement among the circles over time, as people feel welcomed to leadership opportunities at varying levels, there will also be those individuals who stay at a particular level of involvement.

As leaders, it is important to recognize and honor that this parish means something to each one of these people, in each of the circles. This is the way that a church is configured—and we need all of the stories from all of the circles to best be able to recognize the goals and challenges before us, and to discern who God is calling, through you, to lead His people forward in this particular place, at this particular time.

I know that each of you have committed to the Holy Conversations, and will be taking an important role in preparation, and in hospitality. Thank you for all you are doing.

When you arrive at your table, I hope you will allow all of that responsibility to simply be set aside for a couple of hours, and give yourself permission to enter fully into the telling of YOUR stories, as part of your parish story, and part of The Greatest Story Ever Told.

God bless you and the work before us.

Faithfully,
Kay

202   **Becoming the Transformative Church**

›› ››

APPENDIX J

The Office for Transition Ministries the Diocese of Lexington

Dear Nominating Committee member,

On behalf of the Bishop's Office, your sister and brother congregations
in the Diocese of Lexington, and the work of Transition Ministries, I
congratulate you on the deep commitment you have made to God, to
the work of the Kingdom, and to the future of your parish as you accept
membership on the Nominating Committee for Calvary Church. As has
often been stated and was reiterated in the application form for the Nominating Committee, this is not an honorary position, but a holy call to the
hard work of discernment. Rectors are not *hired* in the secular sense, but
called and raised up for ministry. Discerning how the Spirit is moving in
your parish and in the lives of candidates is the task of mutual discernment that will lead to your eventual recommendation to the Vestry. As
one who is privileged to walk this path with our congregations, I know
that the Holy Spirit is present among us, and we have only to heed that
presence as we follow our process to come to a faithful and joyful conclusion to our work. It is demanding work, but it is also joyful work—and
part of that joy is coming to know people with whom we have wor-
shipped and perhaps shared some aspects of ministry over the years, and
some whom we barely know, in a new way, in that very committed working community you are about to enter.

    We will begin with the **Formation Retreat** on Saturday, July 23rd
from 10–4 at Diocesan headquarters at Mission House, 203 East Fourth
Street. We will begin and end promptly, and have a very full agenda for
the day, so please plan to arrive by 9:45–9:50. If you have not been to
Mission House, we are located on the corner of 4th and Martin Luther
King, across from the side of the Living Arts and Science Center. You enter
the parking lot through the stone pillars on 4th Street, and come into the

The Office for Transition Ministries the Diocese of Lexington **203**

›› ››

building through the side portico door off the parking lot. I understand that you each have agreed to full attendance at this meeting. Please know that the work of the committee cannot begin without 100% participation in this retreat. IF, FOR ANY REASON, YOU ARE UNABLE TO BE PRESENT ON THE 23rd FOR THE FULL MEETING, PLEASE NOTIFY ME IMMEDIATELY, AS THE MEETING WILL BE RE-SCHEDULED AT A TIME ALL CAN BE PRESENT.

Please Bring With You:

- A brown bag lunch (we will have a working lunch, so plan to bring your sandwich, salad, or other goodies with you—there will be room in the frig for storage and quick access), and whatever snacks or drinks you would like. Coffee and tea will be available throughout the day.
- A 2" 3-ring binder with paper for note taking. Your complete materials will be ready for you to place in your binder when you arrive at the meeting.
- Casual, comfortable clothing
- Your faith and spirit of adventure

The Purpose Of The Formation Retreat:

- Spiritual grounding. Discernment is a holy process, and each committee's work is grounded in scripture and growing knowledge of each other's spiritual path, from which many of our preferences and passions arise.
- Team building. It is of major importance that we are aware of each other's styles of communication, decision making, group participation, etc. in order to function most effectively.
- Purpose and perspective. What brings you to this committee? Who do you represent? What are your responsibilities? What other perspectives might there be? Are there gaps we need to attend to?
- The parish and the system; past, present and future. We are but one chapter of a long, long story that is continually being written, and we cannot go forward without a glance backward at the parish and diocesan systems and their relation to each other to be aware of what we value, and without being intentional in holding the door open to God's future for us.
- Clarifying the process. What is the Episcopal Process, the Diocesan Process, and why does it exist as it does today? How does it differ

from past processes and why? What can we expect? What if I don't
like the process?

- Making plans . . . for the next steps.

The Process And The Role Of The Consultant

In recent years, the Provincial networks for Transition Ministries and the
Office of Transition Ministry at the Episcopal Church Center in New York
have intensified their research and development of processes that have
proven helpful to the work of transition between rectors and the selection of new rectors. Among those practices are the use of trained interims
in parishes in transition and the work of trained consultants to guide the
intricate process, as well as better guidelines for the process. Those who
might be familiar with older models of what has in the past been called
a "search" process will learn about the new, improved models, and how
technology, better guidelines, and adherence to those guidelines are resulting in better transition periods and better matches. We ask that you come
with a sense of being an open cup, ready and willing to be filled—with
what you will learn from and of each other, and what will be revealed to
you in the coming months about your parish, about the ordained ministry
of your church, and about the Episcopal processes. It matters not how
long you have been an Episcopalian or a member of your parish, what
roles you have played or not played in the past, or what your personal
preferences are. In this work we start as equals on a journey, called to
set aside our personal preferences to best represent the people of God in
a particular time and place—in a process that is constantly evolving and
improving in its efforts to best serve God and His people.

As Transition Officer for the Diocese, I serve as Process Consultant to
our parishes in transition. My job is to be your *guide*—both in following the steps of the process and in being sure all necessary forms are filed,
approvals given, etc. While a parish may go through this process once a
decade, the Diocesan Offices shepherd an average of five such processes
each year! Our guidance and facilitation are intended to enable your most
efficient and effective work. The term "consultant" means "one who gives
professional advice or information; counsel or advice in a particular area
of expertise." In that sense, I am the person to whom questions about the
process should be addressed; the bridge person to the Bishop's office and
the larger process. You will each have my contact information (see below)
and should feel free to check in with me at any time, for any reason. Our
mantra is "when in doubt, ask." There is no question too large or too
small—and much time and frustration can be saved by asking questions
or expressing concerns *directly* when they arise. I can promise you that

when I don't have an immediate answer to your questions or concerns, I do know where to find the answers and will respond to you quickly. If you have any questions about the Retreat—call or e-mail!

You will see my name and e-mail on all correspondence to and among committee members. While most often I will not comment as your e-mails go back and forth, I cannot begin to tell you the number of times that my observation of process through e-mails has prevented innocent missteps in procedure that could de-rail or slow down an otherwise great process.

There are inevitable resistances to any process, and questions which arise. As you will see in your materials and hear many times, we are embarking upon a process we know works. We understand that each of you will from time to time believe that your committee is the exception to a rule, or that there is a better or more creative way to approach some aspect of the work. We have endeavored to provide rationale for all phases of the process—and we certainly do not discount creative thinking or the possibility of alternative solutions. We do ask you to understand that it is expected that we will together follow the process that is utilized in this Diocese, and that any alternative steps be brought to the Consultant for consideration *prior* to committee discussion or action. We will address all concerns as immediately, openly, and honestly as possible. Please be aware that we as Episcopalians live not only under authority—Episcope—but under the *guidance and protection* of a Bishop elected to guard the doctrine, discipline, and worship of our church for generations to come. That task has become more difficult over the years, and many dioceses, including our own, have had the misfortune of learning after the fact of misuses of transition processes which have led to attempts to take property and other devastating issues. It is a sobering reality of our life today. The good news is that when we all understand that we join in this work under a specific process to ensure not only the immediate welfare of your parish, but the future of our faith for our children's children, we know that the work we are undertaking is greater than any one of us, or any one candidate—and that we step forward in His name and for His sake.

Please feel free to call me with any questions you might have between now and our formation retreat. That day, and the commissioning ceremony that will take place before the congregation, will make the beginning of your work as the Nominating Committee. I consider it an honor and privilege to walk this path with you, and look forward to seeing you on July 23rd.

Faithfully,

Kay

APPENDIX J1

Formation Retreat
The Nominating Committee

OCTOBER 2, 2010—MISSION HOUSE

10:00	Welcome and Introduction—Kay Collier McLaughlin, Consultant
	Diocese of Lexington Culture of Courtesy Covenant
	Competency and Commitment (Yon)
10:15	Interactive Spiritual and Process Grounding
	Spiritual Mapping—Where my spiritual journey began and major influence; when and where I became an Episcopalian—major current influence
	Myers Briggs Continuum—By understanding where we fall on this line, and where others stand, we have a better idea of how we as a group will gain and lose energy, dialogue; give and receive information; make decisions; come to conclusions; keep our options open; etc.
	Past, Present, Future—What want to retain; leave behind
	Spiritual Archetypes (Holmes/Alban)—As a microcosm of our parish, we consider our first and second preference among head, heart, mystic, and kingdom spirituality, and what it means to the whole.
	Awareness Wheel—How I make decisions
	Group Formation; Community Making and Dynamics (Peck and Weber)—There are predictable stages in the life of all groups, and we will cycle through them several times in our work together.
	Iceberg Theory—We see what is above the water, but dangers lie under the water—what we don't name and identify
	ICO, Inclusion; Control; Openess—How important is it to me to be included? To you? How much do I need to be in control? Do you? How open am I willing to be with the group? How open are you willing to be?
	Levels of Truth—Suwu Bona: "I see you; I hear you." The words indicate that in certain cultures, not to recognize the truth of someone's story and acknowledge it and them is greatly insulting, for until we truly see someone, they literally do not exist. We want to see and hear each other and others respectfully.
11:15	Who We Are and What We Bring to the Work of Discernment—Deepening our knowledge of each other; owning our gifts and talents
12:00	Group Photo
12:05	Break (includes getting your lunch to the table)
12:15	"Ghosties and Ghoulies and Long-Legged Beasties, and Things that Go Bump in the Night"
	A Brief Historical Context
	Family Secrets—Hurts, disappointments; things we've never been allowed to talk about
	Former Rectors—Strengths and weaknesses—reflecting back on what we've said, what patterns do you observe?
	Congregational Size and Leadership Styles
1:15	The Episcopal Process for Calling a Rector

2:15	The Parish and Diocesan Systems—Family systems and the church
3:00	The Diocesan Process
3:30	The Self-Study And How It Leads to the Rest of the Process (will include a visit with the Convener of another parish's Nominating Committee)
	Holy Conversations Theory and Practice
	Preparation for Data Analysis
	Goals and Challenges—All leading to the development of profile brochure
	Theory and Rationale behind new form of profile brochure/web presence (see samples)
	Further training for the next steps of process as time nears
4:30	Business and Next Steps—Discernment and emergence of leadership (explanation of roles of convener, co-convener, secretary, chaplain) and written suggestions for each
5:00	Closing
11:00	The Episcopal Process for Calling a Rector
11:15	Break
11:30	The Parish and the Diocesan System
11:45	Boundaries, Confidentiality, Transparency, and Communication
12:00	LUNCH AND TABLE CONVERSATION
12:30	The Diocesan Process
1:30	Election of Chair/s; Secretary; Chaplain
2:00	Planning for Holy Conversations—Next steps; web page and newsletter; meeting time
3:00	Closing—Jeremiah 1:4–9

APPENDIX K
Data Analysis Following Interactive Data-Gathering Sessions (Holy Conversations)

Rationale: Honesty and transparency are hallmarks of interactive, face-to-face data gathering, building trust in the process which leads to support of the goals and challenges and the leader chosen to meet those stated goals and challenges.

Supporting process: Participants at tables fill out individual sheets on questions at each session. Participants share at tables, while the outside trained facilitator records key words of the stories and qualities of the stories on newsprint, which are shared with the community in attendance and posted on the walls for all in the congregation to see.

At the conclusion of each session, the nominating convener is asked to store the data until the conclusion of all sessions. At the final session, the data analysis process and approval of goals and challenges by the vestry, bishop, and congregation is shared.

Setting up the data analysis meeting (plan for 2½–3 hours): Space should have sufficient wall space for posting of all newsprint collected. Newsprint is posted by sessions; individual sheets from sessions #1 and #3 (and #4 dependent on total number held) are retained by session. Sheets from Session #2 were placed on the altar and disposed of by the consultant following the service and team de-briefing.

Consultant covers one wall with a large sheet of airplane cloth sprayed with adhesive. 5 x 7 tear sheets of newsprint, one side sprayed with adhesive, are laid on tables in the ready. Blunt-tipped large markers are available in contrasting colors. (It is also possible to use 5 x 7 tear sheets of commercially available miniature legal pads, which come in several bright colors, and differentiating sessions by color of sheets.)

Consultant introduces session with a prayer for openness to the Holy Spirit in allowing the wisdom of the people to come through the work.

- **The process of phenomenological clustering:** Phenomenological research values the first person reports of life experience. The freedom from supposition—of knowing in advance—that this is allowed is known as *Epoche. Things cannot be known in advance or known without reflection for meaning. Each participant has answered questions formulated to provide a common lens on the experiences.* Dr. Clarke Moustakis, one of the guiding figures of qualitative research states that: *Organization and analysis of data begin with regarding every statement relevant to the topic and having equal value.*

- Statements are clustered around themes or meanings and may form phenomenological depictions around stories that represent the same meaning.

- The final step in the phenomenological process is the synthesis of meanings and essences, which in this process results in goals and challenges that emerge from the meaning clusters of lived experiences.

Nominating committee role:

1. As invited by the consultant, study the newsprint for Session #1 for **Qualities** in the stories. Using the markers, write one quality per provided sheet and stick in Session #1 column on large wall cloth. When all appear to have located and shown all qualities, they are asked to take the individual sheets and check them against their work, to be sure that all qualities have been identified.

2. They will repeat this exercise for each session. The nominating committee will not have the individual sheets for Session #2, which were placed on the altar during the Eucharist and Healing Service. The leadership team will have extracted qualities from those sheets which the consultant will have available.

3. The committee then divides into three teams and takes the papers for their question to their table, where they begin *clustering the qualities.*

4. When all clusters are completed, the table groups begin to shape goals and challenges from the clusters.

5. After approximately 30–45 minutes, the groups read the results of their work to the other groups, with rationale for their development. The groups then discuss and decide upon which are goals and which are challenges.

210   **Becoming the Transformative Church**

›› ››

6. Each group is asked to continue to work over the following week on refining the wording of their goals and challenges by e-mail, and prior to presenting to the vestry.

7. The nominating convener (and the entire committee if they so desire) presents the goals and challenges to the vestry, who may (a) accept completely, (b) suggest small changes, and (c) hopefully, not ask for massive change! When the vestry has approved . . .

8. The convener of the nominating committee will send to the consultant/transition officer (who may or may not be the same person), who will submit to the bishop for his/her approval. The bishop may exercise the same options as the vestry, before final approval. The bishop's primary question of the consultant/transition officer: *Is this what the team heard in the Holy Conversations?*

9. Once the approval of the bishop has been received, the goals and challenges may be posted on the parish and diocesan website, and used in a brochure or other information about the parish. At this point, those who participated will be able to see that they were heard and be supportive of the results.

10. Incoming candidates frequently ask, "Are these goals and challenges real?" New clergy in the Diocese of Lexington generally base their first vestry retreat upon revisiting the goals and challenges for any changes since they were done, on how to implement action plans to work on them.

APPENDIX L

Developmental Tasks in the Interim Church

I. Coming To Terms With History

FOCUS:

- Putting history and former tenures in perspective
- Honoring and appreciating what has been good and bad
- Appropriate ventilating, grieving, accepting, and moving on

SUGGESTIONS:

- Tell the church's story, make a timeline for the church, update its written history
- Identify and celebrate watersheds in the congregation's life, significant moments and accomplishments
- Utilize professional denominational resources to teach the grief process and provide for the safe ventilation of feelings
  - List strengths and weaknesses of previous pastors
  - Listen and teach listening skills
- Review covenants or statements that bind members together
  - Update files, records, resource and member lists
- Maintain healthy traditions while questioning problem ones

Unresolved	Somewhat unresolved	Neutral	Somewhat resolved	Resolved
1	2	3	4	5
SIGNS AND SYMPTOMS OF NON-RESOLUTION			**SIGNS AND SYMPTOMS OF RESOLUTION**	
Living in the past			Living in the present: time focus more to present; accepting the past; much less talking about "the good old days," the way the former rector did things	
Selective memory; gaps in memory			Healthy movement through the grief process	
Stuck in grief; old pain revisited			Stabilizing membership, giving, participation	
Declining membership, giving, participation			Articulate about traditions	
Unwillingness to consider the "why" of traditions			Process questions: Where are we going? What now?	
Feelings of apathy, alienation, anger, blaming, and/or depression			Investment in current issues	
"Ghosts" of rectors past			Healthy humor; openness to new and different talents	
Try to find clone or exact opposite of previous rector				

Developmental Tasks in the Interim Church
II. Seeking/Discovering a New Identity

FOCUS:

- Is the congregation's image of itself realistic
- Is the interim time seen as opportunity for growth and renewal
- Does the congregation see itself as an entity without a clergy person
- Is the congregation separating its identity from the past rector's personality and style

SUGGESTIONS:

- Work for ongoing reality testing
- Conduct congregational self-study to gain accurate information
- Hold cottage meetings to talk about what we are like and what we want to become
- Conduct study of neighborhood ministry needs
- Encourage program and resource assessments
- Develop a broad vision of congregation's future, establish goals and objectives

Unresolved	Somewhat unresolved	Neutral	Somewhat resolved	Resolved
1	2	3	4	5
SIGNS AND SYMPTOMS OF NON-RESOLUTION			**SIGNS AND SYMPTOMS OF RESOLUTION**	
Time focus remains in the past			Time focus on present and future	
Resistance to self-assessment			Willingness to do self-assessment/study	
Unrealistic myths still operative			Facing reality	
Emphasis on blaming "someone"			Affirming "who we really are"	
Low trust levels; lack of authentic sharing			Growing excitement; energy about vision	
Identity confusion: Who are we?			Process questions: Where are we going?	
Leaders/others continue to consult previous rector			Openness to inclusion	
Same old programs, even when they don't fit reality of present			Rising trust level, humor, patience with search process	
Resistance to bishop, Diocesan relationship, polity			Forging new relationship and understanding with diocese	
Confusion or disregard of Episcopal polity			Understanding and respect of Episcopal canons and polity	
"White-knuckling" prior visions and goals			Vision and goals fit present reality	

Developmental Tasks in the Interim Church
III. Managing and Facilitating Shifts in Power and Leadership

FOCUS:

- Power and control of directions and decisions of congregation
  - Healthy, realistic decision making
    - Managing conflicts

SUGGESTIONS:

- Honoring past leadership; handling burnout, drop out, and continuing involvement of leaders
  - Assess leadership necessary to reach interim goals and recruit leaders to meet those needs
  - Affirm leaders' different styles and talents; use the Myers-Briggs Type Indicator or other tools
    - Teach family systems, behavior and impact, conflict resolution
  - Re-think process of developing leadership and lengths of terms of office; write position descriptions
    - Recognize and celebrate the leaders who are going out of office
  - Determine whether or not processes are congruent with those stated in denominational polity and governing documents
    - Be open to all members; seek input and share information widely

Unresolved	Somewhat unresolved	Neutral	Somewhat resolved	Resolved
1	2	3	4	5

SIGNS AND SYMPTOMS OF NON-RESOLUTION	SIGNS AND SYMPTOMS OF RESOLUTION
Division/destructive sub-grouping	Open leadership/decision-making structure
Competition and avoidance	Interdependency
Counter dependency	Win-win decisions
Power plays	Clear decisions with follow-through
Win-lose decisions	Shared leadership in maintenance and development
Lack of clear decisions; decisions not carried out or fall apart	New faces elected, acceptance and support of new
Search committee becomes a power center	Both old and new leaders involved
Secret meetings, self-authorized decisions	

Developmental Tasks in the Interim Church
IV. Renewing Denominational Linkages

FOCUS:

- Healthy partnership with the denomination
- Authority, dependency, interdependency, counter-dependency
- Congregation's tendency to see judicatory or denomination through former pastor's eyes
- History of the relationship, dollars and trust; shared mission

SUGGESTIONS:

- Make use of denominational resources: staff, programs, facilities, literature, training, retreats
- Encourage denomination to give clear information about its expectations, requirements, resources, and programs
- Identify common interests of church and denomination
- Identify and affirm church members who hold denominational positions
- Allow for feelings of ventilation about denomination
- Have denominational ministries and programs lifted up in newsletters or during mission moments in worship

Unresolved	Somewhat unresolved	Neutral	Somewhat resolved	Resolved
1	2	3	4	5

SIGNS AND SYMPTOMS OF NON-RESOLUTION

- Resistance to denominational requests or suggestions
- Criticism of denominational personnel and programs
- Failure to meet pledges and budgets
- "We-they" outlook

SIGNS AND SYMPTOMS OF RESOLUTION

- Willingness to accept help and resources
- Appreciation for denomination's traditions and mission
- Stable or increased giving to denomination: dollars and people
- Denominations resources and facilities are used

Developmental Tasks in the Interim Church
V. Commitment to New Directions in Ministry

FOCUS:

- Wide ownership and excitement about the shared vision for the future
  - Getting a good match between pastor and congregation
  - Clear and shared expectations between clergy and congregation
- Clean exit of interim pastor and consultant; good closure for interim period

SUGGESTIONS:

- Bring closure to good interim
- Interim sharing insight with new pastor
- Minister-in-transition support programs (new clergy and priest-in-charge groups)
- Make sure transition rituals are in place
- Exit interview with interim and denominational representative

Unresolved	Somewhat unresolved	Neutral	Somewhat resolved	Resolved
1	2	3	4	5

SIGNS AND SYMPTOMS OF NON-RESOLUTION	SIGNS AND SYMPTOMS OF RESOLUTION
Anxiety and rushing or bypass search process	Focus on the future
Trying to hire interim or familiar as permanent pastor	Enthusiastic preparations for new pastor
Unrealistic or unclear expectations or desire to control new pastor or clone old pastor	Clarity and consensus on leadership style to meet identified goals and challenges
High anxiety; low energy; lack of humor	Appropriate circumstantial anxiety; evident energy and good humor
Inability to agree on choice of a pastor	Increasing ownership and levels of involvement in process moving to consensus
Failure to issue a call; discouragement with process	Appreciation of interim process and leaders
Clinging to interim	Willingness to say goodbye to interim

Resourced from: Temporary Shepherds: A Handbook for Interim Ministry, Interim Ministry Network (ecumenical resources) and Office of Transition Ministry of the Episcopal Church and Transition Ministers of the Episcopal Church

APPENDIX M

Behavior-Impact

A Case Study

Back Story: Two university professors had been in conflict for 14 years, under three different deans and five department chairs. In desperation, the provost called in a consultant to mediate the dispute. After weeks of individual sessions and mediated dialogue, the consultant introduced the disputing colleagues to anxiety behaviors as identified in Bowen Theory/Family Systems, and asked them to 1) help define the behaviors, 2) identify if they had experienced the behaviors in their department, 3) identify if they had been sucked into participating in the behaviors, and 4) identify the impact of the behaviors. After considering their responses, they were asked to reflect on whether or not the impact was what they sought. If not, as adults they had a choice about whether to repeat the behaviors or to choose alternative behaviors for different impact.

BEHAVIOR	DEFINITION	EXP/PARTICIPATE?	IMPACT?	DESIRED?	OPTION?
Triangulating	Indirect comm. around person or group	Contact students and talk to other colleagues	Splits; more triangles; distorted comm.; betrayal	No	Ask to go to source; offer to go with them. Authenticate data. Present facts.
Distancing	Push away; not engaged when present	Angry about something; stop coming or come and not participate	Start triangle anxiety in leadership; loss of talent (can also be needed and constructive down time)	No	Let it be; civility; treat each other as adults; check in and on; welcome but don't expend energy or chase

BEHAVIOR	DEFINITION	EXP/PARTICIPATE?	IMPACT?	DESIRED?	OPTION?
Conflict	Aggressive or passive aggressive; quiet or active	Blaming; competing for students	Fear and anger among students; distract from work; lost opportunities	No	Expert help; reveal data
Over-function	Do too much; think they only one should do	Don't trust anyone else to do	Others left out; talents missed; entitlement		Self-aware; active recruit-recruitment and inclusion
Under-function	Do nothing; shut down	Say will do and do nothing	Less effective department; plays into above		Data on talents recorded and used
Sabotage	Pull carpet out; set up to fail; secretive, masked, or overt approaches	Whisper and rumor; don't speak up at appropriate time and undermine later	Chaos; lose significant potential; fear; frustration; destruction of people and mission		Get out on table; strengthen strong to be stronger
Cut-off	Gone—no chance of conversation, healing, or reconciliation	Leave	No chance for resolution		Invite; not chase; teach reconciliation
Bullying	Can be physical, verbal, emotional—loud or quieter; many forms	Over-talk; sarcasm; put-downs; excessive "expertise"	Fear; shut down; intimidate; limit input for effective decisions		Identify and refuse to accept for self or group

This exercise can reveal important patterns and allow individuals an opportunity to self-assess; to know and own the impact of their own behaviors and thus have an opportunity to make choices about different future behaviors to achieve different future impact. All too often people or groups point to an assumed or known INTENT and fail to realize that INTENT IS NOT THE KEY FACTOR. IMPACT OF THE BEHAVIOR ON THE FIGURAL GROUP IS THE KEY FACTOR, REGARDLESS OF WHAT THE INTENT MIGHT HAVE BEEN. Focusing on the IMPACT allows a leader of anyone in the system to step back and say, "I am unwilling to accept behavior that causes that impact—and there are alternatives."

APPENDIX N
Competency-Commitment

An Effective Partnership

Inspiration and motivation are important words for any leader of any organization. Just how important is illustrated by the efforts most organizations make to provide speakers and workshops which are dedicated to inspiring and motivating individuals of all levels within an organization.

To what is each person to be inspired? For what are they being motivated?

The majority of leaders can remember some time when they came back from a conference *inspired and motivated,* only to have the new energy fade as weeks and months go by. Others have sent employees for training, or brought a particularly fine speaker into the organization to inspire and motivate—but have not seen the kind of lasting results for which they have hoped.

EQ-HR Leadership Development is based on theories that undergird *skill development* in areas which will assist leaders in:

- Understanding the important interface of competency and commitment

- Understanding self in relation to one's own competencies and commitments as a basis for understanding and relating to others' competencies and commitments

- Transferring *content and motivation* into the introduction and practice of behaviors and models which are sustainable over time, and evolves in an organic manner, rather than providing a short-term prescription

	Lo	Hi	
COMPETENCY Skill Building Training	Goof Offs	Producers	Hi
	Do Nothings	Goof Ups	Lo

COMMITMENT
Revival Experiences

What Does That Mean During An Eq-Hr Workshop?

It means that the working groups are opportunities to actually experience oneself interacting with others in a microcosm in which you will likely meet every type of individual you have or will encounter in your life, and receive feedback from them. At the same time, you will receive feedback through your EQ instruments which will allow you to become aware of how you and others assess YOU.

You know that you are *dedicated* to being an effective leader and are *deeply engaged* in the work of leadership. In group, you will open yourself to the possibility that how others see you, as well as how you see yourself, has something important to do with who you are as a leader and how people respond to you in that role. This is not navel gazing! This is data gathering about an important subject—YOU—human being and leader. Feedback from others, as well as your interaction with others in the group and the EQ inventory results, will give you information that allows you to experience yourself as others experience you . . . and to choose this opportunity in a safe environment to practice some new ways of "doing"—all of which lead to the development of new competencies and the improvement of existing competencies. This is practice time—for the "real game" back home!

What Does That Mean Back Home?

When you return home, you will take with you some *new skills/competencies, as well as some you might have neglected, and some you are polishing up a bit.* As the *"high"—the inspiration or motivation* of an intensive experience—wears away with the demands of back-home dailiness, you will have your resource guide to remind you of theories, your EQ to remind you of self- and other-assessments, and your group interactions to remind you of areas of practice—all of which will enable you to continue to develop those competencies.

Competencies require practice for integration, and regular use to keep them ready to go as needed.

Commitment requires more than occasional inspiration and motivation to sustain: it requires a foundation which allows commitment to be sustained, even when the going gets tough (which it always does!).

Competency. Commitment.

Important companions on the journey of leadership.

APPENDIX P
Understanding
How Groups Develop

By Kay Collier McLaughlin

Groups have a predictable lifecycle. This is good news for anyone who has ever led a group and wondered about some of the seemingly quirky, crazy things that seem to overtake a group of perfectly nice, normal human beings who have been together for awhile. And suddenly, a group that had most certainly been crazy seems wonderfully stable and focused on task.

What's it all about?

The good news is that the stages of group development are not permanent—and most groups cycle through them. A long-term group may cycle through them several times over many months, while a short-term group may cycle only once.

The two most-used models of group development are by Richard Weber and Scott Peck. We will list them here in parallel form:

WEBER	PECK
Infancy (forming)	Pseudo-community
Adolescence (storming)	Chaos
Norming and performing	Emptiness
Transforming	True community

Whether one chooses to use terminology from Weber or from Peck, the most important thing is to recognize that there *are* predictable stages, and to be able to identify the stage and know that whether it is pleasant or unpleasant, the group will experience it and move on to another stage.

STAGE 1. Infancy, forming, pseudo-community. A group is birthed, and comes together. This is the polite stage, with everyone on his/her best behavior as issues of inclusion, control, openness, and style become obvious.

Individual goal: establish safe patterns of interaction

Group goal: establish basic criteria for membership

Relationship to leader: dependency

Stage 1 may be smooth and pleasant, or intense and frustrating, depending on the similarities in style and needs in the group, and the tolerance for ambiguity.

STAGE 2. Words like chaos, storming, and adolescence bring graphic images to mind for this stage. This is probably the most difficult of the stages, and one all groups must go through on their way to performance. It can be a startling change in dynamics, as members shift from "pretending" to be a community (pseudo-community) to dealing with the individual differences.

Individual goal: respond to perceived demands of their task, react and attack designated leadership

Group goal: try to create acceptable order/process for decision making while bids for power and control rage

Relationship to leader: counter-dependency—react negatively to any leadership behavior that is evident

STAGE 3: Lower level of frustration than first two. Here the group becomes really cohesive and begins to negotiate roles and work collaboratively.

Interpersonally: members working out of an affection, a deep regard for each other in a deeper, less superficial way

Relation to leader: leadership issues resolved through interdependent relationship

STAGE 4: The experience of group effort creates a powerful unifying bond. The group now has a life and identity of its own.

Re-Cycling Through Or Death:

Groups move through the stages at different speeds, but all must go through them. When the purpose of the group has been achieved, or it is time for it to conclude, the group is faced with one of two forms of transforming:

Redefinition: establishment of new structure and purpose

Disengagement: termination, or death

The natural tendency for any group that has successfully completed a full cycle is to attempt to remain together in some form for the future. The group has bonded together through all of its experiences of joy, pain, frustration, success, failure, etc.

When the purpose has changed or the time has elapsed, the group must stop or disengage. Failure to do so will lead to a frustrating and unfulfilling path, as members attempt to stay in contact rather than bring closure. Even if they were to stay together, the experience will be a new one, not a repetition of the previously experienced one, and therefore will be disappointing.

222   **Becoming the Transformative Church**

>> >>

APPENDIX Q
ICA
Inclusion, Control, Affection (Openness)

The concept known as ICA was developed by William Schutz in his work with groups in the early 1960s. Schutz posited that upon entering a new situation or group, all people have a series of questions they ask themselves about how they might function in this setting:

Questions of Inclusion include:

- Who else is here, and what are they going to think about me?

- How can I be in relation to them? What will it cost me?

- What kind of behavior is acceptable here? How much am I willing to pay?

- Can I trust them with my real self? Will they hold me up if I am falling?

Questions of Control include:

- Who is in charge? Calling the shots here?

- How much can I push for what I want? What do they require of me?

- Can I say what I really think?

- Can I take it if they say what they really think?

Questions of Affection (Openness) include:

- Am I willing to open myself to others?

- Can I show support or caring for someone?

- What will happen if I show support for one person and not another?

- What if no one supports or cares for me? What if they do?

- What if I disagree, show anger—will I still be liked?

Sources

Schutz, W.C. *Interpersonal Underworld* (Palo Alto, CA: Science and Behavior Books, 1967).

Schutz, W.C. *Profound Simplicity,* 3rd ed. (San Francisco: Will Schutz Associates, 1988).

Schutz, William. *A Three-Dimensional Theory of Interpersonal Behavior* (New York: Holt, Reinhart, 1958).

APPENDIX R
Healthy and Unhealthy Boundaries

By Kay Collier McLaughlin, PhD

Robert Frost said it in a poem: "Good fences make good neighbors."

Boundaries are intangible fences which separate one human being from another. Just as a fence delineates where one piece of property ends and another begins, a personal boundary indicates that there is a stopping place, a clear space, between human beings—physically, emotionally, mentally, and spiritually.

Many people have a very clear sense of their boundaries—especially if they have been raised in an environment where there was respect for this separation: people knocked on closed doors before entering; considered someone's room and property personal, not to be invaded without asking, etc. Those who have grown up without personal space and possessions being treated with respect may not understand their own or others' boundaries as well.

Understanding and maintaining good boundaries is about three things:

- Making sure I know my own boundaries and maintain them.

- Making sure I am a respecter of the boundaries of other people, which may be quite different from my own.

- Making sure that I understand how power differential plays into boundary situations, in order not ever to abuse any situation in which I am in a perceived position of power (whether I recognize it as such or not), or allow another person with relatively more power in a given situation to abuse his/her position in relating to me.

Physical boundaries: It is a good thing to be aware of our own sense of personal, physical space, and how close we allow others to come to that space. When a person is touched roughly, or hurtfully, almost every-

one realizes that is inappropriate and will draw back or retaliate. There are more subtle forms of touching that may not be physically hurtful, but should never be allowed without explicit permission (if you are the receiver) and should never be used (if you are the toucher)—standing or sitting too close to another; touching hand, arm, knee, face, or any other part of the body while making conversation; hugging without permission; contact that is overly familiar or intimate. These are all the signs of UN-HEALTHY boundaries—for either the receiver or the toucher (invader). Physically drawing back or removing oneself from the situation or firmly saying "no" are healthy responses.

Emotional boundaries: Many people are unaware that they are entitled to emotional, mental, and spiritual boundaries as well as physical ones. Emotional boundary invasion includes such actions as giving or receiving too much personal information early in a relationship; accepting gifts, food, sex, conversation you don't really want; violating personal beliefs to please others; not being aware of the right to have boundaries; not knowing when boundaries are being violated; falling in love or relationship at first sight; changing self to be whatever someone else needs you to be; allowing verbal abuse; trusting everyone or trusting no one; and believing what someone else says about you (especially negative things). Emotional boundary violation is a little like the slow drip of water on a rock—you may not notice it at first, but the steady and cumulative effect wears one down in damaging ways.

Intellectual and spiritual boundaries: This kind of boundary violation is closely related to needing to be valued or needed so much that one allows their own positions to be de-valued or questioned, and acquiesces to the values and beliefs of others. In this sense, someone else is defining another's reality, setting another's goals and life direction.

Power differential: While every individual is responsible for maintaining his/her own boundaries and respecting the boundaries of others, the person who is in a perceived position of power has a real responsibility to refrain from abusing the trust that is given (if too readily) to a position "over" another. Individuals in perceived to be "lower" positions in any system may fear retaliation by someone who is more powerful than they, monetary or vocational loss, or simply approval. This kind of fear puts persons in more powerful positions in a dangerous place. All leadership would do well to ask themselves who might perceive them to be "more powerful," and how they are managing their own power positions in terms of boundaries.

Setting Boundaries

Many books have been written on this important subject, and can enhance these simple bullet points:

- Start by knowing what is non-negotiable, more negotiable, negotiable, and open to options in your own life. Those values will inform you of the boundaries that are most important to you.

- Write your boundaries down so that you are clear about them in your head and heart *before they are needed*. The concept of boundaries, much less the ability to use the concept, can fly out the window in a high-pressure situation of boundary abuse.

- Practice, practice, practice—saying "no" and taking care of yourself.

Bibliography

Andreas, Brian. *Traveling Light.* Decorah, IA: Story People, 2003.

Center for Emotional Intelligence and Human Relations. *Participant Handbook: Emotional Intelligence and Human Relations Skill Training.* Boonsboro, MD: Center for Emotional Intelligence and Human Relations, October 2012.

Episcopal Diocese of Lexington. *Transition and Nominating Process Manual.* Lexington, KY: Episcopal Diocese of Lexington, 2013.

Friedman, Edwin H. *Failure of Nerve: Leadership in the Age of the Quick Fix.* New York: Church Publishing, 1997, 2007.

_____. *Generation to Generation: Family Process in Church and Synagogue.* New York and London: The Guilford Press, 1985.

Gilbert, Roberta. *The Eight Concepts of Bowen Theory: A New Way of Thinking about the Individual and the Group.* Falls Church, VA: Leading Systems Press, 2004, 2006.

Goleman, Daniel. *Working with Emotional Intelligence.* New York: Bantam Books, 1998, 2000, 2006.

Heifetz, Ronald A. and Linsky, Marty. *Leadership on the Line: Staying Alive through the Dangers of Leading.* Boston: Harvard Business Review Press, 2002.

Intrator, Sam M. and Scribner, Megan. *Leading from Within: Poetry that Sustains the Courage to Lead.* San Francisco: Jossey-Bass Wiley Imprint, 2007.

Peck, M. Scott, M.D. *A Different Drum.* New York: Simon & Schuster, 1987.

Sawyer, David R. *Hope in Conflict: Discovering Wisdom in Congregational Turmoil.* Cleveland, OH: The Pilgrim Press, 2007.

Schneider, John. *Finding My Way: From Trauma to Transformation: The Journey through Loss and Grief.* Traverse City, MI: Seasons Press, 2012.

Schutz, William C. *Here Comes Everybody.* New York: Harper and Row, 1971.

Steinke, Peter L. *Congregational Leadership in Anxious Times: Being Calm and Courageous No Matter What.* Herndon, VA: Alban Institute, 2006.

Wheatley, Margaret. *Finding Our Way: Leadership for an Uncertain Time.* San Francisco: Berrett-Koehler, 2005.

_____. *Leadership and the New Science: Discovering Order in a Chaotic World.* San Francisco: Berrett-Koehler, 1999.

_____. *Turning to One Another: Simple Conversations to Restore Hope to the Future.* San Francisco: Berrett-Koehler, 2002.